GENDER, PEACE AND CONFLICT

 PRIO

International Peace Research Institute, Oslo
Fuglehauggata 11, N-0260 Oslo, Norway
Telephone: (47) 22 54 77 00
Telefax: (47) 22 54 77 01
E-mail: info@prio.no
http://www.prio.no

The International Peace Research Institute, Oslo (PRIO) is an independent international institute of peace and conflict research, founded in 1959. It is governed by an international Governing Board of seven individuals, and its main source of income is the Norwegian Research Council. The results of all PRIO research are available to the public.

PRIO's publications include the *Journal of Peace Research* (1964–) published six times a year and the quarterly *Security Dialogue* (formerly *Bulletin of Peace Proposals*) (1969–) and books. Recent titles include:

Kumar Rupesinghe & Khawar Mumtaz, eds: *Internal Conflicts in South Asia* (1996)

Jørn Gjelstad & Olav Njølstad, eds: *Nuclear Rivalry and International Order* (1996)

Johan Galtung: *Peace by Peaceful Means: Peace and Conflict, Development and Civilization* (1996)

Pavel K. Baev: *The Russian Army in a Time of Troubles: From the Taiga to the British Seas* (1996)

Valery Tishkov: *Ethnicity, Nationalism and Conflict in and after the Soviet Union: The Mind Aflame* (1997)

Ola Tunander, Pavel Baev & Victoria Ingrid Einagel, eds: *Geopolitics in Post-Wall Europe: Security, Territory and Identity* (1997)

John Markakis: *Resource Conflict in the Horn of Africa* (1998)

Clive Archer and Ingrid Sogner: *Norway, European Integration and Atlantic Security* (1998)

GENDER, PEACE AND CONFLICT

Edited by
Inger Skjelsbæk and Dan Smith

 PRIO

International Peace Research Institute, Oslo

SAGE Publications
London • Thousand Oaks • New Delhi

First published 2001

SAGE Publications Ltd
6 Bonhill Street
London EC2A 4PU

SAGE Publications Inc.
2455 Teller Road
Thousand Oaks, California 91320

SAGE Publications India Pvt Ltd
32, M-Block Market
Greater Kailash - I
New Delhi 110 048

British Library Cataloguing in Publication data

A catalogue record for this book is available from the British Library

ISBN 0 7619 6852 0
ISBN 0 7619 6853 (pbk)

Library of Congress catalog record available

Typeset by M Rules
Printed in Great Britain by Redwood Books, Trowbridge, Wiltshire

Contents

Foreword

This book on the role of gender difference in conflict resolution and political decisionmaking resulted from the Expert Group Meeting organized jointly by the United Nations Division for the Advancement of Women (DAW) and the International Peace Research Institute, Oslo (PRIO) at the United Nations Research and Training Institute for the Advancement of Women (INSTRAW), in Santo Domingo, in 1996. The Expert Group Meeting explored further the application of a gender perspective to conflict resolution and decisionmaking.

One of the most important outcomes of the 1995 Beijing Conference was to reach agreement of the concepts of gender and gender mainstreaming. The latter is the process of assessing the implications for women and men of any planned action, including legislation, policies, programmes and research in all areas, and at all levels. This agreement was reflected in the Platform for Action which was adopted. Further elaboration by the United Nations Economic and Social Council (ECOSOC agreed conclusions 1997/2 and 1998/2) implied that the gender perspective should become an integral part of the design, implementation, monitoring and evaluation of all policies and programmes in all spheres, at national and international levels, so women and men can benefit equally. It also implied that the consistent inclusion of women's views and experiences in all policies would inevitably lead to changes in their content and priorities, making them better tailored to the realities of our times, and to the needs of *all* members of society.

By applying a gender perspective to conflict resolution, the Santo Domingo meeting recognized that women and men were differently involved in armed conflicts but that policies and research have reflected a 'gender blind' approach. In practice, this means that men and male norms have been taken to represent the norm for all human beings. To bring a truly gender perspective to conflict resolution therefore means to develop a fuller understanding of women's roles and the changes that might come about with greater participation of women in conflict resolution, including decisionmaking.

There is evidence that women can make a visible difference to political decisions and agenda, political culture and styles of decisionmaking when they constitute a sufficient proportion of a decisionmaking group – a '*critical mass*' of perhaps 30–35%. Although women have been involved in conflict resolution in different arenas and in various roles, they have never achieved a 'critical mass' as decisionmakers. Many women have made important contributions as peacemakers, crossing lines of conflict that men were unable to cross; working with the other side of a conflict on new peaceful solutions; networking with women and other actors in civil society and encouraging women at the grassroots level to get actively involved. These contributions, however, are not recorded and have not had decisive long-term implications.

Most women appear to have a somewhat different understanding of peace, security and violence than most men. This has led to the assumption that if women were involved in a sufficient number in peace, security and conflict resolutions, these definitions would be transformed and so would all related policies, activities and institutional arrangements. Broadening both these concepts and participation in conflict resolution would open new opportunities for dialogue. It would replace the traditional model of negotiations aimed at ceasefire or crisis management by a real conflict resolution model, where the root causes of conflict are addressed, all aspects of human security are taken into consideration, and the process of negotiation is inclusive, involving representatives of civil society, including women's organizations.

The results of the Santo Domingo meeting clearly indicate that, indeed, the incorporation of gender is essential for the better understanding of ongoing conflicts and their root causes and, subsequently, for the elaboration of more relevant means and policies for their peaceful resolution. The meeting also provided an opportunity for cooperation by the two institutions with the distinct but interrelated mandates: the Division for the Advancement of Women, a focal point on women's issues and gender mainstreaming in the United Nations Secretariat and the International Peace Research Institute, Oslo, an institute specializing in conflict resolution. This partnership by itself constitutes a step towards gender mainstreaming in practice and the much-needed collaboration of a policy-oriented, intergovernmental organization with a research institution. More of this type of cooperation is needed.

It is critically important that more research be done to demonstrate how essential the incorporation of gender is in all aspects and at all stages of conflict resolution. This book and the Expert Group Meeting from which it resulted are first steps in that direction.

Angela E. V. King
Assistant Secretary-General
Special Adviser on Gender Issues and Advancement of Women

Acknowledgements

This anthology is a product of co-operation between the International Peace Research Institute, Oslo (PRIO) and the United Nations Division for the Advancement of Women (UN DAW). The first major activity of the co-operation was a UN Expert Group Meeting, jointly organized by UN DAW and PRIO, with the support of the United Nations Educational, Scientific and Cultural Organization (UNESCO), and hosted by the United Nations International Research and Training Institute for the Advancement of Women (INSTRAW) in Santo Domingo, Dominican Republic, on 6–11 October 1996. The chapters of this book are based on papers presented at that meeting. The United Nations published the report of the meeting and its conclusions on 7 November 1996 (reference: EGM/PRDC/1996/REP.1).

We would like to thank Angela King, UN Assistant Secretary-General, Special Adviser on Gender Issues and Advancement of Women, for her support of this project throughout. We also want to thank John Mathiason, then Deputy Director of the UN Division for the Advancement of Women, whose support for the project at the outset was crucial to raising funds for it, and whose participation at the Expert Group Meeting was fundamental to its success. Special thanks are due to Dorota Gierycz, author of one of the chapters in this anthology and Chief of the Gender Analysis Section of UN DAW; she was the one who initially brought PRIO and the Division together and proposed this co-operative enterprise.

Our thanks also go to Martha Dueñas Loza, Director of the United Nations International Research and Training Institute for the Advancement of Women (INSTRAW) in Santo Domingo, together with her administrative staff, who did everything necessary to make the Expert Group Meeting run efficiently and pleasantly. Eva Irene Tuft, one of the authors in this anthology, was at that time Research Consultant at INSTRAW, and was particularly helpful in arranging the co-operation and ensuring it worked smoothly. We were also fortunate to have the intellectual and practical support of UNESCO, whom we also wish to thank, especially Ingeborg Breines, Director of the UNESCO programme on Women and a Culture of Peace.

This anthology is shaped and inspired by the presentations and discussion at that Expert Group Meeting at INSTRAW in 1996. For various reasons not all of the presentations could be included in this anthology, so we would like to thank the ones who are not included among the authors of chapters in this book: Rukia Said Ali, Eugenia Piza Lopez, Carolyn Stephenson and Sandra Whitworth. Observers at the meeting also participated fully in the discussion of the issues and the shaping of the report, and our thanks go to them too: Georgina Ashworth, Berit Kyllingstad Collet, Claire Fulcher, Martha Olga Garcia, Elise Judith Kant, Maja Mischke, Maria Cristina Nogufra, Mary Power, Lucero Quiroga, Maria Cristina Sara-Serrano, Eleni Stamris, Maj Britt Theorin, Cora Weiss and June Willenz.

We also want to take this opportunity to record our gratitude for the financial support that this project has received. The UN Division for the Advancement of Women, UNESCO, and the Norwegian Ministry of Foreign Affairs provided funding for the Expert Group Meeting. In addition, the Norwegian Ministry of Foreign Affairs provided the further financial support necessary for the preparation of this book.

During the extended process of organizing this anthology, we received essential assistance in compiling the bibliography from PRIO's librarian Synnøve Eifring, with further help from Jon Arild Olsen. The editorial assistance of first Susan Høivik and then of Lesley Hauge was invaluable. And Karen Hostens efficiently carried out the chores involved in answering copy-editing queries and tying the last bits and pieces together to take us over the final hurdle and into production and publication. We are extremely grateful to all five of these colleagues for their help, their cheerfulness and their good nature.

Inger Skjelsbæk
Dan Smith
Oslo

Introduction

Inger Skjelsbæk and Dan Smith

When decisions are to be made about politics and peace, what role does gender play? That is the focus in this volume of essays. For decades, much political and social science research remained blind to the very existence of gender – a blindness so obtuse that it sometimes seemed as if it had to be deliberate.

Whether planned or not, ignoring gender difference in research has meant that male norms and male behaviour have been taken to represent the *human* norm. This produces a gross distortion of reality. In most fields and sub-fields in the social sciences, this distortion has now been acknowledged, and serious efforts have been made to rectify the situation. These efforts have faced considerable opposition, though only some of the resistance has been deliberate. International relations (IR) has been considerably slower than, for example, anthropology, sociology or social psychology in coming to terms with the idea that there *is* an issue worth addressing, and then in getting on and addressing it. Since the mid-1980s, nonetheless, there has been exploration of the role played by gender in matters that fall within the scope of IR, and inquiry into the degree to which the range of issues addressed in IR could or should be expanded. This collection of essays is one of several efforts at the turn of the millennium that are attempting to bring IR up to speed.

The ambition in this anthology is by no means to set about re-theorizing the entire field of IR. The chapters that follow have a specific focus: the impact of gender difference in decisionmaking in relation to conflict and conflict resolution – an issue often avoided by IR scholars and other political scientists. Basic gender blindness is probably the main explanation for this, but it may also be that interest has been low because the most influential perspectives on such issues have been overly simplistic. International relations in general, and war in particular, are almost exclusively male fields. True, some women have made their mark in international politics in recent times – for example, Margaret Thatcher, Gro Harlem Brundtland, Madeleine Albright, Golda Meir, Indira Gandhi –

but there are very few such figures. This has allowed some writers to develop a line of argument that holds that, since women are rarely responsible for decisions to go to war, women should be regarded as inherently peaceful. Judging by the small number of researchers who have taken up this question, the mere assertion of women's peacefulness seems to have been enough to deter many from examining it in greater depth. Men in particular seem to have been scared off. We want to contribute to bringing an end to this state of affairs by opening up the question of the impact of gender difference in the study of peace and conflict.

The works of writers such as Boulding (1981), Elshtain (1987), Enloe (1983, 1989, 1993) and Tickner (1992) did a great deal to introduce gender issues in the study of peace, conflict and international politics. They mounted a sharp and forceful critique of the narrow focus of IR and much of peace research – and this in a way that could not be dismissed as mere polemic. And on the back of the critique, they established a challenging new agenda to be assessed and explored. Of course, there have continued to be dismissive reactions to this work, attempts to marginalize and ghettoize it. But there has been an undeniable shift in the centre of gravity of discussion within IR and peace research, with the growing realization that issues of gender raise important and previously ill-considered questions. It is perhaps especially with the end of the Cold War, as IR has come to look more closely at conflict resolution, reconciliation and peace-building, that more and more IR scholars have come to realize the relevance of gender issues.

The process of asking searching questions, mounting the critique and setting out a new agenda does not of itself provide answers or even address the items on the new agenda. Getting to grips with the implications is a task that has been addressed in the second half of the 1990s by research that, for example, looks more closely at geographical areas or focuses on specific issues such as the use of sexual violence in war, or the roles of women in military groups or peacekeeping operations. It is alongside that work that we wish to set this book.

The chapters that follow combine theoretical argument, reviews of policy and of the literature, and a geographically broad range of case studies. We hope with this combination of diverse elements to provide an overview of the field and of the possibilities within it, and to break down the often unfortunate divisions between different kinds of studies. We have put theoretical and empirical research pieces alongside each other to underline how much each needs the other. Theory is rootless without empirical exploration; empirical research is a mere assembling of facts unless there is a theoretical basis to explain how the facts relate to each other. The two together are required for us to see how a steady accumulation of case studies may lead towards an overall reassessment of major issues in conflict resolution and peace-building. The point is not to adjust conflict resolution so that 'and gender' is inserted at appropriate points, but rather to understand that ignoring the gender dimension of social reality makes it impossible to address crucial elements of conflict resolution.

Some of the violent acts perpetrated by men in armed conflicts are perpetrated precisely because the men have become convinced that that is the way to show their masculinity. This view of masculinity as something to be reinforced through violence is linked to a view of femininity that emphasizes passivity in those issues, like war, that are deemed to be men's business. In such a social context, mobilizing people for reconciliation may be impossible as long as the dynamics of the male–female division of labour are ignored.

Women and war

From the beginning of 1990 until the end of 1999, the world saw 118 armed conflicts, in the course of which approximately 6 million people were killed.[1] Few of these wars have been open clashes between two sovereign states. Most have been civil wars, many of them internationalized through the involvement of outside powers as paymasters, suppliers, trainers or combatants. Such wars are generally off the radar screens of world politics, receiving scant attention from the international news media. These are long, slow conflicts, often confined to one region of a country. Such a conflict may remain relatively low on the graph of lethal violence for a long time, but is often capable – as in Rwanda in 1994 – of erupting into unimaginable viciousness. About one-third of the wars that were active in 1999 had lasted more than two decades. The weaponry used is relatively low-tech. Almost all the killing is done at close quarters, by men, some of it by male children.

Data on war casualties are uncertain; it is often not clear exactly who is counted and who is left out of the tally. Despite many reservations about the data, it is generally accepted that in warfare at the start of the twentieth century, 85–90% of war deaths were members of the armed forces. By this common 'guess-timate', a small minority of the war dead were civilians who got caught in the cross-fire or were killed in atrocities. It may be that the proportion of non-combatants killed in war was actually higher, because it is not clear whether this estimate includes colonial wars of conquest, in which the whole of the conquered population suffered. In Europe, however, it seems clear that in World War I civilian casualties did not represent a large proportion of the whole. By contrast, in World War II civilian fatalities have been estimated at between one-half and two-thirds of all war deaths, including all theatres of war, and including death camps, massacres and bombing raids. Today, it is conservatively reckoned that some 75% of all war-deaths are civilian non-combatants.[2]

War has been brought to the civilian population. No longer are civilians the chance victims of accidents or of excesses. They are no longer – in the jargon of the US war in Vietnam – part of the 'collateral damage', consigned to the margins as the perhaps regrettable and probably unintended but unfortunately inevitable casualties of military exigencies. Why do civilians make up such a high proportion of the casualties of war today? Because in many wars, *the civilians are the targets*. Civilians – as well as the economic and industrial infrastructure – were the targets of strategic terror bombing in World War II, culminating in the nuclear strikes on Hiroshima and Nagasaki in August 1945. Civilians were likewise the targets of ethnic cleansing in the war in Bosnia and Herzegovina in 1992–95, and of the genocide in Rwanda in 1994. In both these recent cases, Western media initially tended to depict the violence as the result of a frenzied orgy of hatred. Evidence has since emerged to show that in both cases the killing was in fact planned in cold blood.[3]

When war is brought to the civilian population, women suffer. Data generally fail to distinguish with respect to gender or age. However, the United Nations High Commissioner for Refugees (UNHCR) (1993, p. 87) has reported that about 80% of international refugees are women and children, compared to the 70% of the population of an average Third World country that is constituted by women and children. Clearly then, women and children are disproportionately hard-hit by this aspect of war suffering. Among the reasons is that men are more likely to be involved in the actual fighting; moreover, even as civilians, men are often killed while the women and children are expelled. Detailed accounts of the 1995 massacre of Bosniak men in Srebrenica are an example of this (Danner, 1998).

One form of violence specifically targets women: *rape*. Though men as well as women can be and are raped – especially in all-male contexts such as prisons – accounts of atrocities in war rarely include rape of men, though there are well-documented reports of the sexual mutilation of men. It thus seems that rape in war affects women exclusively. Rape has long been part of war and is often regarded as, if not acceptable, then so inevitable that there is no point in making a fuss about it. In her classic study and polemic, Susan Brownmiller (1975, p. 31) quotes a passage from the memoirs of General Patton in which he recalls telling another officer that, '[I]n spite of my most diligent efforts, there would undoubtedly be some raping'. Patton goes on to report that he requested details as soon as possible 'so that the offenders could be properly hanged'. Though rape is illegal under every military code and is frequently punishable by death, acceptance of the inevitability of rape by soldiers is often so fatalistic as to amount to complaisance.

Rape piles vulnerability on vulnerability, most clearly demonstrated in the case of refugee women who are attacked and raped, as with the Somali women and girls in refugee camps in northeastern Kenya in 1992 and 1993. The rapists were reportedly armed bandits, including groups from the former Somali army.[4] Here, as in most wars throughout history, the raped women and girls were the deliberately chosen victims of male rapists, at the same time as they were the incidental victims of war.

Today, a further dimension has been added with the increasing awareness of the use of rape as a deliberate weapon of war. In Bosnia and Herzegovina, 'All the warring parties have been implicated, though to varying degrees' in 'rape being used as a weapon to further war aims' (UNHCR, 1993, p. 70). The Bosnian Serb army was the main offender, and Bosniak women were the most numerous victims, often of multiple gang rape, and often in camps especially set up for that purpose (Amnesty International, 1993; United Nations, 1994). Rape as well as murder was used in the genocidal attacks on Rwandan Tutsis in 1994. According to one investigation, virtually every Tutsi woman who survived a massacre was raped (Human Rights Watch, 1996). A less publicized case occurred in 1992 in Burma, where the army's campaign to expel 250,000 *Rohingya* Muslims and force them into Bangladesh plumbed extreme depths of brutality and inhumanity, including the systematic use of rape. In one refugee camp of 20,000 people, 'Almost every woman interviewed said she was gang-raped before being allowed to cross the border'.[5]

This deliberate and systematic use of rape is an extension of the use of rape as a means of torture, of which there have been numerous accounts over the years in many states. Rape is used not simply to attack the woman but, through her, to attack another target – somebody whom she is believed to be protecting, for example, a male comrade in arms. The attack exploits not only the physical vulnerability of the woman, but also her subsequent sense of shame and defilement, and all too often the likely rejection by her partner, family and community. In 1972, over a period of nine months, Pakistani soldiers raped 200,000 women in the breakaway Eastern Pakistan, which became Bangladesh. After the war, the government of Bangladesh had the greatest difficulty in trying to persuade the husbands of raped women to accept their wives (Brownmiller, 1975, pp. 78ff.). Thus mass rape is a way to terrorize individuals, communities and, if done on a large enough scale, an entire ethnic group. Those who are ruthless enough to launch a war in which civilians themselves are the target are therefore likely to find that rape can be a convenient and effective weapon.

In war, women have become central as victims, but marginal as agents. Nor has this changed with the shift in emphasis towards attacking civilians as an end in itself. As Enloe (1993, p. 51) notes, 'One of the most striking characteristics of militaries themselves is that they are almost exclusively male'. This is a question of both numbers and culture. As to numbers, Table 1 shows the available data. Over 580,000 women serve in the forces of 25 states. Three states (China, Russia and the USA) between them account for slightly under 85% of the world's military women, who comprise a little more than 2.5% of the world's more than 22 million regular military personnel. In most countries where women serve in the military, they are a small minority. Only in seven countries – Australia, Canada, China, New Zealand, Russia, South Africa and the USA – do the data show that women make up more than 10% of the regular military personnel, though it is likely that Israel, which provides no figures, should be added to that list.

TABLE 1   *Women in the armed forces, 1998*

	Number of women in armed forces	Women as a percentage of total armed forces
Australia	7,400	13.4
Bahamas	70	8.1
Belarus	2,100	2.5
Belgium	2,570	6.2
Brunei	600	12.0
Canada	6,100	10
China	136,000	5.5
Cyprus	445	4.5
Denmark	1,020	4.2
Finland	500	1.6
France	22,790	7.2
Germany	1,440	0.4
Greece	5,520	3.3
India	200	0.02
Ireland	200	1.7
Japan	9,100	3.9
Netherlands	1,920	3.4
New Zealand	1,370	14.4
Norway	185	1.2
Portugal	2,300	4.6
Russia	145,000	14.4
South Africa	16,998	24.3
Spain	3,800	2.0
Sri Lanka	1,000	0.9
UK	15,860	7.5
USA	199,900	14.5

Source: International Institute for Strategic Studies, *The Military Balance 1998/99* (Oxford: Oxford University Press, 1998).

Note: If a country's forces are not shown in this table, that does not necessarily mean its forces exclude women – only that *The Military Balance* has no information on this. The percentage calculation is based on the proportion of women serving in the regular armed forces of all services, excluding paramilitary units and reserves.

Where and when women have been recruited into the armed forces, there has always been controversy about their proper role. It is widely felt that women should not be in the military – and further, that if they are there, their roles should be strictly limited. That women are unsuitable for combat roles has long been taken for granted. Marlowe (1983) offers a representative view. Writing as a senior US army psychiatrist, he argues that men and women have different capacities for 'certain kinds of things':

> One of these things is fighting, certainly in the forms required in land combat. The male's greater vital capacity, speed, muscle mass, aiming and throwing skills, his greater propensity for aggression and his more rapid rises in adrenaline make him more fitted for physically intense combat. (Marlowe, 1983, p. 190)

An argument along these lines might barely be sustained for the infantry, but it can hardly be relevant with regard to the rest of today's mechanized and increasingly computerized military forces. The physical intensity of combat even in modern mode is undeniable, but the strength that is required is not dependent on muscle mass, adrenaline or other features of explosive strength. What is required above all is stamina, and here women often outdo men.

All the same, women in the military are confined to 'support' roles – medical, secretarial and clerical, transport and communications – in which they neither carry weapons nor are expected to use them. It is at the margins that the definitions and distinctions have been most blurred. US and Israeli armed forces deploy women in direct combat roles. There were women in combat roles in some units of the Bosnian government army in the 1992–95 period, including the 17th Brigade, which was often reported as one of the most effective Bosnian units.[6] Many insurgent forces have employed women in support roles, whereas a smaller number have employed women in combat. Among these are the Liberation Tigers of Tamil Eelam, the secessionist forces in Sri Lanka, who were said to have more than 3,000 women fighting in the early 1990s. The Sandinista forces in Nicaragua employed women in relatively large numbers, both during the insurgency against Somoza in 1978 and 1979 and in the 1980s' war against the 'Contras'. The Farabundo Marti Liberation Front in El Salvador recruited large numbers of women guerrillas, as did the Eritrean People's Liberation Front during its 30-year war of independence against Ethiopia that ended in 1991. The armed wing of the African National Congress in its war against the South African apartheid regime included smaller numbers of women. Women have served in several of the armed organizations that have fought for the Palestinian cause over four decades. In many other revolutionary and insurgent forces, women carry out functions that are not quite those of the frontline fighters, but which cannot be regarded as non-combatant, such as courier and intelligence work.

Fears that recruiting women would change the internal culture of the armed forces are often expressed by politicians and by military servicemen. Nobody knows what a mostly female modern military force would be like – and no modern armed force has offered to conduct the experiment to find out. In fact, however, the point of recruiting women is not to change the forces' culture but simply to utilize their skills and motivation and thus to obtain a wider recruitment-base.

Gender differences: theory

The nature of gender differences has been variously conceptualized within the scholarly literature. According to how we perceive men and women to be different, we behave, think and design policies that reflect our point of view. A large section of this volume is therefore devoted to describing different ways in which gender differences are conceptualized, and what the implications of these differences might be.

Dorota Gierycz places the themes and arguments in this book in a global context, using the UN as a viewing aid. She describes the steps taken in the build-up to the Fourth World Conference on Women in Beijing in 1995 and shows how the theme of 'women and peace' has received increasing attention over the years. This increased interest coincided with the ending of the Cold War and democratic transformations in many countries around the world – according to Gierycz, not an accidental development. With greater attention to the theme of women and peace has also come a conceptual shift. The focus is no longer on women in isolation, but on the interaction between the genders. Whereas some conceptualize gender differences as the same as sex differences, the United Nations has defined gender differences as *the socially constructed roles played by women and men that are ascribed to them on the basis of their sex.* It was with this definition in mind that the Beijing Conference was convened. The heated debates about gender and peace were related to opposing understanding of the nature of gender differences. The last sections of Gierycz's chapter address the possible contributions that women in political decisionmaking and conflict resolution can make. Research indicates that it takes a minimum of around 30%, often referred to as a critical mass, in order to expect changes. Gierycz suggests that further research in this field should focus on: (1) how best to prove the gender difference hypothesis beyond doubt, (2) how to take advantage of this difference in policy formulations, and (3) how best to ensure a gender balance in decisionmaking and conflict resolution at all levels.

Dan Smith argues that political strategies against gender inequality go astray if they rely on essentialist conceptions of femininity. Smith defines essentialism not as a theory or a philosophy, but as a mind-set that sees individual and social identity in terms of an unchanging inner core or essence, and which then explains people's views and behaviour by reference to their identity. His starting point is that discussing the impact of gender difference means thinking about a fundamental component of our individual and social identities. This makes a critical approach to essentialism necessary, because most people tend to discuss identity problems in essentialist terms, as if we each had a simple and unchanging identity. The more complex truth is that our identities are complex and changeable. Smith argues that, by appealing to simple notions of identity, essentialist strategies can be effective instruments of political mobilization, but their emphasis on perceptions of in-groups and out-groups makes them unreliable instruments for progressive movements. Moreover, he argues, since identity is volatile, the success of an appeal to one aspect of a complex identity is inherently ephemeral. Smith traces the assumptions and errors of essentialism. His conclusion is that we must acknowledge that reality is more complex, more interesting and more rewarding than the monochrome world presented by essentialist modes of thinking.

Inger Skjelsbæk discusses femininity, peace and war. On the basis of a series of oral testimonies she looks at women's reactions to and participation in three different conflict areas – El Salvador, Vietnam and former Yugoslavia. This study highlights three different social psychological constructions of femininity: victimized, liberated and traditional. These constructions were based on the ways in which the women responded to how the conflict was organized along gender lines; what men and women represented on a symbolic level in the conflict; and, finally, on the women's intra-personal experiences of themselves in the conflict. She concludes that one simply cannot claim that femininity is inherently peaceful. The responses the women convey in the research material are sometimes peaceful, sometimes not. However, this does not make an argument against including women in political decisionmaking on war/peace issues – it is simply a warning against one-dimensional expectations.

Michael Salla's chapter is a variation on Skjelsbæk's theme. He sets out to deconstruct the stereotypical dichotomy that men are war-oriented and women are peace-oriented. Salla suggests that a better avenue to examine the male/female versus war/peace distinctions is to look at how social power structures interact with these stereotypes. Using Foucault's conceptualization, Salla argues that power should not be explored merely in terms of the distinction between power *over* and power *to*; rather, we should focus on the mechanisms that underlie the various forms of power. According to Foucault, power does not become manifest only through agents and institutions: rather, it is embedded in social structures that define knowledge, identity and regimes of truth. These, in turn, manifest themselves in institutions and agents. From this view, Salla argues that altering the gender composition in political decisionmaking bodies will not necessarily lead to peaceful solutions to conflicts, because exercising power is not solely the province of agents. Examples of male pacifists like Martin Luther King, Mahatma Gandhi and Leo Tolstoy show that it is relational thinking which gives hopes for peaceful solutions to conflicts. Salla emphasizes that relational thinking comes in two forms: one guided by conscience and moral principles, and the other by attachment to human relations. It is especially with the latter that the outcome may be violent, because human relations are valued above all else.

Errol Miller's chapter provides a different conceptualization of gender and its relations to patriarchy. Using a constructionist perspective, Miller argues that gender cannot be understood in isolation from race and class. Like Salla, Miller argues against the assumption of female unity and male unity across cultures and races. White women may have more in common with white men than with black women. Miller problematizes the notion of patriarchy, and argues that this should be understood in terms of genealogy, gender and generation combined. He focuses on kinship relations in particular, holding that these cut across gender. Patriarchy must therefore be understood as the marginalization not only of the women in the kinship collective, but also as the marginalization of men in other collectives. The nation-state is a manifestation of patriarchy perceived in this way. Kinship groups struggle for power, and the ruling kinship is made up of both men and women. It would therefore be wrong to say that the patriarchal structure of the nation-state is based exclusively on gender. Against this background Miller rhetorically asks: why is it then that women are underrepresented in parliaments in liberal democracies, when they constitute at least half the voters? He outlines some possible approaches: (1) recognizing women's integrity and rationality, (2) recognizing that the marginalization and oppression of women in society is linked to other forms of marginalization and oppression; and (3) taking account of the complexities of gender relations.

Gender differences: practice

If more women are involved in political decisionmaking, will it make a difference? Will the political empowerment of women contribute to a more peaceful world? These are the questions addressed by *Drude Dahlerup*. She argues that women's participation in politics on equal terms with men must be regarded not only as a matter of justice, but also as a potential for change. Differences in values and interests among men and women may have significant implications for changes, although the path to change is by no means straightforward. Dahlerup warns against exaggerated expectations of women who enter into politics. It takes a critical mass for a minority to have influence on the ruling majority, she holds, basing this on organizational studies. Dahlerup's own studies of Scandinavian politics support this proposition. With more and more women involved in politics, there has, according to the Scandinavian politicians she has interviewed, been a whole range of changes – from the political climate, through what times are regarded as most appropriate for meetings, to specific items on the political agenda. Despite these effects, Dahlerup believes that a critical mass must be accompanied by critical acts that can change the position of the minority considerably and lead to further changes in policies. Such critical acts – for example, quotas for women, or developing a platform for change – can be carried out by both men and women.

The chapter by *Anuradha Chenoy* and *Achin Vanaik* presents a case study of the status of women in politics in South Asia. The authors set out to investigate whether altering the gender balance in those decisionmaking bodies concerned with peace, security and conflict resolution will create hopes for more peaceful solutions to conflicts. They argue that it is the doctrine of realism which dominated both interstate relations between India and Pakistan as well as internal conflicts in the region. The doctrine of realism presumes patriarchal structures, which again contribute to rigid conceptions of womanhood. It is true that there have been female prime ministers in four of the South Asian countries. These women have, however, been recruited to their positions as daughters, wives, or mistresses of famous political leaders. These women have not changed the political decisionmaking climate in their countries. Like Salla and Miller, Chenoy and Vanaik argue that the way to change the political climate is not simply to 'add women and stir'. What is needed is a new paradigm for international security, one based on the realization that gender is a constituent of political experience and is basic to the identity of the state and structure of the international system. Rethinking national security would then not only imply greater equity between the genders, but would also redefine the relationship between state and non-state actors, between state and society and therefore also between the structures of decisionmaking in these two areas.

Eva Irene Tuft argues for a complex gender approach in the conflict resolution process in Colombia. For the past 40 years, Colombia has suffered internal warfare. As the conflicts have become increasingly multifaceted so the responses must also be. Tuft emphasizes that including a gender dimension in the conflict resolution process can open the way to such a multidimensional approach. The consequences of the conflict are both direct and indirect; the latter category includes socio-economic, socio-political and socio-psychological consequences, which are different for the two genders. For instance, more men than women are victims of direct violence, whereas more women are victims of socio-economic violence. A gender analysis must not be based on a static understanding of gender differences. A gendered approach to conflict resolution would mean addressing gender-based and other forms of inequality and discrimination simultaneously. The participation of other actors than those directly involved in the armed conflict would be essential. Women's organizations, research institutes, and the international community need to put the theme of gender on their agendas.

Svetlana Slapsak provides a rich, historical and cultural background to contextualize women's responses to the Yugoslav war. Her argument is that during the conflict all those involved, including women's groups, turned to ancient myths and images of womanhood and manhood. Slapsak begins by explaining the portrayal of women in epic poetry and women's responses to this, followed by an outline of women's roles in the death cult. When the early feminist protests against the war began in Serbia, Croatia and Slovenia in 1990–91, the imagery of women's roles in the death cults was played upon. Peasant and urban women united in this effort. Slapsak also describes the status of feminism during the Communist regime and after. Feminism and dissidence were perceived and portrayed as parts of the same movement. She argues, however, that feminism was a more united movement than other social movements. Denunciation of rapes served to unite women's groups across republics. The fact that many women have defended mixed marriages, mixed origin and the like shows that the common explanation of the Yugoslav conflicts in terms of religion, history and collective memory simply is not correct for the female half of the population.

Kumudini Samuel points at the many paradoxes and complexities that characterize women's involvement in conflict resolution in Sri Lanka. On the one hand, the roles and positions of women in Sri Lanka have changed due to the prolonged conflict. The killing of men has created a growing group of female-headed households and families where the woman is the primary breadwinner. On the other hand, the traditional roles as wives and mothers are still strongly valued both by men and women. Samuel provides a brief background to the ethnic conflict and emphasizes its multidimensional characteristics. She then goes on to describe the many women's initiatives in connection with attempts at conflict resolution. Women's groups have worked closely with the human rights community and have linked women's human rights to human rights issues in general. She describes eight women's groups that have worked both independently and in cooperation with each other. The group 'Women for Peace' managed to organize a petition demanding negotiations; this in turn led to the first round of political negotiations between the government and the Tamil militant leadership in late 1984. In 1995, the 'Mothers and Daughters of Lanka' group and the 'Women for Peace' were in a predominantly Sinhalese delegation that visited the Northern province controlled by the Liberation Tigers of Tamil Eelam. This was the first such visit in four years. Both the nationalist groups and the women's movements have played on women's roles in their respective struggles. The Tamil nationalists addressed the woman question in the early 1980s as part of their nationalist agenda as a means of eliminating barriers to women's participation in the struggle. They also promised women equal status with men in the liberated society for which they were fighting. Some activist women's groups embraced this and suggested a new liberated femininity, whereas others, such as the 'Southern Mothers Front', played on their roles as mothers. Samuel emphasizes the important role women's groups have played and continue to play in conflict resolution efforts, as well as stressing the importance of having more women involved in political decisionmaking at all levels of society. She argues that even though a woman is president, there has been no general increase in the number of women in politics in Sri Lanka.

Conclusion

The various contributions in this volume clearly demonstrate the inherent complexities of integrating gender perspectives to our understandings of peace and conflict. Some critics might argue that the gender dimensions are so inherent that the gender impact can never be clearly assessed, simply because we cannot isolate its cause and effect. What the authors in this volume show, however, is that an awareness of gender differences can be an avenue for identifying new ways of thinking and dealing with questions of politics and peace, while they also warn against expecting unidimensional changes. Gender difference does not have a monolithic cause or outcome: it is one of several organizing principles of our social worlds. What we do claim is that analyses of peace and conflict which do not include gender reflections are simply incomplete. The contributions in this volume should be taken as examples of how to make studies of peace and conflict more comprehensive.

Notes

1 These estimates update those in Smith (1997b).
2 The much-cited estimate that over 90 per cent of war-deaths today are civilian is based on a confusion. When first given an authoritative airing (Ahlström, 1991), that estimate of casualties included wounded and refugees.
3 On Rwanda, see Sellström & Wohlgemuth (1996, pp. 50–52), Adelman & Suhrke (1996, p. 66); on Bosnia and Herzegovina, see Danner (1998).
4 'North Eastern Kenya: Rape of Somali Women Refugees', *Women's International Network News*, vol. 20, no. 2, Spring 1994 (based on a report by the Women's Rights Project of Africa Watch, Washington, DC).
5 'Burmese Muslims Fight Army Assault', *The Guardian*, 13 February 1992; see also UNHCR (1993, p. 70).
6 'Weary Muslims Weigh Costs of War and Peace', *The Guardian*, 31 August 1994.

1

Women, Peace and the United Nations:
Beyond Beijing

Dorota Gierycz

Introduction

Since the creation of the United Nations Commission on the Status of
Women (CSW) in 1947, elements of the issue 'women and peace' have
been part of its agenda. However, unlike such questions as the political
participation of women, or development, 'women and peace' was generally not considered a priority. That it has been retained on the
Commission's agenda has been due largely to the pressure of the Eastern
European countries. The Commission's approach to this issue has been
political rather than substantive: rather than dealing with women's perspectives, it has involved a projection of a wider political debate into what
was considered an intergovernmental women's forum. For example, discussion on the situation of Palestinian women living in the Occupied
Territories, and of women under apartheid – two standing items on the
agenda of the CSW – followed the traditional pattern of East–West confrontation over the 'Palestinian problem' and 'apartheid'. Women-specific
aspects of both matters, such as their roles in the daily survival of their
families and societies, or their contribution to peace efforts, remained
almost completely neglected until the late 1980s.

Consideration of the issue of 'women and peace' has also been affected
by the division of functions between different organs of the United Nations
and the various parts of the Secretariat servicing them. With peace and
security matters allocated to the political departments of the UN and to the
intergovernmental organs that they serve, many delegations did not see
sufficient grounds for discussing them within the context of social and
developmental departments, which is where the Division for the
Advancement of Women and its predecessor units have been situated since
1946. Thus, the repeated mandates given by the Commission on the Status
of Women in the area of 'women and peace' have been viewed by many
governments as redundant, demanded for purely political reasons.

One pertinent fact has often been overlooked: representation at the

Security Council and the First Committee of the General Assembly and the composition of the respective departments within the Secretariat servicing their activities have been almost exclusively male, at least at the decision-making levels. Likewise, the CSW and the Third Committee of the General Assembly constituted the only forum where women's perspectives and experiences in peace-related areas could have been articulated.

Evolution in approaches to gender analyses in the areas of peace and security

In Copenhagen and Nairobi

In the preparatory process for the Second and the Third World Conferences on Women in Copenhagen and Nairobi and during the Conferences themselves, government discussion on the subject continued to be shaped by the climate of the Cold War. It was characterized by a lack of clear focus on women's approaches to peace, security, disarmament, conflict resolution and their situation under occupation and apartheid. Those issues continued to serve as an extension of the political confrontation between East and West. In addition, in Copenhagen, in 1980, the debate focused on the emergency situations and the human rights violations in some countries/ territories such as Bolivia, Chile, El Salvador, Lebanon, Namibia and South Africa and their effects on women. In Nairobi, in 1985, the intergovernmental dialogue emphasized some themes, such as the role of women in education for peace, in peace research, in decisionmaking and in non-governmental activities related to peace, and took into consideration, at least to a certain extent, women's perspectives and experiences. Those themes were less politicized. The provisions of the Nairobi Forward-looking Strategies under the theme of Peace (paras 232–262) reflect the stage of consideration of those issues at the international level in the mid-1980s.[1]

Despite its limitations, the Conference in Nairobi was the first UN Conference, which included a number of feminist perspectives in its final document. The holistic definition of peace found in the Nairobi Forward-looking Strategies is a case in point. The Strategies, in paragraph 13 state that

> Peace includes not only the absence of war, violence and hostilities . . . but also the enjoyment of economic and social justice, equality and the entire range of human rights and fundamental freedoms within society . . . Peace is promoted by equality of the sexes, economic equality and the universal enjoyment of basic human rights and fundamental freedoms. Its enjoyment by all requires that women be enabled to exercise their right to participate on an equal footing with men in all spheres of the political, economic and social life of their countries, particularly in the decision-making process, while exercising their right to freedom of opinion, expression, information and association in the promotion of international peace and cooperation.[2]

It should also be noted that the Strategies placed the issue of violence against women under the heading of peace, thus emphasizing the link between all forms of violence, ranging from the personal violence to the violence of war and their implications for peace at all levels. The existence of this interdependence has been long denied by the intergovernmental fora. The adoption of the Strategies by consensus raised hope that the holistic approach to peace and its inextricable linkage to human rights, gender equality and the elimination of all forms of violence against women would become a part of discussions in all relevant bodies inside and outside of the UN system, thus influencing emerging policies. However, this was not the case. The only real step forward at the government level was a reluctant acceptance that these views should be further studied and developed within the context of the UN programmes dealing with women's issues. They were, however, broadly discussed by the interested non-governmental women's organizations and feminist scholars and increasingly put into practice by the women's movement.

At the end of the Cold War

In 1990, the first UN review and appraisal of the implementation of the Strategies[3] reflecting the views of governments identified several priority elements of the 'women and peace' theme, including the participation of women in decisionmaking and non-governmental activities related to peace, and education for peace. The approach to those issues was mainly focused on the collection of data on the level of women's representation in various decisionmaking bodies at the local, national and international levels and on their contribution to education for peace, mainly derived from women's traditional social roles as first educators. The reports prepared by the United Nations Division for the Advancement of Women for the Commission on the Status of Women on education for peace and on other aspects of the participation of women in decisionmaking, in parliaments, governments, trade unions, non-governmental organizations (NGOs) and in the civil service (in 1988, 1989 and 1990) followed that approach and reflected the state of the art to the degree limited by the availability of sex-disaggregated data. They also pointed to the existing obstacles and incentives to women's participation as well as to possible ways of strengthening women's contribution to those areas.[4]

In the early 1990s the topic of 'women and peace' was mainly discussed in the context of political participation of women, in particular in decisionmaking, which became one of the most visible aspects of the work of the Commission. Although the practical progress in this area remained very slow, there was a noticeable increase of interest in addressing this issue by both governments and NGOs. There was also growing recognition of the fact that the enormous gap between the *de jure* and *de facto* situation of women in decisionmaking – particularly in peace and security areas – had to be narrowed. Numerous government discussions, expert group meetings and publications began to reflect the view that there could be no progress in democratization, participatory governance and breakthroughs in peace, security and conflict resolution without the full and equal participation of women.[5]

On the eve of Beijing

Further discussion of what had been traditionally called 'women and peace' took place in the new political climate that arose from the end of the Cold War. The changes leading towards establishing democracy, market economies and improved cooperation between East and West, however, brought uneven results in terms of government interests in peace-related issues within the context of the Commission on the Status of Women and the work of the Division for the Advancement of Women. Some governments reduced their interest in 'women and peace' on the grounds that it was no longer politically valid. Others tried to explore it as a potential contribution to ongoing international dialogue. They began to pay more attention to newly emerging areas and women's roles, highlighting the link between the participation of women in all spheres of life as full citizens and the prospects of building new, democratic societies and fostering peace processes through more gender-balanced participation in conflict resolution and decisionmaking at the national and international levels.

With the attempts to establish and maintain peace in the future by international peace forces under the auspices of the UN, the new roles for women in such a force were addressed, first at non-governmental and later at the governmental level.[6] As it was envisaged that the role of an international peace force would go beyond the traditional military peacekeeping and would also encompass some new non-military and police responsibilities (peacemaking, negotiating peace settlements, supervision of elections), the question of the participation of women in such broad peacekeeping activities was brought to the discussion.[7] That, in turn, promoted questions on the participation of women in military and police forces at national and internal levels. These were given most attention by governments within the context of the second review and appraisal of the Nairobi Forward-looking Strategies in 1995.[8] Seventeen governments reported on this topic which, previously, had hardly ever been addressed seriously by governments.

The end of the Cold War was also accompanied by important changes in the focus of NGOs and feminist researchers. In the past, women's participation in non-governmental peace activities had mainly concentrated on organizing anti-nuclear or pro-disarmament demonstrations, promoting peace education and alternatives to a militarized society, and on avoiding or ending violence. In the new political climate increased attention and importance was attached to the participation of women in all aspects of peacekeeping, negotiation and peacemaking, including decisionmaking. Women have also addressed the implications for human rights of the paradoxical reality that women are excluded from those areas of decision-making, yet suffer the consequences of war. A more open political climate and the increasing recognition by governments of the need for the involvement of non-governmental organizations and other actors in civil society, including women's and feminist groups, in the government debate at the UN and elsewhere created a more conducive atmosphere for the incorporation of their ideas into the debates and documents. Governments devoted more attention to the issue of war-related violence against women and to the fact that in certain armed conflicts women were subjected to rape and forced prostitution as a 'weapon' to humiliate the adversary. The realization that women have rarely been involved in decisions on war and peace, but have always been victims, increased the interest of governments in the issue of women's participation in decisionmaking, in conflict resolution and in all stages of post-conflict reconciliation.

The visible role which women played in the United Nations Transition Assistance Group (UNTAG) in Namibia in 1989–90 further strengthened the argument that women could play a significant role in all stages of peace and security operations, in particular if they achieve a 'critical mass'. In the case of UNTAG, women constituted 60% of the professional staff recruited for the operation. Although the highest-level positions were occupied by men, five women served at the Director level (D-1/D-2) and women held three out of ten senior field posts as regional directors. They often performed non-traditional roles dealing with the local police, working in dangerous areas and pursuing dialogue between polarized groups.[9]

These new approaches were reflected in the work of the Division for the Advancement of Women in the preparatory process to the Fourth World Conference on Women in Beijing. In this period the Division which acted as the Secretariat of the Conference addressed women's roles in decision-making on peace, security, peacekeeping and conflict resolution. This was explained in the context of the human rights of women, women's citizenship and self-reliance. The Division also began to analyse the difference which women can make in the peace process if they act as a group. The focus of the analyses, however, started to shift from 'women' to 'gender' as the socially constructed roles played by women and men that are ascribed to them on the basis of their sex. Consequently, gender analysis emerged as an important methodology applied to studies on decisionmaking and conflict resolution prior to the Conference in Beijing and as a leitmotif of the 1995 Beijing Declaration and the Platform for Action.

On the platform for action and beyond

Among other matters, the Platform for Action addressed the issue of the participation of women in decisionmaking and in conflict resolution.[10] In addressing these areas, the Platform for Action emphasized that women's right to participate constitutes their basic human right as well as their right and responsibility as citizens. It stressed that women's active involvement in conflict resolution at all levels should replace the prevailing attitude to women as helpless victims, subject to humanitarian assistance. The Platform for Action also pointed to the need for mainstreaming a gender perspective throughout all critical areas.

While there was general understanding of what was meant by a gender perspective, no effort was made to articulate its concept and practical implications in detail in the period leading up to Beijing. Thus, translating the concept into practical action became particularly important in implementing the commitments of the Conference afterwards. As a starting point, in UN usage, gender was applied to the socially constructed roles played by women and men that are ascribed to them on the basis of their sex. Gender analysis is done in order to examine similarities and differences in roles and responsibilities between women and men without direct reference to biology, but rather to the behaviour patterns expected from women and men and their cultural reinforcement. These roles are usually specific to a given area and time. That is, since gender roles are contingent on the social and economic context, they can vary according to the specific context and can change over time.[11]

Gender analysis as part of the application of a gender perspective moves the analysis beyond a focus on women as an isolated group, and to the consideration of an issue and its relationship to men and women. Such an approach allows that advantages and disadvantages experienced by either group can be made visible, and for steps to be taken to address disadvantages with a view to preventing or eliminating and redressing them.[12] The next step towards defining and implementing the concept of mainstreaming a gender perspective was made by the UN Economic and Social Council. In its agreed conclusions 1997/2 of July 1997, the Council defined the mainstreaming of a gender perspective as the process of assessing the implications for women and men of any planned action, including legislation, policies or programmes, in all areas and at all levels and as a strategy for making women's as well as men's concerns and experiences an integral dimension of the design, implementation, monitoring and evaluation of policies and programmes in all political, economic and societal spheres so that women and men benefit equally and inequality is not perpetuated. The ultimate goal is to achieve gender equality.

The Council also spelled out the principles for mainstreaming a gender perspective in the UN system and made specific recommendations for the implementation of gender mainstreaming across all areas of activity. The Council also made it clear that gender difference should be diagnosed in all areas and an assumption of gender-neutrality should not be made; that the responsibility for translating gender mainstreaming into practice rests at the highest levels of decisionmaking; and that it requires systematic capacity-building measures, including the creation of accountability mechanisms, the provision of training for gender mainstreaming and the strengthening of the role of gender units and focal points in all UN entities.

The Secretary-General conveyed the agreed conclusions 1997/2 on gender mainstreaming to all heads of departments, funds, programmes and regional commissions and to the heads of specialized agencies and international trade and financial institutions. The Special Adviser on Gender Issues and the Advancement of Women, Ms Angela E.V. King holds follow-up sessions with senior managers and staff in various UN entities, including political departments.

It is premature to assess the impact of these decisions in the areas related to peace, security and conflict resolution. The first steps, however, have been made. The Department of Political Affairs organized gender-sensitivity training for its staff. Its main objective was to sensitize women and men in the department to the relevance of gender in their daily work. The Department of Peacekeeping Operations is undertaking the preparation of a long-term study on mainstreaming a gender perspective in multidimensional peacekeeping operations. The study should provide an opportunity to assess the impact of gender difference on the design, conduct and outcome of the selected peace and security operations. Its results should be applied to the future operations, so the positive gender-related aspects can be strengthened and the negative aspects diminished.

Participation in decisionmaking as a human right of women

The human rights dimension of the political participation of women, which had been part of UN consideration from the outset, became particularly visible in the preparatory process to the 1993 United Nations World Conference on Human Rights, held in Vienna. According to the established international human rights norms, every person, without discrimination, has the right to vote, to hold office and to perform public functions.[13] This norm also includes the equal right of women with men to participate in politics and decisionmaking at national and international levels, in accordance with the international standards of equality reflected in articles 7 and 8 of the Convention on the Elimination of All Forms of Discrimination against Women, the right which is most relevant to the participation of women in peace-related activities.[14] While recognized as a legal norm, there remains a wide gap between the *de jure* and *de facto* situation of women in particular in the area of decisionmaking, one of the widest among all areas of human rights.

Women have the right to vote and hold office in almost all countries of the world, except Kuwait (where a 1999 decision gives women the right to vote from 2003) and the United Arab Emirates. Despite this, relatively few women have been elected through the democratic process to national legislatures and even fewer have reached top executive posts or decisionmaking positions at national and international levels. In 1997, the average representation of women in parliaments (both houses combined) globally was 11.7%. It declined from 14.8% in 1988. There are some countries where women have had the right to vote for a long time, but there are still no women in parliament. Bhutan, the Comoros, Djibouti, Kiribati, Mauritania, Micronesia, Palau, Papua New Guinea, Saint Kitts–Nevis and Saint Lucia are cases in point. In Eastern Europe, with recent changes towards democratization and the introduction of free elections and of multi-party systems, there has been a sharp decline in the number of female parliamentarians over the previous record. Generally, female parliamentarians are concentrated in social, health and educational committees and commissions of parliaments. They are rarely members of the parliamentary bodies dealing with peace, defence and security (Inter-Parliamentary Union, 1995a, 1995b, 1996, 1997).

As regards women in government decisionmaking positions, they made up 6.8% of cabinet ministers worldwide in 1996 compared to 3.4% in 1987. They also remained heavily concentrated in such areas as social affairs and education, health, and women and family ministries (14%). Their presence was much lower in political areas (3.4%), including in such ministries as defence, interior or foreign affairs and the executive offices of heads of state and government (3.9%).[15]

In international organizations, whether governmental or non-governmental, women are also in the minority and are concentrated at the lower-level posts, in administrative positions. They are almost totally absent from organizations and structures directly involved in peace and security matters and peace negotiations. From both the perspective of women as citizens and from the perspective of those organizations claiming to be pluralistic and democratic, this situation is unacceptable. Even in the UN, which is expected to create a model for national public services, the participation of women is low: women hold 18.8% of senior posts (Director, Assistant Secretary-General, Under Secretary-General and Secretary-General).[16] Throughout the history of UN peacekeeping there have been only three women in charge of the UN missions: Margaret Anstee, Special Representative of the Secretary-General in Angola, 1992–93, Angela King, the Chief of Mission in South Africa and later Deputy Special Representative, 1992–94 and Elizabeth Rehn, Special Representative of the Secretary-General in Bosnia and Herzegovina, 1998–99. Although intergovernmental organizations are, to some extent, influenced in their personnel policies and appointments by Member States, they also enjoy some independence in hiring staff and experts for short-term technical and professional positions. These positions, which do not involve leadership or political functions, do not entail the political consent of governments. Not being bound by any particular cultural tradition, international organizations should be able to be more gender-balanced and equal opportunity employers. This is not the case. Thus, at the international level the conceptualization and implementation of international policies related to peace and security is carried out with very limited participation of women.

The human rights argument is also closely linked to the ongoing debate on democratization and the meaning and content of democracy (Gierycz, 1996). In this context questions are asked whether countries which drastically ignored women's right to participate could be called democratic and why, despite the decades of women's suffrage in almost all countries of the world, women did not use the vote as a tool and did not demand their equal share of power and participation in decisions.

The human rights dimension of democracy also encompasses the relation between majority rule and the protection of minorities, and those who are different in terms of race, ethnicity, colour, religion or sex, political, social and cultural affiliation, or due to disability, way of life and sexual orientation. History has demonstrated that the blind rule by the majority, even when democratically elected, can bring the most destructive and undemocratic results if the rights of those who differ from the majority are not protected; if their voices are not heard and their interests are not represented at the decisionmaking level. This aspect of democracy is particularly important for women, since all existing political structures have been historically created by men, and women are political newcomers constituting a minority within political elites.

A participatory aspect of democracy is also particularly important for the representation of group interests and equality between men and women. If political and cultural pluralism are perceived as assets, then the articulation of group interests and differences should be encouraged rather than suppressed. Thus, the reflection of a variety of group interests, and ideological and political perspectives at decisionmaking levels, serves as a legitimization for decisionmakers and indicates to what extent societies are democratic. The fact that women have specific interests and that their perspectives have not been reflected in mainstream political structures led to the recognition that those interests can best be represented by women themselves. Since societies are composed of both men and women, men and women should equally represent their interests at the decisionmaking levels. This interpretation contributed to the establishment of the Norwegian model, which requires 40–60% representation of each sex on public boards and commissions (Skjeie, 1991a, 1991b). A similar concept formed the basis for the notion of 'parity democracy' elaborated by the Council of Europe and for the 'Plan of Action of the Inter-Parliamentary Union to correct imbalances in the participation of men and women in political life' of the Inter-Parliamentary Union (1994).

Although the human rights approach to the participation of women retains its value, the discussion on power-sharing and participation in decisionmaking evolved further and was complemented by the argument of a 'difference', which women could make if they were represented in large enough numbers in the decisionmaking arena (constituting what has been termed a 'critical mass', estimated at a level of at least 30–35% in decisionmaking bodies) (Klein, 1946; Dahlerup, 1988a; UNDAW & PRIO, 1996). This theory has been further applied in analysing a qualitative difference which women's participation could bring to the peace process and conflict resolution.

Such an approach to gender analysis is most valid in relation to the peace, security and conflict resolution areas in implementing the Platform for Action and beyond.

Gender analysis: differences women can make

Historical roots of gender differences

Throughout history government structures, principles of governance and decisionmaking processes have been developed almost exclusively by men. Women have been confined to the 'private' sphere, mostly to domesticity. Therefore, the baseline for most contemporary patterns of governance, decisionmaking and related activities originates from the models created by men. Their implementation as public policy structures and *modus operandi* remain strongly 'gendered'. As political 'newcomers' women have had to adjust to existing structures and look for ways to include their interests and accommodate their working styles.

It is worth recalling that until the twentieth century, women for the most part were not considered citizens even in countries with strong traditions of democracy and participation. Women had no voting rights; they were denied the right to influence public matters and to enter into civil contracts. It was taken for granted that in most public, political and civil arenas women's interests were to be represented by men, who knew better what was appropriate for women, since men, historically, were accustomed to represent non-citizens: slaves, foreigners, minors, women and the disabled (Halvorsen, 1992).

The status of 'non-citizens' associated with women throughout history was reflected in all spheres of life, ranging from their lack of electoral rights and lack of access to public education, in particular to universities, to their limited civil capacity, for example in relation to inheritance, marriage or choice of domicile. Switzerland, France and the Scandinavian countries provide instances where some universities were opened to women in the nineteenth century, while others, like the Faculties of Law in Spain, Hungary and Bulgaria, admitted women only in 1930 (Halvorsen, 1992). Even today, in some parts of the world, women still do not enjoy full rights of citizenship. For example, in many countries with Islamic law, women are subject to male guardianship, which means that they are unable to exercise their civil rights without their guardians' consent. In many countries in Africa and Asia, women still can not inherit or own property on a level of equality with men (An-Na'im, 1995).

Despite the progress achieved towards equality in the second half of the twentieth century, in the areas of peace and security, even in societies which are considered to be democratic, the main decisions are made and implemented by relatively small, homogeneous groups. These groups operate to a great extent in secrecy and are composed almost exclusively of men who are mainly linked to military and industrial interests. Such groups promote concepts of peace, which they perceive as the absence of war, and of security, based on deterrence and military force, which have been developed throughout most of history by male political elites.

Even where there is increasing democratization and public participation, the possibility of directly influencing these areas by civil society remains limited. Thus, the members of civil society, including women's groups, try to exercise their influence through various activities at the non-governmental level: by actions in support of, or against, national or international peace-related policies or events; within the framework of peace research and education; as members of issue associations; and through many functions as conscientious citizens.

Since mainstream peace and security policies remain strongly 'gendered', women are concerned that they cannot influence them and that existing structures do not provide for the articulation of their interests and views. Thus, they have had to seek independent movements and activities which would allow them to present their viewpoints and to press their goals. The European Movement of Women against Nuclear Armament, Women for Peace, Strike for Peace, the Great Peace Journey or the American Peace Link are cases in point.

Military service is another area with strongly 'gendered' roles. In the majority of countries women are still excluded by law from combat and combat-related duties and men are obliged by law to undergo military service. Besides, many men and women think that the military is 'men's business'. The historical reservation of military roles to men is largely the result of social construction, separation between men's and women's roles and stereotypes of men as 'the protectors' and women as 'the protected' (Stiehm, 1983). What is often overlooked is that the military is an integral part of any political system. The military accounts for a certain proportion of public expenditure, constitutes an important employer and provides career opportunities and training which can lead to other than military careers. Since the military constitutes an important element of state order, decisionmaking and governance, all citizens, women and men, should be concerned about the kind of military that they have and decide for themselves whether they want to join it or not. By being outside the military women cannot be involved in the decisionmaking relating to the use of military forces, changes in military institutions and overall control of its performance.

Where women made a difference

In accordance with the theory of 'critical mass' (Hernes, 1984; Boman, 1987) in order to bring substantive differences into decisionmaking in terms of content and priorities, as well as style and working climate, participation must be at least 30–35%. Such a minimum level of participation would enable a minority to influence the culture of the group and the outcome of discussion.

At the national level

Although the evidence that women's participation makes a difference in terms of political agendas, managerial style, attitudes to conflict prevention, monitoring and negotiation is anecdotal, there are many examples to be cited. Women have achieved a critical mass at the national decisionmaking level only in a few countries, particularly the Nordic countries. The experience shows that when women in those countries acted in solidarity they were able to make a visible impact on political decisions and political culture. For example, they have changed people's attitudes towards female leaders and they have placed on public agendas such issues as social support services, equality, health care, women's reproductive rights and protection against violence (Dahlerup, 1988a).

According to public opinion polls, surveys and other sources of information in some countries in North America and Western Europe, women are less militaristic, more concerned with the preservation of peace and more opposed to any form of increased militarization or nuclear energy compared with men. Women more strongly supported measures to protect the environment, to help the economically disadvantaged and to improve race relations.[17]

The same sources pointed to women's different political style which has been noted among female politicians at the local level. Whenever women have joined the decisionmaking bodies in sufficient numbers they have created a more collaborative atmosphere, characterized by mutual respect, independent of prevailing political differences. Women seek consensus or acceptance rather than a win-or-lose solution. They are more focused on solving than on discussing problems. The experiences of local councils in Stockholm, in New Jersey and in south London are cases in point. All those characteristics would be most useful if applied to conflict resolution and peace processes at the national and international levels (Boman, 1987; Wills, 1991).

Women in developing countries have also influenced public agendas. For example, women's groups in Mexico and Brazil have campaigned against rape and domestic violence and succeeded in achieving important changes in the legislation and in the functioning of the judiciary and police, making them more gender sensitive. In India, women organized the Chipko movement to secure a ban on felling trees, to replant the available land and to manage it properly. In Kenya, the Green Belt Movement focused on planting trees, contributing significantly to the reduction of deforestation. Beside their impact on the improvement of the environment, both movements constituted a challenge to the traditional male-dominated power relations at the family and community levels. They also placed women in the centre of the ongoing discussion on environment-related policies, decisionmaking and the human rights of women.

Women from both parts of Cyprus organized a number of joint meetings and seminars aimed at the development of dialogue instead of hostility at the community level and promotion of understanding despite the division of the island. In peaceful efforts to overthrow the dictatorship of Ferdinand Marcos, women in the Philippines, including nuns, stopped tanks deployed to attack rebelling troops.

The main points on the present governmental disarmament agenda – full test ban treaty on nuclear weapons; full elimination of chemical and biological weapons; zero option for nuclear weapons – which have been long advocated by the women's movement, correspond closely to the recent women's disarmament agendas which include: a full ban on nuclear weapons and the destruction of nuclear weapons arsenals; the ratification of all treaties related to the elimination of nuclear weapons; a reduction of other weapons worldwide; the reallocation of resources from military to peaceful purposes; peaceful conflict resolution; education for peace, reduction of violence and protection of the human rights of women.[18]

The press coverage of the 1996 presidential elections in the USA showed a gender difference clearly indicating that women preferred the Democratic Party of the incumbent president. Comparing the platforms of both parties, those results confirmed the earlier findings that women in general and women legislators lean more towards education, human welfare, the environment, the right to choice, including abortion rights, and cuts in massive military spending.

There is also evidence that women's votes in the 1995 elections in Poland were decisive for the victory of a social democratic presidential candidate, who declared himself on the human rights of women, for the right to choose and for the separation of state and church. Women also appeared to have retained the Austrian Social Democratic Party as the strongest partner in the ruling coalition in the last elections because they feared the increasing influence of a very conservative group.

The organization 'Soldiers' Mothers of Russia' against the war in Chechnya, 1995–6, and against corruption and violence in the Russian army has gained broad recognition. Its actions included travelling to Grozny and demanding the return of their sons, reaching out to Chechen mothers to share their concerns and sorrow and negotiating the release of military men held by Chechen forces. Although the organization was based on a conservative concept of 'motherhood', its courage and opposition to authoritarian rule gained broad international support, in particular because the conflict in Chechnya at that time had not been subjected to public criticism in Russia except by small groups. The organization contributed largely to bringing the violence in the Chechen conflict to the public agenda, especially during the 1996 presidential elections in the Russian Federation. This probably influenced the outcome of the Russian elections and strengthened the position of General Lebed. He surprised many by performing well in the first round of the presidential elections, after he had taken similar positions.

Women's parties which focus specifically on attracting the female electorate were recently created in Russia, Lithuania, Ireland and South Africa. It is premature, however, to assess their popularity and impact. The only women's party with a longer tradition and a more visible influence on policy-making is the Women's Party of Iceland.

At the international level

The issue of gender difference with respect to peacekeeping was discussed at the UN in connection with the Secretary-General's Agenda for Peace.[19] A critique of the Agenda was undertaken from a gender perspective. It led to the conclusions that lasting peace could not be achieved through arms build-up and military enforcement without respect for and the application of democratic principles, including the full participation of women in all stages of peace negotiations, peacemaking and peace-building. The need for the prevention of hostilities, the application of peace settlement procedures of Chapter VI of the UN Charter and peace-building linked to sustainable development was emphasized rather than the reliance on military peacekeeping based on Chapter VII of the Charter.

The preliminary research on UN peace and security missions also pointed out that those missions which had a more gender-balanced composition, in terms of their management and staff (like Guatemala, Namibia and South Africa), appeared to have been more effective than missions where few women were involved. Further, 'focus group' discussions with male and female participants in some of these missions helped to identify the following specific women's contributions to peacekeeping.[20]

- When a critical mass of women in UN peacekeeping missions exists, local women in the host country are mobilized through a positive demonstration effect. For example, the success of local women and NGOs in being able to defuse violence in South Africa probably contributed to the conclusion that UN military personnel were not needed in preparing for elections.
- The participation of women in UN peacekeeping missions focuses attention on the need for an up-to-date code of conduct for UN peacekeepers, particularly in the areas of human rights, gender issues and sexual harassment.
- In performing their tasks, women were perceived to be compassionate, less threatening or insistent on status, unwilling to opt for force over

reconciliation, willing to listen and learn, and to contribute to an environment of stability and morality which fostered the peace process.

- The presence of women seems to foster confidence and trust among the local population, a critical element in any peacekeeping mission.
- Women are successful as negotiators, active in proposing constructive solutions, action-oriented and often willing to take innovative approaches to establish a dialogue between polarized groups. They sometimes use unorthodox means such as singing to defuse potentially violent situations. Women's participation helps to break down traditional views and stereotypes of women in countries and local communities where they serve among peacekeepers.
- Contrary to some expectations, many women willingly accept the challenges of working in all types of situation including in dangerous and isolated areas.
- Civilian women peacekeepers work effectively with both military and police personnel.

These were all indications that a major factor in the success of the above missions was the inclusion of different perspectives and approaches by men and women to conflict resolution.

Another issue which was analysed from a gender perspective at the United Nations was a culture of peace.[21] The discussion focused on the social transformation which was necessary to depart successfully from the prevailing culture of violence and to build a new culture of peace. It also emphasized the critical role which women could play in this process due to their experiences of personal and structural violence resulting from their historically vulnerable and subordinated roles.

Beyond Beijing

At the present state of knowledge and discussion on 'gender difference' and its applicability at the policy-making levels the following queries can be raised. Gender analyses should not be equated with 'women's issues' or limited to women's perspectives only. Men's perspectives should be given equal attention and they should be looked into together. Analysing men's perspectives would allow reflection of differences in views among their various groups, often along the lines of men in the position of authority and men in alternative non-governmental movements. That in turn would help to identify potential allies in pursuing certain goals. For example, in some countries, the main division of opinions on such issues as ongoing armed conflict, human rights of women or abortion is not between women and men, but rather follows lines of religious belief, life philosophy, political orientation or economic status.

Both women's and men's perspectives and experiences should be taken into consideration, keeping in mind that neither women nor men constitute a homogeneous group – a fact which has often been over-looked in the past. Looking into a diversity of views within each group may provide better clues for understanding why, for example, women do not necessarily vote for women; what the divisions among the female electorate are and which issues bring women together beyond party affil-iations and ideological differences.

Gender perspectives are not static, but changing. Considering the pace of change in our times due to the impact of modern technologies, mass com-munication and globalization, the changing nature of once-established gender perspectives should be systematically examined.

Recognition of gender differences as a socially constructed set of per-spectives, formed in the past, should not lead to the stereotyping of female and male behaviour. It is becoming more and more apparent that 'mas-culinities' and 'femininities' are not necessarily representative for men and women respectively. As Robert Connell (1995) indicates, the range of char-acteristics identified as typically male is broad and not necessarily representative for each and every male, as some of them are adopted by females, and vice versa.

Trying to apply the theory of 'gender difference' in practice, in the areas of conflict resolution and monitoring, in decisionmaking and in peace and security dialogue, it would be essential to analyse which of the existing gender attitudes of decisionmakers, developed by men through-out the ages, enabling them to exercise governance and power and to make major decisions at the national and international levels, constitute obstacles to more innovative and constructive approaches in these areas. For example, it could be investigated to what extent the dissociation of military from civilian lives and lack of understanding of 'daily preoccu-pations' by full-time politicians are impediments to their abilities of understanding, envisioning and projecting the requirements for lasting peace; to what degree, in some long-running military confrontations, does the separation of gender roles prevent the leaders from going beyond a ceasefire, to achieving lasting peace, as this cannot be done without the involvement of civil society, most of whom are women. Further research may also be needed to focus on women's attitudes in monitoring and negotiating conflicts, in decisionmaking and crises man-agement which, if included in policy formulation and implementation, would make them different; and the extent to which the difference that the presence of a 'critical mass' of women has made in some instances at the grassroots level can be applied at the policy level. Thus, further research agendas can focus on:

- how best to prove the gender difference hypothesis beyond doubt;
- how to take advantage of this difference in policy formulation by gov-ernments, intergovernmental and non-governmental organizations, research institutes and professional associations, in particular in the areas of peace, security and conflict resolution;

- how best to ensure gender-balance in decisionmaking and conflict resolution at all levels within a realistic, but the shortest possible, timeframe.

Notes

1   United Nations, 1993b. *The Nairobi Forward-looking Strategies for the Advancement of Women*, DPI/926-41761, September 1993, p. 8. New York: United Nations.

2   Ibid.

3   Report of the Secretary-General: *Progress at the National, Regional and International Levels in the Implementation of the Nairobi Forward-looking Strategies for the Advancement of Women*, E/CN.6/1990/5. New York: United Nations, 1989b.

4   Reports of the Secretary-General: *Access to Information and Education for Peace*, E/CN.6/1988/5, 29 December 1987; *Full Participation of Women in the Construction of Their Countries and in the Creation of Just Social and Political Systems*, E/CN.6/1989/7, 20 January 1989; *Equality in Political Participation and Decision-making*, E/CN.6/1990/2, 13 December 1989. New York: United Nations.

5   Reports of the Secretary-General: *Equal Participation in All Efforts to Promote International Cooperation, Peace and Disarmament*, E/CN.6/1992/10, 12 December 1991; *Women and the Peace Process*, E/CN.6/1993/4, 28 December 1992. New York: United Nations.

6   United nations, 1995a. *Looking Back, Moving Forward: Second Review and Appraisal of the Implementation of the Nairobi Forward-looking Strategies for the Advancement of Women*, E.95.IV. New York: United Nations.

7   Boutros-Ghali, Boutros, 1995. *An Agenda for Peace* (DPI/1623/PKO) (second edition). New York: United Nations Department of Public Information.

8   *Looking Back, Moving Forward* (see note 6).

9   United Nations, 1995d. *Peace: Women in International Decision-making*, Report of the Secretary-General, Economic and Social Council, E/CN.6/1995/12, para. 27; United Nations/Department for Policy Coordination and Sustainable Development/Division for the Advancement of Women, 1995. *Women 2000: The Role of Women in United Nations Peace-keeping*, p. 7. Vienna: United Nations/Centre for Social Development and Humanitarian Affairs/Branch for the Advancement of Women.

10   The critical areas of concern G. Women in power and decisionmaking, and E. Women and armed conflict, respectively; in United Nations, 1996a. *The Beijing Declaration and the Platform for Action*, Fourth World Conference on Women, Beijing, China, 4–15 September 1995, DPI/1766/Wom. New York: United Nations, Department of Public Information.

11   United Nations, 1996e. *Implementation of the Outcome of the Fourth World Conference on Women*. Report of the Secretary-General, A/51/322. New York: United Nations.

12   Ibid.

13   See, *inter alia*, the provisions of the 'Universal Declaration on the Human Rights' (United Nations, 1948) and the 'International Covenant on Civil and Political Rights' (United Nations, 1966), both in Centre for Human Rights. Geneva, ed., 1993. *Human Rights: A Compilation of International Instruments*, vol. 1, parts 1 & 2, ST/HR/1/Rev.4, pp. 2 and 30. New York: United Nations.

14   United Nations, 1996d. *Convention on the Elimination of All Forms of Discrimination against Women*. New York: United Nations, Department of Public Information.

15 Unpublished database compiled by the UN DAW; see also United Nations Centre for Social Development and Humanitarian Affairs, 1992. *Women in Politics and Decision-making in the Late Twentieth Century*. Dordrecht: Martinus Nijhoff, and 'Power in influence' in United Nations, 1995e. *The World's Women 1995: Trends and Statistics*, E.95.XVII.2. New York: United Nations.

16 It reflects the percentage of women at D-2 and higher level posts, subject to geographical distribution, which comprise: D-2, Director; ASG, Assistant-Secretary-General; USG, Under-Secretary-General and SG, Secretary-General (as of 31 March 1999).

17 United Nations, 1992. Equal Participation in All Efforts to Promote International Cooperation, Peace and Disarmament. Report of the Secretary-General, E/CN.6/1992/10, 12 December 1991. New York: United Nations; Virginia Wills, 1991. 'Public Life: Women Make a Difference', Expert Group Meeting on the Role of Women in Public Life, Vienna, 21–24 May. EGM/RWPL/1991/WP.1/Rev.1.

18 Those priorities were also reflected during the discussions of the 1994 and 1995 Expert Group Meetings organized by DAW in New York and DAW/UNESCO in Manila respectively (see notes 19 and 20 below).

19 It was discussed at the Expert Group Meeting on 'Gender and the Agenda for Peace' organized by the United Nations Division for the Advancement of Women, 5–9 December 1994, New York, and during the preparatory process to the meeting involving a series of consultations with women and men who participated in peacekeeping missions. See United Nations Division for the Advancement of Women, 1994. *Gender and the Agenda for Peace*, GAP/1994/WP.6.

20 Report of the Secretary-General: UN DAW, 1994. *Gender and the Agenda for Peace*, GAP/1994/1 (see note 19); United Nations, 1995c. *Participation of Women in Political Life and Decision-Making*, E/CN.6/1995/12; *Women 2000: The Role of Women in the United Nations Peace-keeping*, no. 1, December 1995.

21 It was discussed in the context of the Expert Group Meeting on 'Women's Contribution to a Culture of Peace' organized by UNESCO and DAW, 25–28 April 1995, in Manila.

2
The Problem of Essentialism

The appeal of essentialism

How are people persuaded to support a political position, a movement, a programme, a candidate? Among a variety of possible political and communicative strategies, one that has proven effective is to appeal to a common identity. To take two examples from very different places in the political spectrum, consider first a remark by US Senator Robert Dole, part of his closing statement in his first debate with President Bill Clinton during the 1996 US presidential election campaign. Summing up himself and his candidacy, he said, 'I know who I am and I know where I'm from'.[1] Standing opposite the US President often denigrated as 'Slick Willy', this was a shrewd appeal to conservative, homespun, white American values. Dole's reference to his identity and origins was intended to offer the viewers reassurance that, if he knew himself, they could trust him and know what and how he thought. From a more radical point on the political spectrum, consider this evocation by the Australian anti-nuclear campaigner Helen Caldicott (War Resisters' League, 1981): 'I appeal especially to the women . . . because we understand the genesis of life.' The reason she adduced for this special understanding was that 'Our bodies are built to nurture life.' Perhaps most telling about this appeal is not that Helen Caldicott made it, but that a major pacifist movement was so struck by it as to immortalize it in their calendar.

The strategy underlying statements of this kind is to mobilize people on the basis of who they are, and the views and preferences they are assumed to hold because of who they are. It is an appeal that aims to circumvent the intellect and touch not simply the audience's emotions but their very identity, their sense of who are. The appeal is to the essence of the target audience, based on a clear sense of what that essence is. The name for the strategy, and for the philosophy of politics and the perspective on people that lie behind it, is essentialism. It has proven capable of mobilizing large numbers of people in movements and campaigns for a wide variety of objectives – among them peace and disarmament, justice for oppressed groups, and civil and political rights. Nonetheless, this chapter will argue that, for political movements and campaigns seeking these goals, essentialism is ultimately unhelpful and destructive.

The unavoidable encounter

An encounter with essentialism is unavoidable in any discussion of the impact of gender difference in political decisionmaking and in conflict resolution. The reason is that discussing gender in politics means thinking about a fundamental component of our individual and social identities. The way that most of us, most of the time, approach such discussions is shaped strongly by essentialist ways of thinking. They are a common means of cognition, of organizing and rationalizing our experience of our social worlds. They are not the result of scholarly research; rather, they both form and draw on what people often call 'common sense'. We tend to group people by, for example, their race, nation, ethnicity, religious belief, gender, sexual preference or social class. And then we often generalize about the views and behaviour of the people in each group. We may see one group as essentially untrustworthy and mean, while another is thought to be hard-working and noble. One group may be characterized as bad drivers and poor financial managers, while another is regarded as mechanically adept and well suited for managerial positions. One group may be deemed better at concrete thought, another at abstraction. One group may be regarded as inherently competitive and prone to conflict, while another is inherently peaceful. Such sweeping generalizations are an ordinary part of the way in which we commonly organize our knowledge and understanding of our social environment. They are also the stuff of essentialism.

Though the discussion of essentialism is an important part of thinking about the impact of gender difference, it is not straightforward. As an object of discussion, essentialism has many of the features of a wet bar of soap: it seems to get all over the place but is often hard to take hold of firmly. Its assumptions have lain behind a great deal of ethnographic research. As an approach to studying ethnic difference, it has long been challenged and more or less dismissed (Atkinson & Hammersley, 1994), though it was the dominant mode of ethnography in the former USSR and remains influential in that region (Tishkov, 1997, pp. 1–7). Essentialism also rears its head in the study of psychology. Critics of Freudian theories and some other approaches have accused them of being reductive and essentialist. The criticism is that some psychoanalytic theories treat differences between men and women as innate and derived from sexual sources, when they are explained as well or better by reference to social position and power (Lippa, 1990, pp. 365–368).

Despite these and other academic uses of essentialism, it is not an across-the-board theory, nor is it a single and coherent worldview. Essentialist views in one field do not necessarily entail or imply essentialist views in another. This is what makes it hard to grasp. It is not so much a theory or a philosophy as a largely unrecognized mind-set. It has not generated a coherent body of scholarly literature scholarship to which one can refer in order to derive definitions. Thus, while essentialist arguments and prejudices permeate political discourse and have to be discussed, doing so risks giving them a coherence they lack, ascribing to them a misleading consistency and a logic.

If, despite those reservations, an attempt is made to characterize essentialism and its discursive function, it must be seen as a mind-set that claims to recognize the unchanging essence of individual and social identity, and which then connects views and behaviour to identity. It reduces the diversity of a society or a population to one or at most two criteria (usually nationality and gender), which come to be seen not only as the definitive components of that group's make-up and identity, but also as unavoidable and given by nature (Calhoun, 1997, p. 18). The alternative view is, in social science terminology, normally known as 'constructivist'.[2] It differs from essentialism in three main ways. First, constructivism argues that the way that people are is not given by nature but is constructed through social, economic, cultural, historical and political factors. Secondly, whereas essentialism views people as unchanging, constructivism views people as always changeable, if not actually always changing. And, thirdly, where essentialism views people's identity in terms of one or two dimensions, constructivism points to the multiplicity of individual and social identities we bear.

One way of understanding the argument about essentialism is by looking at the classic debate about 'nature' and 'nurture', which concerns the degree to which we are shaped by innate characteristics or by learned ones. Many people understand this debate in commonsense terms, in which a universal human nature has a cultural overlay that accounts for the differences between genders, races, ethnic groups, etc. This view can be related to 'trait theories' of personality in social psychology – theories that identify innate personality traits in individuals, but see behaviour as determined by the interplay between these traits and the situations in which people find themselves (Lippa, 1990, pp. 172–179). The distinction between an ontological core and its cultural patina is hard to sustain, in part because it is hard to know of what that core consists. One argument is that the evidence of pre-human history shows that culture was not 'added on, so to speak, to a finished or virtually finished (human) animal', but was a central determinant in the production of the human animal (Geertz, 1973, p. 47). This view – '[T]here is no such thing as a human nature independent of culture' (ibid.) – could be taken to be the bedrock position of constructivism. We are what we have learned to be, in the broadest sense of the word 'learned'. What culture consists of and how the term is to be understood are, however, a great deal less clear than this bedrock contention.

The reason that essentialism is worth engaging with lies in its stress on unambiguous group identity and group loyalty. Not itself a theory, essentialism offers a variety of theories. Each of them proposes that a given identity is clear and unchanging and its roots are primordial. Essentialism is therefore characterized by exaggerated claims about the stability and clarity of individual and social identities and their meaning. Denying the possibility of ambiguity or change in identity, it projects supposedly timeless and unambiguous conceptions of identity. By contrast, reconciliation and the creation of peace out of conflict, or of justice out of unjust situations, or of equality where there was inequality, depend on people changing. Thus, as the basis of political strategies for peace, justice and equality, essentialism is unreliable. Even as a means of political mobilization it can cut two ways. For example, emphasizing the idea that women are mothers may help get some women out to a demonstration to close a military base, while it may equally well persuade larger numbers that their true role is to stay at home. Underlying its flaws as the basis of a political strategy for justice, peace and equality are inaccurate assumptions about people, identity and society.

Politics and identity

Recent years have seen a major expansion in the literature on the relationship between identity and politics. The focus in political science on actors' interests is now balanced – and sometimes, misleadingly, altogether replaced – by a recognition that social and political struggles are not fought out purely over questions of interests. Who people are, as well as what they stand for, lies at the heart of the major political and social movements of the past two centuries (Calhoun, 1991). It has thus become important in the social sciences to explore previously disdained problems, not least the linkages between personal and collective (or social) identity, and between identity and action. Drawing on scholars such as Horowitz (1985) and Gurr (1995), both peace research and security studies have increasingly emphasized the large number of armed conflicts in which the division between opponents is to a significant degree defined by ethnic difference, or other types of difference in identity. At a more grandiose level, Huntington (1993, 1997) has won a great deal of attention with his thesis that future conflicts will be shaped by a clash between the world's great civilizations. The thesis is, however, based on a weak foundation made up of sweeping generalizations.[3] Its flaws point up the drawbacks of focusing on differences of identity at the expense of other salient kinds of difference and other important factors that lead to violent conflict. To understand the onset of violent conflict – and equally to understand other important social processes – it is necessary to avoid making a fetish out of identity, interest or any other single dimension. The task is to incorporate all the different strands into an explanation of how people and social forces are mobilized;

part of this task is to understand how the process of mobilization plays on people's sense of identity (D. Smith, 1997a, pp. 197–200).

Individual identity is not fixed but is constructed and reconstructed in a narrative of 'I' that is modified continually, if each time only marginally (Giddens, 1991). People are not 'the kind of unitary rational being that liberal humanists once convinced most of us were' (Davies, 1990, p. 501). Individual identity is ever shifting, and highly situational. As individuals, we have a repertoire of identities we can and do call on in different situations. The choice between the various possibilities may be more or less conscious (Hogg & Abrams, 1988, p. 24). Some choices may be dramatic and obvious – becoming a parent, for example. Others are relatively modest, expressed in decisions about clothes, hair, cosmetics. Some people switch accents depending on the social situation they are in. Choice of conversational style, for example, whether and how much to use profanities and choice of jokes, are also ways of making marginal adaptations in our outward identity. These adaptations may be made in order to fit into a particular social occasion or group, or in order to stand out from it. They could be made for reasons as varied as avoiding embarrassment or securing one's career. Over time, selection within our repertoire of identities shows a bias in one direction or another, and the repertoire itself changes. Some options are lost, others enter the repertoire. Over time, as we know from our knowledge of our long-term friends and from looking back over our own lives, small changes cumulate into transformation.

Identity politics has been justly criticized for making individual identity the dominant factor in politics.[4] As a form of political calculation, it means that 'What is to be done is replaced by who am I?' (Bourne, 1987, p. 1). People are mobilized more for who they are than for what they believe in. But the 'I' that is called upon is the 'I' that is part of an 'us'. In other words, identity politics appeals to that part of individual identity that is shared in a collective identity.

The question to ask about this kind of politics is, 'Which collective identity?' It is a question that is never asked in the process of political mobilization on the basis of identity; indeed, the question is often actively suppressed, sometimes violently. The idea that individuals share in more than one collective identity is inconvenient for a political strategy based on mobilizing just one collective identity. Yet it is by no means a new insight to acknowledge that collective, or social, identity is multiple and that the different identities overlap (Smith & Østerud, 1995). We each have a composite social identity constructed through a combination of levels (for example, nationality, class, gender, faith, other aspects of worldview such as political allegiance, profession, sexual orientation). On each level, there is a variety of categories: for example, two genders (some say more), many professions, a handful of social classes, many hundreds of ethnic groups, numerous religions and variants of each, a great variety of political causes to support, over 200 states, thousands of cities and regions, five continents (sometimes counted as six, occasionally as seven) and one world. No level of identity is exclusive of another but, on each level, each category is in principle exclusive. Thus, an individual might be Norwegian (but could not also be Swedish), and therefore Scandinavian (but not also from the Mediterranean), from Tromsø (but not also Bergen), white (but not also black), middle class (but not also working class), Catholic (but not also Hindu or Shinto) and socialist (but not also conservative).

It is important to underscore the reservation that each category of identity is *in principle* exclusive of any other. Increased mobility and migration have increased the number of multicultural societies, and thus the number of individuals with multiple categories of social identity. A Norwegian citizen of Turkish parentage could justifiably claim to be Scandinavian or Mediterranean depending on the circumstances. Children of marriages between people of more than just one racial, ethnic or national group can also have access to either one of their parents' racial, ethnic or national identities – and sometimes to a third or fourth one. The child of a marriage between an English person and a Scot could claim to be English, Scottish, Anglo-Scottish or British. If the child later emigrated, a range of further hyphenated identities would be possible. Access to a range of identity categories may, depending on the case, be a privilege, an irrelevance, or a source of oppression. During 1992 and 1993 in Bosnia and Herzegovina, for example, the decision to opt for either Serb or Muslim identity was forced upon people at gunpoint. Depending on their decision, they were either killed or had to prove their allegiance to their identity-decision by killing another.

The way that identity politics can take on such a vicious and directly personal nature opens the way to noting another of its important features. Each category of identity can have a variety of meanings. Over time, these may be volatile and often contested. What it means to be a man, or a woman, or a Briton, or an American will differ from time to time and place to place, and even from person to person. Moreover, the salience of each level of identity is also volatile and contestable (Hogg & Abrams, 1988, p. 26). The degree to which a Jewish, British, heterosexual woman feels that her core identity resides in her Jewishness, Britishness, sexual orientation, gender or profession will vary with circumstance. It could be, for example, that an attack on one component of her composite identity could make her feel that that is the key component. Sexist behaviour by a male boss towards a female colleague may lead her to respond with a feeling of women's solidarity. But if the boss is Jewish and the woman under attack responds with an anti-Semitic insult, the observer's response is likely to be more ambivalent.

Part of the process of identity politics is a battle to assert the salience and meaning of a given identity. One form this can take is an effort by contending political groups to summon support on the basis of claims that the members of this or that collective identity should all stand together. This is the appeal of patriotism in time of war. It is the appeal of revolutionaries in time of crisis. It is the appeal of nationalists in the battle for independence, and the appeal of nationalists too in a time of war and ethnic cleansing.

The battle over the salience and meaning of an identity also takes the form of attempting to influence behaviour. Conservative political ideology often includes an effort to assert that the role of women is to remain in the home and look after the family. The targets of this effort are both men and women. There are places where women who attempt to defy such restrictions on their freedom and behaviour are directly punished – in Afghanistan under Taliban rule, for example. There are also cases when the attempt is made directly to reward women who accept the restrictions – in Norway since 1998, for example.[5] But whether backed by open incentive or punishment, or simply by the indirect pressure of social norms, the effort to get women to stay at home is an effort to get both women and men to accept a definition of the 'proper' and 'essential' nature of each gender.

It is in the nature of political mobilization that the arbitrary nature of an appeal to identity cannot be acknowledged. Thus, the political insistence that one category of identity has the highest salience and a particular meaning is accompanied by a denial that there is any real choice in the matter. To be Serb is, in the mythology of Serbian ethno-nationalism, to be one kind of person with one kind of experience and one kind of view. To be a woman is, in conservative gender politics, to be unhappy except as a homemaker. But it is pure myth to think that women's place is naturally in the home. If that were the case, it would not be possible to explain why so many women have laboured in the fields over so many centuries. It would not be possible to explain why women make politicians and government ministers who are as competent (and sometimes as incompetent), as democratic and authoritative (and sometimes as dictatorial and authoritarian) as any man. Indeed, people who make essentialist generalizations about women's role are usually unable not just to explain but even to acknowledge the diversity of women's experiences and abilities.

Identity as a norm

When the issue of identity is raised, the commonsense way of understanding it – our own identity and that of others – is to begin by thinking of it in the singular: the appropriate question seems to be 'What is my identity?' rather than 'What are my identities?' The latter question would, for most people in ordinary conversation, imply the possibility of aliases, fraud, lies and disguise. Because of this, the ordinary way to think of identity is in terms of 'an essential authentic core', an 'I' that is clearly opposed to a 'not-I' (Minh-ha, 1997, p. 415), and thus, by extension, a core that is part of an 'us' that is clearly opposed to a 'not-us'. At any time we may regard any component of our composite identities as 'the real us', the core person, and at some other time, some other component is privileged in that way.

This core is not real, yet it is powerful and appealing, a 'mythical norm' lurking 'somewhere, on the edge of consciousness' (Lord, 1997, p. 375). Seen in this light, identity is not simply a question of who we are, but of who we ought to be. The mythical core is normative, a pressure upon each of us to conform to what we suppose we ought to be as men or women, as members of one nation or another, or along any other single dimension out of the many that make us who we are. Thus, when a politician berating modern society for a decline in traditional family values asserts that what women really want is the role of housewife and mother, the argument is not simply descriptive. By asserting this supposed reality, an appeal is launched at those women who do not want that role, or who want something more, to change their wishes and their needs. And the assertion contains, only half-hidden, the further claim that those women who should change their needs and wishes are not truly women unless they do make that change.

Identities in flux

Two things make essentialist politics effective. The first is that we tend to think of identity in a unitary rather than a composite way. The second is that some components of our composite identities, taken singly (e.g., as a patriot) or in a pair (e.g., as a patriotic man or as a patriotic woman), can have striking normative power. The appeal of a group identity can be at times almost irresistible for many people, based on the urge to experience the security and solidarity of membership of the group. Thus, essentialist politics mobilizes people not just on the basis of who they are but, more subtly, of who they think they want to be or ought to be. One of the paradoxes of essentialism is that, seen through essentialist eyes, the world is inhabited by monochrome people whose identity is simple and straight-forward. Yet essentialism is effective precisely because identity is neither simple and one-dimensional, nor fixed and unchanging. Essentialism insistently recognizes only a limited range of the spectrum of collective identity. It gives that part of identity a privileged place in political discourse, simultaneously defining the identity, projecting it and appealing to it for support. We humans are able to respond to the appeal because we have the capacity and the tendency to regard now this, now that component of our complex identities as the one that is the most important. In other words, just like our sense of what is right and wrong, our sense of our own identity is in part subject to the influences of political discourse and debate. Yet the malleability of identity, which gives essentialism its political bite, must be denied by essentialist discourse.

Essentialist generalizations are in many ways commonsense notions about identity. The essentialist appeal can be successful in part because we are often reluctant to recognize our own ambivalence about who we are. Most of us do not like to live with doubt about the fundamental things in life. We generally find it easier and more comforting to think of ourselves and our identity in simple, relatively fixed terms. This is likely to be particularly true if our sense of 'self' is under pressure from external events. If, for example, we are insecure at work, a common response is more assertive behaviour. Likewise, a family will tend to bind together more closely under the impact of bereavement.

War does something similar on a larger, social scale. As Tickner (1992, pp. 47–48) has noted, war is a time when gender polarization sets in. The differences between male and female social characteristics become more emphasized, as men take on the role of warrior and women keep the home fires burning. But this is not always a simple, unidirectional process. Skjelsbæk (1997, pp. 49–51) shows that, although women are largely excluded from fighting forces worldwide, there are cases when women actively take part in war. And, like their male counterparts, the women in those cases do not all experience war as uniformly horrifying and oppressive. In World War II, the huge shift of men from productive labour into the armed forces of Britain and the USA led to a correspondingly large shift of women into industrial and agricultural labour. However, most of the images that appealed to them from the cinema screens to help warm their support for the war effort reminded them of women's true role, as heroine after heroine waited with quiet courage for hero after hero to return home. And in the case of the 1980s war in El Salvador, in which women were active in combat roles, the effect of peace on women's role was aptly summed up by this sentence in a report in *Ms* magazine: 'Now that the war is over, Esmerelda has had her IUD removed' (cited by Enloe, 1993, p. 1).

Fundamental political or socio-economic change has a similar effect of putting pressure on established norms and conventions of identity. One example of this is the emergence of nationalism as a major political force in the nineteenth century. Many scholars have identified the impact of modernity as one of the key determinants (see Smith & Østerud, 1995). Nationalism met a multidimensional need for a relocation of social identification from the local to a larger scale. Different writers stress different aspects of this need that was at once functional (Gellner, 1983), political (Greenfeld, 1992) and cultural (Anderson, 1983; A.D. Smith, 1971, 1986). Underlying the relocation of group identity from a small unit such as a village to the much larger unit of the nation were the disruption of traditional ways and the breaking up of rural communities. These were inherent to the onset of modernity. A new worldview was needed if social and personal stability were to survive. That was the role of national consciousness and nationalist ideology.

In the late twentieth century, the continued vitality of nationalism still seems to owe much to the impact of major socio-economic change, such as the collapse of state socialism in the former USSR and Eastern Europe. Such large-scale upheaval creates stress and pressure on existing social identity formations; this may lead to a relocation of identification, or to a reassertion of pre-existing identities, or a potent mixture of the two – a relocation that is understood by those who participate in it as a reassertion. The result may be the forceful resurgence of group identities that have been unimportant to people for years.

In the same way, the pace of economic, technological and social change in the five decades since World War II has served to destabilize assumptions about gender roles. In the OECD countries, there have been both greater opportunities than before and a greater need for women to join the paid workforce in a variety of jobs and professions. The need has been both macroeconomic – a need for a larger labour force – and microeconomic – as family incomes are increasingly augmented by and sometimes dependent on the women's earnings. This change in gender roles is often unsettling and has been accompanied by a series of other social changes, relating not least to major changes in sexual attitudes and behaviour. Among the responses to these changes has been both the feminist movement since the late 1960s, and a backlash by those, both women and men, who attempt to assert more traditional gender roles. In the backlash, the effort is made to project a clear sense of what it is to be a man and what it is to be a woman. It is impossible to assert the inviolability of pre-existing gender roles without asserting that they are natural, based on the natural characteristics of men and of women. Gender traditionalism is inevitably essentialist. By contrast, it is far from inevitable (though not unknown) for feminist arguments to be couched in essentialist terms; when they are, it is usually with an odd combination of essentialism about men, more varied awareness of women, and open questions about gender roles (Davies, 1990, pp. 502–503).

The errors of essentialist discourse

It is not possible for arguments shaped by an essentialist discourse to understand their own historical roots or place. Were they to do so, they would automatically sacrifice their implicit claim to be expressions of a natural – or primordial – and unavoidable truth. They can get to grips with neither their longevity nor their impermanence. Nationalism almost always projects the existence of the nation for which it speaks several hundred years into the past and claims the same long life for national traditions, even when those traditions may be barely one century old (Hobsbawm & Ranger, 1983). As in nations, so between men and women: the evident change in gender roles through the ages and from one culture to another is routinely obliterated by essentialist appeals for women and men to resume their rightful, traditional roles and places.

Essentialist arguments repeatedly err by simplifying patterns of identity and regarding identity formations and allegiance to them as fixed and frozen. However, the problem with essentialism as a type of discourse is not that it makes generalizations about social groups and their behaviour. Observed anthropological generalizations about groups are legitimate, interesting and often – if we are honest – entertaining. As between women and men in any given society, there are generally observable differences in behaviour. These reflect social position and are not unimportant in explaining political leanings, cultural preferences, styles of political activity, and so on. It is legitimate and even necessary to acknowledge these empirical generalizations and assess their weight and meaning. Equally, between different nations there are observable differences in patterns of behaviour and attitude. Likewise between different classes, professions, religions, and so on. The problem about essentialism is not that it identifies these differences, but that it exaggerates and freezes them.

Though there are observable differences in behaviour between men and women, there are also differences among men and among women. Even in relatively homogeneous Western society, there is more than one form or code of masculinity (Connell, 1995), more than one way to be a man. Likewise, there are multiple possibilities for women. At the same time, the men and women between whom there are observable differences in behaviour as men and women must also be understood on other identity levels. The sample is united and divided in different ways – not only by gender but also by nationality, class, age, religion, profession, and so on. Which element of her social identity is it that shapes the behaviour and attitudes of a person when she votes? Even to ask the question is to realize its irrelevance to understanding her behaviour and attitudes. It is not just one feature that determines her behaviour. Yet, in the appropriate essentialist discourse, the point is precisely that one or two features of social identity can be called upon to explain and characterize the whole person.

At the same time as crosscutting patterns of social identity are evident, changes and exceptions are equally visible. That the English restrain their displays of emotion has long been taken for granted, not least by the English. Understatement, restraint, the stiff upper lip, phlegmatic behaviour – these are part of the staple diet of national archetypes. At least, they were until the very public mourning for the death of Diana Princess of Wales in August 1997. The outpouring of grief surprised everybody, not least the English. But then it became possible to note that, in fact, public displays of emotion did not suddenly begin in August and September 1997, and the response to Diana's death was treated as the expression of a change (and not the cause of it). The English 'are becoming less Victorian and more like the insubordinate, flashy demonstrative people of an earlier Britain' (Marr, 1998). None of this means that the image of restraint and reticence is or was wholly wrong: far from it, but the image is neither wholly nor permanently true.

In a different context, something similar is evident in discussions of gender gaps in politics. Clear gender differences have been recorded in opinion and voting behaviour on, for example, male and female support for high military spending in the USA (Tickner, 1992, p. 61). This does not, however, form evidence that proves anything about all women or about all men. Opinion polls and studies show that proportionately more women than men tend to oppose high military spending – but they also show that many men oppose it and many women support it.

At its simplest, the point here is that generalizations allow for exceptions. Social identities and their behavioural and attitudinal attributes are plastic and volatile. Therefore, they do not admit of universal, comprehensive rules. Those who do not understand that, understand nothing about identity. The first error of essentialism is to regard identity as a fixed category. We know it is not true. The common concept of maturity expresses the simple idea that people do change. In general, social identities are more persistent, but their meaning too is in constant if slower flux. The possibility of change lies within the relationship between social identities and the social conditions of their existence. As social and economic realities change, the ways in which they are interpreted necessarily change, and thus also the content and meaning of group identity. On the basis of simplistic and frozen notions of social identity, essentialist discourse builds crude political assumptions and claims. It insists that political views are or ought to be derived from identity, which has already been erroneously conceived as one-dimensional and fixed, and tries to deflect the uncomfortable truth that people often think before they vote. This approach to politics is a negation of the role of values, understanding and intellect. Of course, loyalties based on a shared group identity do surface and help shape electoral behaviour and other political choices. But it is simply not empirically true that identity is in general, a sole or even the main determinant of political behaviour. It is true that there are times and places when and where it is the main determinant. But that is a different claim, which acknowledges that the identity element of politics is neither given nor timeless but contingent and constructed.

In essentialism, valid empirical generalizations – having been treated as universals, built into essential truths, and turned into political platforms – are recycled as imperatives. Those who do not conform to the expected or desired pattern of behaviour are designated renegade – not true members of their group. The bitterest moments in the struggles of nationalist movements often come when, with words or with weapons, the activists fight against their own kind. At one point it was common among Margaret Thatcher's political opponents to say or imply that she was not a true woman – or, as some of her supporters would put it, was more of a man than most men.

The errors of essentialism culminate in what should be recognized as its tragedy. Compared to reality, it is a bleak and uninteresting view of human life that emerges from the narrow, cramped framework of essentialism. It denies the richness of individual and social identities. Rather than acknowledging that there are many ways to be women and to be men, it insists there is only one of each. Or promotes but one model of acceptable heterosexuality. Or states that there is only one way to be British. Surely anybody who has read any history, any anthropology, any novel, anybody who has ever watched a film or a play, must see how threadbare is the vision of life purveyed by essentialist discourse. It homogenizes complex social groups and deals in terms of one-dimensional people. Thankfully, the world is not really like that.

The dangers and failings of essentialism

Essentialism has a great capacity to shape reality. The simplicity and non-reflexive nature of the discourse allows it to work equally well on both sides of potential lines of division. Any account of the wars of Yugoslavia's disintegration must include the way that Serbian nationalism from 1986 onwards steadily called into action opposing nationalist ideologies – first Slovenian, then Croatian and finally Bosniak nationalism (Little & Silber, 1995). Within Yugoslavia, Serb nationalism thus did much to create its own adversaries. The problem with Huntington's (1993, 1997) vision of future conflicts being shaped by a clash of civilizations is not that he may be analytically right. Rather, the problem is that on both sides of the major clash he discusses – between the West and Islam – are political leaders, ideologues and intellectuals who express views that are similar to each other in one crucial respect. Both sides expect – or behave as if they expect – clash and confrontation. The visions are tenuously linked to reality, but the proponents on each side have the advantage of the proponents on the other side – bitter enemies but best friends, for they need each other. One myth of confrontation easily generates another opposing one. This is why nationalism is contagious.

Essentialism thus fosters the conditions in which it survives and flourishes. But in this, there is a hidden danger. As Ernest Renan put it in his famous lecture, 'What is a Nation?' (1882/1990), those who would use ethnographic politics must be careful, for it has a habit of returning to haunt the one who first raised it. That holds true for essentialism in general. The call to unity on one side of a dividing line – which itself may be what first makes the division politically salient – sets an uncontrollable process going. Judith Butler points to the tension within feminist arguments between wanting to mobilize women as women and wanting to question the content and meaning of the social category 'women' (Butler, 1993, p. 188). Once the capacity of essentialist discourse to summon its own adversaries into action has been recognized, it must be difficult to see this tension as likely to be in any way productive. Mobilizing women as women, however progressive the cause, must run a strong risk of playing directly into the hands of gender traditionalism, especially if traditional gender concepts are the basis of the mobilizing appeal. The strength of the appeal of gender traditionalism is likely to swamp the more delicate, interesting and potentially fruitful process of questioning the content and meaning of social categories.

To call to women in particular to participate in peace movement activity because, as the child-bearing gender, they have a special feeling for peace, is dubious in several ways. It is not at all clear what it is supposed to say to women who do not have and, perhaps, do not want children. It makes the untenable assumption that women everywhere have the same experience of and attitudes towards children. It may, it would seem, tell women who support a particular war that they are not womanly, as well as telling men that they have no special feeling for peace. It may also encourage a line of thought that, if women are child-bearing, they should also be child-rearing, which means staying in the home and out of politics. There is little logic in that association of physiology and social role – but neither is there in many essentialist claims, and once the essentialist door has been opened it is extremely difficult to control what comes in. Appealing to women for political support and engagement on the basis of Victorian notions of proper female roles reinforces gender stereotypes and discrimination against women (Segal, 1987). At the same time, by defining people out of a group that might be interested in given questions, the language of essentialism is as alienating to the out-group as it is appealing to the in-group. For every person who is mobilized by essentialist rhetoric, another is demobilized, and a third is mobilized in a contrary direction.

This leads to two further and final points. Hitherto, this chapter has treated essentialism as a successful strategy for political mobilization. So it is, but its success is limited in two ways. First, there is no political strategy that is 100% successful: strategies shaped by essentialist discourse are no exception. Nationalists always claim to speak for the nation, but it is never true that they speak for every member of the nation. That is why the concept of 'renegade' becomes such an important aspect of nationalist ideology, to describe those who, for example, have been won over to the culture of the power identified as the oppressor. There will always be those to whom the essentialist appeal does not appeal – Scots who do not support autonomy for Scotland, let alone independence; women who are turned off by any argument that appeals to them as mothers and home-makers; men who are unmoved by appeals to their manhood.

Secondly, to the extent that essentialist strategies are successful, it is because of the plastic and volatile nature of identity formation. It is for that same reason their success is ephemeral. People who are mobilized in the name of national unity may find that, after a time, the nationalist theme is no longer so appealing. The reason need not be that they no longer feel themselves to be part of the nation, but simply that being part of the nation has become less important than, say, their wish for a reasonable degree of prosperity. Similarly, women who are moved as women to support a political cause may later find that, although their gender remains central to their sense of identity, the meaning of being women has changed – with the same effect, that the former political appeal no longer works.

Alternatives to essentialism

The destructive heart of essentialism is its refusal to recognize the richness and complexity of identity. The alternative is then to recognize reality, to acknowledge the richness and variety of identities.

There are some political issues in which progress is only possible if individuals can change, often in large groups. Peaceful conflict resolution, reconciliation between traditional enemies, justice between different races and gender equality are some of the issues in which this is true. This does not mean that there must be total unanimity before change is possible, but that very large numbers of people must change their attitudes and behaviour, or else social and political change is out of the question.

Where then is that change supposed to come from? If people are immutable, there can be no such change. Any philosophy and any discourse that hold that people are unchangeable and unchanging are, therefore, profoundly pessimistic approaches to the key issues of power and peace. That is one reason for rejecting the validity of essentialist discourse in the service of progressive ends such as racial justice or gender equality. The deeper reason, however, is simply that people do change, that identity is not the fixed and seamless quality that essentialist discourse would have us believe. We human beings are not the way that essentialism paints us. Men and women alike, we are far more complex, interesting and contradictory, with far more capacities, and much more creativity. The challenge is to recognize ourselves for what we are, and not for pale, essentialist shadows.

Notes

1   Broadcast on 6 October 1996. I only heard this statement because of my bad habit of keeping the television on while doing other things – on this occasion, preparing this paper for the UN/PRIO Experts Group Meeting in Santo Domingo.
2   There is plenty of room for terminological confusion here, because in social psychology and philosophy the term 'constructivism' is used in relation to the 'constructs' of our minds, whereas in social science the term is used to deal with the 'constructs' of social practice. Social psychology and some social scientists use the term 'constructionism' to refer to what is here called 'constructivism'.
3   For effective refutations of Huntington's original article, see Ajami (1993) and Rubenstein & Crocker (1994).
4   There is an important terminological distinction between *identity theory*, which is theory based on research about identity, explaining among other things how identity comes to shape political views, and *identity politics*, which is an approach to politics, political strategy and political mobilizing that is based on exploitation of common identity.
5   The coalition government elected in 1997 – primarily an alliance of the Christian People's Party and the Centre Party – accepted the right-wing Progress Party's proposal to provide direct cash support for those who stay at home to look after children.

3
Is Femininity Inherently Peaceful?
The Construction of Femininity in War

Inger Skjelsbæk

Introduction

At the heart of the science of psychology is the study of personality and different forms of *identity*. Ever since the 1860s, when Wilhelm Wundt conducted the first psychological experiments in his laboratory in Leipzig, the science of psychology has sought to understand how individuals form and are transformed by their social environment. The central aim has been to study the mechanisms which lead to normal behaviour, and to abnormal behaviour.

The study of international politics has a somewhat similar approach to its main focus – national and international *conflicts*. The researcher tries to describe and explain when, how and why conflicts are transformed into war, and thereby learn more about how it may be possible to avoid wars. Traditionally, scholars of international politics have not paid much attention to the relationship between individuals and the conflict in question: their focus has been on states and nations. Nor have psychologists paid sufficient attention to how states and nations relate to the construction of individual identity. This chapter seeks to integrate an understanding of the construction of gender identity within the heart of the study of international politics, namely war.

The basic premise is that gender identity is negotiable, that is it is not given by nature. 'Doing gender means creating differences between girls and boys and women and men, differences that are not natural, essential or biological', according to West and Zimmerman (1991, p. 24). Masculinity and femininity are *negotiated interpretations* of what it means to be a man or a woman. These interpretations determine male and female actions, behaviour, perceptions and rationality. On the basis of this understanding, I focus on how women's experiences in war are determined by the fact that they are women, and how women's responses reveal characteristics of their femininity. The chapter is based on a study of oral testimonies from women from three different conflict areas: former Yugoslavia, El Salvador and Vietnam.

Two clarifications

First of all, the scholarly literature on women and war is limited. Leafing through historical accounts of war, you are not likely to find the word *women* in the index.

> Women have been left out of history not because of the evil conspiracies of men in general or male historians in particular, but because we have considered history only in male-centred terms. We have missed women and their activities, because we have asked questions of history which are inappropriate to women. To rectify this, and to light up areas of historical darkness we must, for a time, focus on a *woman-centred* inquiry, considering the possibility of the existence of a female culture *within* the general culture shared by men and women. (Showalter, 1988, p. 345)

Women's experiences have been relegated to the shadows of more 'significant' historic events. In these scenarios men play the lead roles, while women are in the background. A woman-centred approach to war can provide insight into an 'other' experience of war. It will also nuance the overall picture of war and its impact. Until we take women's experiences and perceptions into account when conducting research on conflicts, our descriptions and analyses will remain incomplete.

Secondly, attempting to describe how femininity relates to peacefulness is difficult. It is by no means evident what 'femininity' and 'peacefulness' actually are. How then, can we analyse the relationship between the two? Femininity can, as will be shown later in this chapter, be seen as being composed of the actions and rationality of motherhood. Likewise, peacefulness can be said to be distinguished by specific actions and rationalities. In this chapter, peacefulness will be understood as *the lack of will to use violence* (actions) *or to sustain enemy images of the other* (rationality).

From essentialism to social constructionism

In order to get a better understanding of the notion of femininity we need to clarify how social identities are conceptualized within the social psychological literature. Two opposing views characterize different understandings of gender and conflict: an *essentialist* and a *constructionist* approach. These views represent differing ontologies and epistemologies. The essentialist view is based on an ontology which regards the world as rule-governed, one in which our epistemological task as researchers is to uncover and identify the rules and systems of this world. Researchers in this tradition believe that there is an objectively existing reality 'out there', and that they must detach themselves as much as possible from the subject matter. By contrast, the social constructionist view is based on the ontology of an ever-changing world. The epistemological goal of the researcher then becomes to look for changes in our environment, and to attempt to see how reality becomes constructed.

Essentialism

Essentialism is based on the philosophical notion that some objects, no matter how described or defined, may have certain qualities which are timeless and immutable.[1] Sayer (1997) makes a distinction between what he characterizes as strong deterministic essentialism and moderate non-deterministic essentialism, arguing that belief in a certain level of essentialism is crucial to enable us to organize our social worlds. Further, he argues that even if certain things can be perceived as having essence this does not mean that everything must be seen as having essence in the same way. For instance, the fact that H_2O is the essence of water does not necessarily imply that masculinity and femininity may have an 'essence' along the same lines. Conversely, arguing that the essence of masculinity and femininity may be regarded as constructed will not necessarily imply that H_2O is *not* the essence of water.

I sympathize with Sayer's distinction. It would be senseless to argue against the existence of essential biological differences between men and women. Physical differences can be observed and measured: the male brain is larger than the female brain, men are physically bigger and stronger than women, the genitalia and the composition of hormones differ. However, it would be equally senseless to argue that the behaviour, attitudes and perceptions of *all* men are essentially the same and that these are essentially different from the behaviour, attitudes and perceptions of *all* women across time and space. While recognizing biological differences, we must also recognize that the implications of these differences are open to debate.

Essentialism is not as prevalent today as it was in the early years of psychoanalysis, but it has remained pervasive in political rhetoric, commonsense thinking and scholarly literature. Essentialism assumes that gender identities are unchangeable. Gender identities and differences are perceived as the result of *stable underlying factors*. Biology therefore becomes the primary source for explaining differences in male and female behaviour, attitudes and thinking. What it means to be a man or a woman is seen as having the same, unchanging implications across time and space. Both men and women have embraced this line of thought. For men in power, the essentialist position can be taken to mean that there is something about men's power status which originates in their gender identity – that is, the 'true' nature of men. The fact that women have stayed at home and taken care of the house and children is also explained in terms of women's 'true' nature. This interpretation suggests that, throughout history, men and women have tended to do what they are naturally good at. Gender difference thus becomes a matter of nature rather than nurture.

'[S]ome things have essence and some – for example gender or ethnicity – do *not*', says Sayer (1997, p. 455). Essentializing gender is necessarily
deterministic. It further assumes that *all* men are masculine and *all* women
are feminine. A closer look at the phenomenon of attraction will show
how this approach becomes problematic. A central part of femininity is
being attracted to males, thus all women should be attracted to men.
Women who feel attracted to women are seen as abnormal. The implication
is that there is something wrong with their biological constitution, since
this is where their gender identity is supposed to originate. Not surpris-
ingly, the homosexual community is strongly opposed to this line of
thought. Still, large amounts of money are spent on medical research
aimed at finding out where in the body homosexuality 'originates' –
thereby echoing the essentialist position.

What is arguably the main problem with the essentialist position is,
however, that it does not allow for change. It holds that we remain essentially the same people throughout life. A criminal will always be a criminal,
no matter how much he wants to change. Likewise, the essentialist position
assumes that all men share certain unchangeable characteristics which are
qualitatively different from women's shared (and equally unchangeable)
characteristics. Some feminist writers have argued that women are morally
superior to men because they are inherently more peaceful and globalistic
than men (see Kaplan, 1997, pp. 32–33 on women and nationalism). As will
be shown, this assumption becomes problematic when we turn to the
empirical material examined in this study.

Social constructionism

A different approach to the understanding of masculinity and femininity is
through the lenses of social constructionism. Enloe (1990, 1993), is one of
many exponents of this line of thinking. Her starting point is the following:
'Conventionally both masculinity and femininity have been treated as
"natural", not created. Today, however, there is mounting evidence that
they are packages of expectations that have been created through specific
decisions by specific people' (Enloe, 1990, p. 3). Enloe clearly distinguishes
herself from the essentialist manner of thinking. The constructionist[2]
approach is based on an ontological scepticism to what is considered natural or given. It is as much a critique of traditional positivistic research as
it is a coherent paradigm. '[W]hereas positivism asks what are the facts,
constructivism[3] asks what are the assumptions; whereas positivism asks
what are the answers, constructivism asks what are the questions', say
Hare-Mustin and Marececk (1988, p. 456).

Social constructionism is based on the epistemological understanding
that our social worlds are constantly changing. Social constructionism
argues that the locus of gender identity is not within the individual but in
the *transaction* between individuals (Bohan, 1993, p. 7). Gender differences
may be conceptualized as the *construction of masculinity and femininity in*

their distinction from each other. Because this position is linked to a world-view different from than the essentialist position, it is worth going through some of the basic premises for constructionism.

1 Constructionism has a critical stance towards taken-for-granted social knowledge (Burr, 1995, p. 3). The social constructionist is inherently sceptical about uncritically accepted perceptions about social phenomena. When something is claimed to be true and objective, the social constructionist immediately asks, 'Are there alternative ways of describing the same state of affairs?' (Gergen, 1994, p. 72). If the essentialist says that gender differences are rooted in biology, then the social constructionist would try to explain gender differences by other means. The overall goal is not to create competing descriptions, but to create multiple ones.

2 Constructionism regards social knowledge as historically and culturally specific (Burr, 1995, p. 3). The social constructionist regards knowledge about social phenomena as rooted in history and culture. This knowledge is perceived not as cumulative and linear, but as being in constant flux. Gender differences will then be seen as differing from culture to culture and in different historical contexts.

3 Constructionism is based on the belief that social knowledge is sustained by the social process (Burr, 1995, p. 4). The individual is not perceived as a *tabula rasa* who is completely formed by a given context. Our social worlds are pre-organized through previous social interactions. When we enter the social world as male or female there are patterns of behaviour and thinking which are 'available' to us. Parents may choose to dress their baby daughters in pink and baby boys in blue; boys may be given cars to play with while girls are given dolls, sons may be encouraged to study natural science and daughters to study languages. All these choices parents make emphasize differences between the genders. When the young girl or boy grows up, the opportunities and experiences he/she has had will be part of the background which determines future experiences and choices.

4 Constructionism is based on the belief that knowledge and social action go together (Burr, 1995, p. 5). Our descriptions and perceptions of reality take various forms. What we believe to be true will to a large extent determine our actions. If we believe that men and women have different levels of intelligence, then it does make sense to treat boys and girls differently. If, however, we do *not* believe that men as a group score differently on IQ tests than women as a group because men have higher intelligence, we will come to different conclusions.

The social constructionist position argues that our identities are not given by nature: We *become* who we are through our interactions with our social surroundings. The implications and meanings of our gender identity are not fixed, but constantly changing. This does not mean that male and female identities change arbitrarily. Changes follow other patterns of the structures of a given society. Socio-economic changes as well as religion, ethnicity and class will act to determine the meaning and implications of gender identity, just as gender influences the meaning of religion, ethnicity and class.

The major strength of the social constructionist position is that it conceptualizes the possibility for change. Its optimistic potential makes this position attractive as a rationale for analysing conflicts from a gender perspective. If we want to believe that conflicts can be avoided and that peaceful outcomes of violent struggles are possible, we will have to believe that people can change.

Despite deep-rooted differences between the essentialist and the social constructionist positions to the gender dimensions of peace and conflict, they both agree on the need to focus on women's experiences in war. The essentialist claim is that women will, if given power, naturally seek peaceful solutions to conflicts because this is seen to be part of women's essential nature. Social constructionists will investigate how femininity and masculinity become constructed within the context of war and thereby seek to change behaviour and value hierarchies which lead to war. The following analyses will take this social constructionist understanding as the starting point.

Methodology

I have conducted a study where I investigated a collection of oral testimonies. These were gathered by PANOS, an international NGO based in London, Paris and Washington, DC. According to PANOS, the goal of an oral testimony is to facilitate reflections about both self and the conflict in question (Warnock, 1995). An oral testimony is therefore more than a mere reflection of experiences: it is also a constructed perception of reality.

Throughout 1993–94 PANOS ran a project on 'Women and Conflict', on the theme of *Arms to Fight – Arms to Protect: Women Speak Out about Conflict*, which presents women from 11 different conflict areas.[4] The common media image of women in war is that women are helpless victims of a situation over which they have no control. The impression that emerges throughout the PANOS testimonies, however, is that these women are far from helpless, naive or inarticulate. Quite the contrary. They are active participants taking on new responsibilities, whether this is by their own choice or because they feel that it is imposed by the situation. The consequence is that they view themselves with new eyes.

The use of oral testimonies in social psychological research is not common, and it does have its pros and cons. The major advantage is that testimonies like those gathered by PANOS have a particularly authentic character. These oral testimonies were gathered by local women in the various countries where the project was run. The interviewers were recruited through the local PANOS network; the interviewees were women the interviewers knew, and who were willing to tell their stories. The interviewees were able to tell their stories in their own language, talking with someone whom they trusted. The oral testimonies were then translated into English in the local countries, when possible, or translated in the PANOS London office. The major disadvantage of this approach is that, as a researcher, I have not had any influence over the information gathered or the form of the testimony. I have not had the opportunity to ask detailed questions about specific points I find particularly relevant, interesting or difficult. My understanding is completely determined by the form and content of the testimonies that have been collected by PANOS. Nor have I had the opportunity to visit the countries in question and familiarize myself with the cultural setting. These are valid objections, but here let me stress that the major aim of the study has been to investigate a psychological question concerning gender identity. The science of psychology has a tendency to formulate universal principles about human nature, and my aim has been to investigate one such alleged universal assumption. The cultural component of this effort is important, but even more important is evaluating how the oral testimonies can shed new light on a social psychological problem.

The construction of femininity in the wars in former Yugoslavia, El Salvador and Vietnam: a comparative study

My study focused on women's experiences in Croatia and Bosnia, El Salvador and Vietnam. I chose these conflicts because they represent the diversity of the oral testimonies. The many differences that characterize these conflicts, such as the time of conflict, the image of the enemy and the general participation of women, allowed me to speculate on general trends of the gendered, in this case female, experience in war.

Former Yugoslavia – victimized femininity?

By the time the Dayton Peace Agreement was signed on 21 November 1995, the most lethal conflict in Europe of the years 1990–95 was over (Smith, 1997b, pp. 24–25). It is impossible to determine the number of deaths, but some 263,000 people may have died in the period from 1992 to 1995 (Sivard, 1996, p. 18).

For women, this war has meant mass rape, torture and sexual violence in its most grotesque forms. Six mass-rape camps have been identified (Smith, 1997b, p. 34).[5] According to the European Fact-Finding Team, more than 20,000 Muslim girls and women were raped in Bosnia since fighting began in 1992.[6] The report of the Coordinating Group of Women's Organizations of Bosnia and Herzegovina, on the other hand, estimates this figure to be closer to 50,000,[7] while other reports indicate that as many as 60,000 women have been raped.[8] The collection and publication of these figures and others promoted a chain reaction of hatred and hostility in which Muslims, Croats and Serbs all took part, and which, in turn, led to more rapes being committed.[9] Manipulating the figures for rapes thus became a powerful tool in political mobilization: in consequence, we will never know the truth.

Rape has been committed in concentration camps, in rape camps, in public places and in people's homes. These events have put women's sufferings at the forefront in the coverage of the conflict, and major efforts are being made in investigating this specific kind of war weaponry: sexual violence.

The outbreak of the conflict came as a cruel and complete surprise to all the women in this sample.[10] Their descriptions of the outbreak can be seen as variations on a single theme: sudden outbreak, extreme violence and panic. A life of apparent harmony was abruptly changed. 'The most frightening thunderstorm had begun', said Ifeta from Sarajevo. Their descriptions of what time of day, what kind of weather it was, what they were doing, etc. at the time of outbreak all point up the sudden nature of the conflict:

> It was evening. The town was under a blanket of thick black smoke, the smell of smoke and burning rubber was suffocating. (Marcia, Croatian Catholic)

> It was a nice spring morning, in May 1992. . . . The sun itself is blinking and bowing before that spring beauty. After I went the habitual round through the grain field, I came back into our yard to wash myself and to take water from the well. At that moment the Serbians came into our village. Two of them stepped into our yard. My husband yelled: 'Run into the house!'. Chetnicks shot him and they shot me too. . . . My husband was dead, lying in a puddle of his blood . . . I was taken by chetnicks right away and dragged through the village although I was wounded and covered with blood. . . . Panic was in the village. (Anonymous Bosnian Muslim)

The conflict radically changed the lives of all the women in the sample. I tried to understand how the gendered aspects of the conflict influenced the experiences of these women and how the women responded to the conflict situation. Several aspects emerged.[11] At the structural level, their experiences were characterized by a massive absence of men. The women had lost husbands, sons, fathers, uncles and other family members. Rabija explains:

> Males, mostly younger and middle-aged, left the village in those days and ran into the near woods. The ones who had arms, and those were only a few, went to defend the 'positions'. (Rabija, Bosnian Muslim)

The women argued that the disappearance of the male population could be seen as being rooted in traditional understandings of male/female relations. The men 'disappeared' in order to protect the remaining population, which consisted of women, children and the elderly. Within this gender structure, women and children can be seen as symbols of the motherland, which the men are protecting. The result, however, was that many men were killed and many women were left unprotected.

The most dramatic effect of this segregation is that many women were raped. The high rape rate has forced us to see rape as a powerful weapon of war and part of the ethnic cleansing process, and not merely as the outcome of individual aberration. When these women were raped, the act was intended to affect the ethnic group to which the individual woman belonged as much as it was intended to affect the individual woman herself. The women themselves describe the connection between rape and political struggle quite clearly:

> I think it was planned in advance and arranged in order to destroy the soul of a nation. (Sabina, Croatian Muslim)

> He [the rapist] said to me a few times: 'Would you like to give birth to a Serbian baby?'. In the middle of May 1993 he noticed that my stomach was growing and asked me if I was pregnant. I said: 'I think that I am.' 'Really nice, there will be more little Serbs in the world', he said. (Vesna, Croatian Catholic)

In former Yugoslavia the identity of a child has traditionally been determined by the identity of the father. With the rise of nationalism in the early 1990s, ethnicity became *the* mode of being in former Yugoslavia. Ethnic identity became the point of reference for all social and political interaction. Mixed identities were seen as weak identities. Erasing the mother's ethnic identity becomes a 'rational' way of coping with this difficult situation.

At the individual level, this leaves the women struggling with intense feelings of fear, absence of joy and despair. It seems that only their children can give them comfort. Their descriptions of their children are therefore particularly interesting. They emphasize how their children respond to the conflict, but also how happy they become when they think of them.

> [T]hese kids are keeping me alive. When the nightmares overcome my mind – it is sufficient to listen to their voices in the morning, to hear them calling me 'neno' [granny] – and I am illuminated with happiness. (Anonymous Bosnian Muslim)

Generalizing across the oral testimonies does not imply that the women in the PANOS group represent the experience of women in former Yugoslavia as a whole. In order to make a generalization for women in former Yugoslavia as a whole I would have had to investigate the background of the individual woman in the sample and determine how each woman was situated within the ex-Yugoslav cultural context. This, however, was not the intention: my aim was to investigate how the sum of the individual experiences in this sample can say something about femininity as a psychologically socially constructed identity. Against the background of the 11 testimonies in the ex-Yugoslav PANOS sample I have concluded that the women in this sample represent a *victimized* femininity. This is based on the following points:

1   As a group these women have lost their husbands and other male family members. They have been left with full responsibility for remaining family members in a very difficult life-situation. The structural division between men and women has placed the women in a highly vulnerable position.
2   As women they became symbolic figures of the ethnic group they represent. In the process of ethnic cleansing, rape was used as a weapon, directed primarily against women of the ethnic groups the aggressors targeted. Although this has had consequences for all women in the conflict, there seem to be more Muslim women among the victims.[12]
3   At the individual level, these women reacted to the situations with strong feelings of depression and absolute helplessness.

The women in this sample describe themselves as utterly helpless and despairing at the time of the interview. The new situation of war meant nothing other than rape, insecurity and grief for these women.

El Salvador – liberated femininity?

The war in El Salvador broke out in 1980 and ended in 1992 with the signing of the Peace Accords negotiated by the Salvadoran Government, the FMLN (Farabundi Martí National Liberation Front) and the United Nations. The history of El Salvador is the story of a struggle between coffee-producing peasants and a powerful land-owning elite consisting of 13 families. Rapid urbanization and the instability of the international coffee market in the 1920s led to a massive influx of peasants to the cities, hoping for a better life. Their dreams rarely came true, and instead they saw themselves becoming inhabitants of city slums. Political involvement and discontent grew out of these poverty pockets (Coleman, 1993, p. 7).

Ardila (1996, p. 339) claims that political involvement is a sport in Latin America more popular than soccer and cycling. He also says that men and women are equally involved in this 'sport of the masses'. Women's political mobilization has had a long history throughout Latin America. Women have been active in wider political movements and organized strikes; they participated in street demonstrations and joined political parties even before they had the right to vote (Jaquette, 1991, p. 3). However, it has been difficult to find exact statistics and figures about women's involvement in the civil war. After much searching, I found that, in fact, 30% of the FMLN combatants and 40% of the revolutionary leadership were women in the early years of the conflict (Montgomery, 1982, p. 151). Whether these figures remained stable or changed during the course of the conflict I do not know, but pictures (in Montgomery, 1982; MacLean, 1987) and the women's testimonies give the impression that women's involvement was massive.

The build-up of this conflict was slow and conscious. The outbreak did not have any of the 'thunderstorm' characteristics of the war in Croatia/Bosnia.[13] The women made no mention of date, time, weather, etc. The conflict itself was seen as the inevitable result of a long process of struggle between the wealthy and the poor.

> I do remember the beginning of the war and the reasons for it. It was because the 'campesinos' and people in other kinds of work were asking for wage-raises and the 'campesinos' demanded land to work and credit so they could cultivate the land. (Suyapa)

The fight against poverty and inequality became a motivation for the conflict as well as a legitimization of the conflict itself.

> [I]n this country we can see some people are, we can say, on three levels: the richest, the ones in the middle and we, the poorest. So, the poor people claimed their rights, because what they were doing there was unfair, it all depended on the rich who didn't agree with that, that the poor would start listening because they couldn't stand injustice anymore, so that's how it grew into conflict. (Maria)

In the slow build-up to the conflict both men and women participated. For the women in the PANOS sample, this meant that they met the outbreak well prepared and trained. Their experiences were thus the exact opposite to those of the Croatian/Bosnian women – these women were active participants and not on-lookers to the conflict.

Moreover, the Salvadoran women share their conflict experiences with men. The gendered structure of the conflict is characterized by a new unity between men and women, and not separation as in the conflict in former Yugoslavia. This unity seems to have been attractive to these women. The slight romanticization of the conflict which can be detected in their testimonies reflects a feeling that they regarded the conflict as a refuge from the gender culture they knew from childhood.

This conflict is also different from the conflict in former Yugoslavia at a symbolic level. The *ideology of liberation*, which can be said to characterize the struggle as a whole, was also meant to include women's liberation. This conflict ideology was particularly attractive to the El Salvadoran women in the PANOS sample.

> I began to grow up, to relate to a lot of people. . . . I learned more because I didn't know much, to learn to read, to write, political talks, military, to live a life which wasn't confined in the house taking care of hens. (Amanda)

Liberation for these women meant liberation from *machismo* culture, but it also meant liberation and equality for all people. At the individual/personal level, these women learned new skills and were given new responsibilities normally reserved for men. This gave a new sense of confidence and strength. Women's participation in the struggle can therefore be seen as *tokens* of equality at several levels: between men and women, and between the struggling groups in this conflict. However, these women were not only puppets in an ideological struggle orchestrated by men: they were contributing to a struggle they themselves believed in. I interpret the women's experiences and responses in the conflict as having created a *liberated femininity*. This does not mean that this is a generalization which is true for all women in El Salvador – it applies to the women in the PANOS sample. By the term 'liberated' I want to emphasize the following points:

1   Contrary to the common segregation between the genders which normally happens at the outbreak of a conflict, these women experienced the build-up as well as the conflict itself together with men. Men and women undertook many of the same activities and missions. During the years of conflict it seems that the women were also liberated from *machismo* culture, as well as being liberated in various ways from their children. Many of the women describe how they sent their children off to relatives or organized child-care in order to be able to participate in combat.
2   Women's participation in combat also served as a token of equality. Women were determined to free their country not only from social inequality, but also from inequality between men and women. Women's participation was therefore motivated by a double agenda.
3   At the individual level, these women describe a new sense of feminine collective consciousness which developed through the years of conflict. One woman tells how women in El Salvador after the conflict now dare to break off relationships they do not want. This was more difficult before the conflict.

The return to peace has, however, not been easy. *Machismo* culture has proven highly resistant to change, despite the wartime promises of favourable changes for women. As a central part of the women's efforts to create changes they emphasized the need for education and equal opportunities in public life for both men and women. When asked about their aspirations for the future, they always referred to the need for security and education for their children.

Vietnam – conservative femininity?

Since 1945, Vietnam has been the site of several wars. In the wars against the French (1945–54) and against the USA (1965–73) women played a

central role. Information about their participation is, however, mostly limited to the war of 1965–73. Women's participation in this war reached
different levels in the North and in the South. In the South, women were
not conscripts in the militia. In the People's Liberation Forces (PLF), a sub-
group of the National Liberation Front (NLF), 40% of the regimental
commanders were women (Bergman, 1975). In the local guerrilla forces,
the participation of women was even higher.

In the North, nearly all Vietnamese women were involved in the militia and formed the core of self-defence teams (Bergman, 1975, p. 171).
They operated and managed cooperatives and factories, and carried out
repair work on the Ho Chi Minh Trail. Legislation was also passed to
ensure that where women were the majority of the workforce they must
be represented at top management level. During the war, women even
held senior management positions, but after the demobilization of a large
number of troops, many women returned to the more traditional female
jobs. Since reunification, the representation of women has declined at the
national, the provincial and the district levels of government (Bennett et
al., 1995).

The Vietnamese testimonies were presentations of post-conflict life and
of war in retrospect, as these women were interviewed almost 20 years
after the end of the war.[14] Yet, despite the time-lag, their descriptions of war
were vivid and detailed. The overall message conveyed throughout the testimonies was that the wars were *necessary*. Their losses were for a greater
cause – the liberation of their country. This was reflected in their descriptions of the conflict, where the use of heroic vocabulary is striking. One
noteworthy aspect of this vocabulary is how they describe their involvement in the conflict as a 'contribution' and speak of the deaths of family
members or others as 'sacrifices':

> I had the responsibility to take part in different activities aimed at complet-
> ing the National Liberation cause. . . . I might not directly take part in the
> National Liberation but I must indirectly take part by participating in social
> activities on the home front so that I can make a contribution. (Pham Thi
> Diem)

> Most of the women whose husbands were soldiers hoped that after the war,
> they would be able to live with their husbands in peace. But unfortunately,
> my husband sacrificed when I was head of the women's union branch. (Bui
> Thi Hien)

The wars in Vietnam resulted in massive mobilization of women's direct
participation in warfare. The women participated because there was a
great demand for labour-power, but also because they wanted to fulfil
their obligations to the state and the family.

> [I] have always thought that I had to replace my husband, who died for this
> Nation, in being responsible for bringing up our children and taking care of
> our parents. Furthermore I had the responsibility to take part in different

activities aimed at completing the National Liberation cause, which my husband hadn't finished yet. (Pham Thi Diem)

Women's fighting was to some extent based on conservative concepts of femininity. Some of their efforts can be regarded as extensions of work traditionally done by women. Pham Thi Xot, who had participated in revolutionary activities since 1960, explains:

> Women mixed into local people. . . . We put the mine into a basket to make it explode on the route which the enemy always would patrol around . . . women had a favourable condition, because women could easily approach the enemy, sometimes we dressed in disguise as legitimate citizens coming from urban to countryside. The enemy looked down upon us. We accessed the enemy more easily than men. . . . We fought in unexpected ways. Fighting that way unnerved the enemy, more than battles full of explosions. (Pham Thi Xot)

She is proud of her contribution, both of the struggle itself, and her particular way of fighting as a woman. The aftermath, however, has been a long journey of sorrow and grief for these women. The loss of male relatives has not only been a personal loss; it has also had social and practical consequences. The women have had to raise their children alone and handle practical issues which are normally taken care of by men. Because the ideals of fidelity are strong, few have settled anew or remarried.

The picture that emerges from Vietnam is one in which the concept of femininity has not been profoundly altered, as was the case in El Salvador. The conflict did change the duties and responsibilities of these women, but it does not seem to have changed the way the women in the sample regard themselves as women. I have therefore chosen to call their responses to the conflict a (re)construction of a *conservative femininity*. This is based on the following points:

1   The conflict provided more arenas for women to act in. It is, however, important to note that the women seized this opportunity in a distinctly gender-conservative way. As they describe it in the testimonies, they did not do exactly the same things as men, but found new and more 'feminine' modes of combat – like the woman with the mine in a basket.

2   The fact that the women did participate in combat, albeit in a distinctly feminine way, did have symbolic implications. In a country which had been haunted by successive wars over decades there was a need to mobilize everyone who could fight. The efforts of the women came to symbolize that everyone was involved in the struggle against the enemy.

3   Unlike the case of the women from El Salvador, the Vietnam conflict has not changed the way these women perceive themselves as women at the individual level, but rather the contrary: the Vietnamese women

found a space where conservative femininity could be given new ways of expression and significance. A central part of this conservative femininity is a strong loyalty to the family, the husband and the state. This is also reflected in their relations with their children. The account of Bui Thi Hien from North Vietnam is one example:

> Although my children were still small and my husband was absent, responding to the appeal of our party all of the women raised up in arms to defend our motherland. I myself and women nationwide replaced our husbands and children to fight for a common goal – Freedom and Independence. (Bui Thi Hien)

Through Communist/feminist rhetoric, this woman indicates how the overall goal – freedom and independence – was more important to her than her role as a mother for her children. Like the El Salvadoran women, also these women sent their children away so that the mothers could participate in combat. Some of the older women in the sample express deep disapproval of the young women in Vietnam today who (according to them) do not feel any obligation towards the country or their husbands.

The thoughts and reflection presented by these women must, however, be regarded in light of the fact that these testimonies were censored by Vietnamese authorities. More in-depth knowledge of Vietnamese society would probably have revealed more about the language between the lines than I have been able to in this presentation. From a social-psychological perspective, however, the value of these testimonies remains unaltered. They portray an understanding of femininity constructed in the transaction between Vietnamese authorities and the individual women.

Is femininity inherently peaceful?

War can be regarded as the cornerstone of masculinity. Boys become men through, among several things, military service (Enloe, 1983) and by participating in war (Elshtain, 1987). By contrast, participation in war or military service is not normally considered a significant event in the social identity construction process of women. For girls it is often other events that mark the transition from girlhood to mature womanhood. Despite this, I feel we may regard women's participation in combat as a potentially significant event in the development process from girl to woman – as has been shown in the oral testimonies.

If we regard *motherhood* as the central marker of the transition from girlhood to adult womanhood, and war-related activities as markers of the transition from boy to man, then it becomes particularly relevant to study motherhood in the context of war. Motherhood can be regarded as the most central aspect of femininity. It is a complex phenomenon composed of *actions* (giving birth and taking care of a child) and *rationality* (the reasons for taking care of/raising a child). When femininity is conceptualized as inherently peaceful, it is the concept of motherhood which is emphasized and cited to legitimize the claim. As we shall see, this claim becomes difficult to legitimize in the face of what emerges from the PANOS testimonies.

The investigation of three different conflicts has led to the construction of three different forms of femininity in war (*victimized* femininity in Croatia and Bosnia, *liberated* femininity in El Salvador, *traditional* femininity in Vietnam). The constructions are generalizations that capture trends across the three groups of oral testimonies: they do not indicate that *all* women in the particular area perceive and present themselves along the same lines. The findings are local, but the implications can be made global.

The actions of motherhood

When motherhood is conceptualized as the antithesis of violence, this is based on an essentialist understanding of motherhood. 'The mothers of the world, who provide the care for most young children, are fundamental and formative peace educators', says Reardon (1993, p. 133). She goes on to say that peace education is an activity where the mother feels a responsibility for creating positive human relations in the family, the community and the world. Reardon's argument supports the essentialist claim that women are more peaceful than men.

There is, however, one crucial element, often pointed out by peace scholars, which complicates the assumption that mothers are inherently peaceful: namely, that mothers frequently encourage their sons and husbands to participate in war. In fact, many women are disappointed and even embarrassed if their men do not fight (Boulding, 1976; Elshtain, 1987; Ruddick, 1989a). Ruddick (1989a) describes maternal non-violence as an intoxicating myth which prevails even in the face of massive historical contradictions. 'Everywhere that men fight, mothers support them', she claims rather provocatively (Ruddick, 1989a, p. 219). This calls for a different understanding of mothers and peace, an understanding rooted in a constructionist view of motherhood. Ruddick's book, *Maternal Thinking: Towards a Politics of Peace* (1989a), provides an explanatory framework for this conceptual change.

Her claim is that thinking is deeply rooted in practice. 'Practices', she says 'are collective human activities distinguished by the aims that identify them and by the consequent demands made on practitioners committed to those aims' (Ruddick, 1989a, pp. 13–14). The practices of mothering are fundamentally characterized by an attempt to foster growth through protection, nurturing and training. It is precisely these activities which carry a *potential* for peace. Because Ruddick (1989b) places her emphasis on practice, and challenges essential understandings of gender, she opens the way for an understanding whereby both men and women share an equal potential for peacefulness.

Throughout the PANOS testimonies, the activities of motherhood are frequently discussed, and the women focus on different aspects of motherhood in their accounts. They also deal with their children in different ways. With regard to the victimized women in Croatia and Bosnia, we have seen that motherhood became their only source of optimism and their sole reason to keep on living. In their accounts of how their children react to and/or deal with the conflict, they express a sense of motherhood as an antithesis of war. These women protect their children by taking them, and themselves, away from the conflict situation. They regard themselves as victims, but it is important for them that their children will not be victims. The El Salvadoran and Vietnamese women also sought to protect their children. However, this very wish to protect their children and ensure for them a better future made them eager and willing to participate in combat and support the war.

On the basis of these observations, we cannot conclude that the actions of motherhood are essentially peaceful. The aspects of protection, nurturing and training – to use Ruddick's terminology – may have a violent or a peaceful outcome, all depending on the context of the actions of motherhood.

The rationality of motherhood

The rationality of motherhood has been a central theme in feminist scholarly literature. Feminists have challenged conventional, male-related understandings of rationality and reason (which are seen as universal, abstract, theoretical) and have proposed alternative ways of thinking. Among the best-known theorists in this field is Carol Gilligan, who has carried out work on moral thinking among girls. She replicated the infamous Lawrence Kohlberg experiments[15] and found that girls often have a different approach to moral dilemmas than do boys. Girls will, more often than boys, consider aspects of contextual character – network thinking – in order to solve ethical dilemmas, whereas boys will rely on absolute and hierarchical principles more often than girls will. Gilligan concluded that girls more often than boys express an *ethics of care* already at an early age: 'The images of hierarchy and web . . . convey different ways of structuring relationships and are associated with different views of morality and self . . . leading to different modes of action and different ways of assessing the consequences of choice' (Gilligan, 1982, p. 62). Reardon links this line of thought to peace movements: '[W]omen in the peace movement tend not to focus on specific weapons in isolation from the overall arms development dynamic . . . they tend instead to see the interrelationship among circumstances and trends' (Reardon, 1993, p. 143). Reardon has formulated a feminist security concept where dimensions of care are linked together. The main components are sustainability, vulnerability, equity and protection. The concept stretches from global to personal phenomena.[16] There are, according to Reardon, three key questions every policy-maker must ask: Will the decision threaten or cause harm to others?

Will the decision strengthen or weaken positive, constructive relation-ships? Will the decision detract or add to the total security of all? (Reardon, 1993, p. 168). She concludes that '[W]omen are the ones who are, and have been, raising these questions in the interest of all' (ibid., p. 169). This might well be true for some women, but it does not mean that *all* women would raise these or similar questions had they been in a posi-tion of power.

Throughout the PANOS testimonies, we have seen that women express different rationalities of care – some peaceful, some not. The victimized women of Croatia and Bosnia did indeed show a new kind of care for their own children, as well as those of others. They have no desire for their children to experience war again; what they want is for their children to grow up in a safe, secure environment. On the surface, then, it would seem that the women of former Yugoslavia express precisely the kind of peace-fulness that Reardon suggests. The paradox, is however, that in order for these women in the PANOS sample to achieve the safe future they want for their children, the solution they see is to protect their children from Serbs. They do not want a future together with Serbs, or one in which their chil-dren live with Serbs. The pattern which emerges is that these women express a rationality of motherhood which is based on protection and care but which at the same time preserves enemy images, on their own and on their children's behalf. For the women from El Salvador, the rationality of motherhood means that they want to see a better future for their children, and they want to protect them. This has led the mothers to become involved in direct combat. For the women in Vietnam we could note a similar pattern. It was precisely motherhood and the rationality of care both for their family and for the country which motivated these women to participate in combat. The PANOS sample has thus shown how mother-hood can have both a peaceful and a war-prone potential.

Conclusion

We have seen that women's experiences in war are determined by the gender culture in which they live and by the nature of the conflict. Whether they are victimized, liberated or express a conservative femininity, they have had strategic and symbolic functions in the different conflicts. These functions have led to changes on the personal level as well, where some women have become totally disheartened and depressed, while others have gained a new sense of self-confidence. How then, do their responses to the different conflict situations reveal characteristics of their femininity? *Is* femininity inherently peaceful?

The conclusion to emerge here is that femininity as such is *not* inherently peaceful. Women can be equally war-prone as men – and, most likely, men can be equally peace-loving as women. A more constructive approach to the war-prone/peacefulness distinction might be to look at differences in values and discourses. There is general agreement that the dominant discourses and value-systems which lead to war are male-related (Ruddick, 1989b), but they are not *essentially* male. The value systems do to a large extent *coincide* with gender, but, as we have seen, some women might also be exponents of militant and war-prone values, even in the context of motherhood and care.

Simply giving women access to male-dominated areas, such as combatant status in war or political power, will not necessarily change the likelihood of war as long as the value system remains stable. However, because women can be regarded as potential bearers of peaceful thinking, it is worth experimenting with more women in power. This might increase the likelihood of changing the value system which justifies war. And so, to our original question, the conclusion must be that femininity should be regarded as *potentially* peaceful.

Notes

I am indebted to PANOS–London, and to Olivia Bennett in particular, for having given me access to oral testimonies from the *Arms to Fight – Arms to Protect* project. I would also like to thank all the participants at the United Nations Expert Group Meeting in Santo Domingo, 7–11 October 1996, for stimulating discussions and comments. An earlier version of this chapter has been published in Norwegian in *Internasjonal Politikk*, vol. 1, no. 56 (pp. 55–74); Iver B. Neumann and Kristian Krohn Hansen deserve special thanks for having provided me with comments and critiques which have been very useful when I prepared this English-language treatment of the material.

1   Definition taken from the *Dictionary of Modern Literary and Cultural Criticism*. Edited by Joseph Childres & Gary Hentzi:<http://www.scrippscol.edu/scripps/~core/definitions/ess.html>

2   Seminal works which have contributed to forming this body of theory are Mead, 1934; Kuhn, 1962; Berger & Luckmann, 1966.

3   The term 'constructionism' is often used interchangeably with the term 'constructivism'. However, in psychology the term constructivist can have a specific meaning. It is often used to denote a set of cognitive theories which emphasize the individual's psychological construction of the experienced world. Both constructivism and constructionism unite in their emphasis on knowledge and perception as constructed and in their challenge of the traditional view that the individual mind is a device for reflecting the character and conditions of an independent world (Gergen, 1994, p. 67).

4   Bosnia and Croatia, El Salvador, India, Lebanon, Liberia, Nicaragua, Somaliland, Sri Lanka, Tigray, Uganda, Vietnam.

5   Brcko, Doboj, Foca, Gorazde, Kalinovik, Visegrad.

6   Figures presented in UNICEF document 'The State of the World's Children 1996'. <http://www.unicef.org/sowc96pk7sexviol.htm>

7   Figures presented by Silva Meznaric (1994) in her 'Gender as an Ethnomarker: Rape, War and Identity Politics in the former Yugoslavia'. She does not comment on the ethnic composition of these figures.

8   These figures were presented by Elenor Richter-Lyonette, of the Geneva-based NGO Women's Advocacy. She was one of the key speakers at a FOKUS seminar held in Oslo, 17 June 1996. Neither Meznaric nor Richter-Lyonette comments on the ethnic composition of these figures.

9   The information in this paragraph is based on Dr Vesna Nikolic-Ristanovic's paper 'From Sisterhood to Non-Recognition: Instrumentalization of Women's Suffering in the War in the Former Yugoslavia', presented at the conference *Women's Discourses, War Discourses,* at the Ljubljana Graduate School of the Humanities, 2–6 December 1997.

10   The Croatia/Bosnia group consisted of 11 testimonies. The average age of the women was 36 years. Five of the women had higher education (secondary school or above), four had primary-level education and the remaining two did not comment on their education. Compared to the women from El Salvador and Vietnam these women were well educated. This meant that financially these women were more independent than the women in the total sample. This point is important, because it creates a background of experience quite different from the other cases. Only one did not have children. Four were married, one was a widow, two were divorced, two were single and the remaining two did not indicate their civil status. They were all refugees. Some lived in refugee camps, and some lived with friends or relatives when the testimonies were gathered. All of them had left their homes.

11   I interpreted their responses at three different levels: (1) the *structural* level: how the conflict was organized along gender lines (who, what, where?); (2) the *symbolic* level: what men and women represented (why?); and, (3) the *individual* level: their intra-personal experiences (how?). In the summaries of the three conflicts the numbers 1, 2, 3 correspond to the different levels.

12   This is the conclusion in the 1994 Bassiouni Report, a report requested from the UN to document human rights violations in the territories of ex-Yugoslavia.

13   The most striking feature of the El Salvadoran testimonies was their length. These women were extremely articulate; individual testimonies were between 20 and 30 pages long. The group consisted of nine women; average age 35 years. This meant that at the outbreak of the conflict these women were in their teens and early adulthood. Five had more or less completed primary school, one had some advanced studies, two were illiterate and the last one did not indicate her education. All of them had children; some had children by several different men. Eight of them described themselves as combatants; only one described herself as a refugee. Some of the combatants had also been refugees in Honduras for longer or shorter periods of time.

14   With an average age of 50 years, the Vietnamese women in the PANOS sample were older than the Croatian/Bosnian and Salvadoran women. This meant that some had experienced the war(s) directly in combat, whereas others experienced it indirectly, through parents' participation. Out of the sample of 11 women, only two were well educated, with an education beyond secondary school. Four had primary school education. This does not, however, mean that they had been literate all their lives. Some got their formal schooling as adults, through the Communist Party, whereas some had attended school at a young age (not everyone commented specifically on their schooling, but throughout the course of the testimonies it was possible to get an impression of their academic background). One was illiterate and the remaining three did not mention formal schooling at all. Almost all of them had children (only one did not mention children). Five were married, three were widows and two had been widows, but had remarried. Seven said that they had been combatants or otherwise politically active, whereas four said that they had not been politically active. Those who were not politically active represent the youngest women in the sample. Because these women had never had the opportunity to compare their experiences with others, they were very eager to participate. The testimonies were fairly long and detailed, but not as extensive as the El Salvadoran ones.

15 These experiments were based on a series of moral questions along the following lines: is it always wrong to steal, or can there be exceptions? Is it always wrong to tell a lie, or can there be exceptions? etc. Kohlberg's system was mainly tested out on young boys; when he tested his system on girls he found that they did not reach the same level of abstraction as the boys – the universal ethical principle level (Fischer & Lazerson, 1984).

16 For a thorough description of these components see Reardon, 1993, pp. 166–169.

4
Women & War, Men & Pacifism

Michael Salla

Introduction

Among the enduring stereotypes encountered in analyses of the roles of men and of women in decisionmaking processes on war and peace is the view that women are less likely than men to adopt decisions that lead to the organized use of force in resolving domestic and international conflict. It is also suggested that, primarily as a result of socialization, women are 'peace-oriented' while men are 'war-oriented'.

Such stereotypes have elicited a range of responses from feminists. Some have argued that these views should be adopted; many have subsequently argued that women have a unique role in furthering peace through a greater participatory role in domestic and international institutions. On the other hand, others have rejected both stereotypes, arguing that responsibility for war rests with both men and women.

In this chapter I begin by outlining the 'women and peace' stereotype and feminist criticisms of it. Next I examine another criticism which argues that those advocating the stereotype employ a narrow and restrictive definition of power, one that overlooks how the exercise of power at the societal level of analysis is more fundamental than that exercised at the institutional level. I then go on to explore the question of men and pacifism and how this impacts on the 'women and peace' stereotype, and ask how decisionmaking might be influenced by pacifist males and women more generally if the 'women and peace' stereotype is accepted.

My conclusion is that there is likely to be an important difference between the anticipated outcomes of decisionmaking processes concerning the use of force by pacifist males and women more generally. Responsibility for peace and war cannot be demarcated in ways suggested by those promoting the 'women and peace' stereotype. Analyses of decisionmaking processes and the participation of men and women in these, and the outcomes emerging from these processes, cannot be divorced from the wider societal processes and 'power networks' that allow the implementation of the decisions taken. This in turn implies that while the inclusion of women in institutional decisionmaking processes may lead to greater participatory involvement of women in public and economic life, this need not signify a challenge to the power networks that support the organized use of force in solving domestic and international problems. The source of the problem lies not at the institutional level of analysis where decisions are made, but at the societal level where decisions are supported and implemented. The significance of an enhanced participatory role for women in institutional decisionmaking processes for the furtherance of global peace would therefore seem to be tenuous.

The 'women and peace' stereotype

In *Women and Peace*, Betty Reardon writes:

> Over the past several years, research into women's ways of knowing, reasoning, and decision making has demonstrated that, at least in Western countries, women's thinking is different from that of men; and it has been argued . . . that this difference can shed new light on, and often produce unprecedented solutions to, some of the world's major problems. (1993, p. 141)

Carol Gilligan similarly argues, in her *In a Different Voice*, that women think differently primarily as a result of socialization:

> From the different dynamics of separation and attachment in their gender identity formation through the divergence of identity and intimacy that marks their experience in the adolescent years, male and female voices typically speak of the importance of different truths, the former of the role of separation as it defines and empowers the self, the latter of the ongoing process of attachment that creates and sustains the human community. (1982, p. 156)

Others have subsequently argued 'that women, more than men, are socialized in "relational thinking", to think more than men about human relationships and the social consequences of actions' (Brock-Utne, 1989a, p. 15; see also Spender, 1982; Ruddick, 1983). In contrast, men have typically been socialized to be abstract thinkers where autonomy is valued, and abstract principles of justice, good, etc., are separated and given priority over human relationships (Kolb & Coolidge, 1988/1995, p. 261). As Nancy Hartsock explains, men's developmental processes lead to conceptions of identity that are 'surrounded by rigid ego boundaries . . . discontinuous with others' (1989, p. 137). The result is, according to Deborah Kolb and Gloria Coolidge, the 'male pattern [of communication] typically involv[ing] . . . linear or legalistic argument, depersonalization and a more directional style' (1988/1995, p. 269).

The implication of relational thinking is that not subordinating human relationships to abstract principles makes it less likely that lives will be expended in the pursuit of justice, liberty and other abstractions. As Gilligan elaborates, 'women's development delineates the path not only to a less violent life but also to a maturity realized through interdependence and taking care' (1982, p. 172). Reardon, Brock-Utne and others have argued that women are generally more peace-oriented in terms of 'nurturing international understanding', 'building consensus through cooperative efforts', 'open and regular communication', 'reducing military budgets' and desiring a more equitable distribution of resources (see Reardon, 1993, p. 56; Brock-Utne, 1989a, p. 1). It has been argued that '[a]ttitude studies consistently show that women are more peaceful and rejecting of violence than men'.[1] Anne Tickner further argues that since women have not identified with state institutions, due to being 'situated far from the seats of power', women are less likely to support war as an instrument of state policy, and to more clearly focus on structural violence at the national and international levels (Tickner, 1994, pp. 50–51).

The argument that women have a different mode of thinking suggests a 'special' role for women in eradicating the most important problems afflicting humanity throughout the globe. The precise origin of this 'special' role lies in socialization rather than biology, thereby making it possible for all to develop a relational mode of thinking. As a consequence, eco-feminists argue that women's 'connection' with nature (as a result of socialization) gives them a more acute understanding of the needed balance between human development and the ecological system (see King, 1989, p. 285; Tickner, 1994, pp. 50–52). Including women in institutional decisionmaking at all levels of government then becomes the *sine qua non* for bringing about policy outcomes that can enhance global peace.

'Wars begin in the minds of men'. This view is exemplified in the following poem:

> Women have seldom been the great creators
> Rather we have been the containers, the protectors, the lovers of life.
> A few men seem possessed by the devil
> > But many more . . . have remained as boys, just boys
> > Heedlessly playing. But the spring of the toys they are winding is death.
> We must take power from these madmen, these prisoners, these perilous children.
>
> (quoted in Burguieres, 1990, p. 4)

The issues raised from the above perspective are critical for the furtherance of global peace and for indicating the roles to be played by women and by men. The key idea emerging is that women are socialized to think in relational terms and will consequently exercise decisionmaking in a way that is identifiably different from that chosen by men. As Charlotte Gilman wrote earlier this century, 'Government by women . . . would be influenced by motherhood; and that would mean care, nurture, provision, education' (quoted in Berg, 1994, p. 336). Mary Burguieres refers to these views as the 'women and peace' and 'men and war' stereotypes (1990, p. 1). She argues that these stereotypes have been criticized by feminists in two ways: either to reject the 'women and peace' stereotype while accepting the 'men and war' stereotype, or to reject both stereotypes.

Rejections of the 'woman and peace' stereotype and acceptance of the 'men and war' stereotype come in two strands. In the first, more assertive or aggressive images of women are promoted, and feminine equivalents of the images used in promoting the 'men and war' stereotype need to be revived. This is done in order for women to be able to compete on more equitable terms in social systems dominated by masculine values of competitiveness, aggression and individualism. Berenice Carroll has argued that these feminists 'question the male monopoly of violence more than they question the use of violence itself' (quoted in Burguieres, 1990, p. 5). The second strand argues that more assertive or militant images of women need to be revived, in order for women to compete with men in individualistic, aggressive and competitive societal systems, without going as far as adopting the bellicosity of the 'men and war' stereotype. Adrienne Harris argues that 'the opposition between masculine war-making and nurturing peaceful women . . . [is] deeply problematic . . . Artemis and Athena, mythic representations of women of mind and action, wisdom and authority . . . have been neglected' (Harris & King, 1989, p. 137). According to Judith Steihm, this leads to rejection of dichotomous conceptions of society into protectors and protected, that is, men protecting women and children, and instead promotes the notion of citizen defenders where 'citizens [are] equally liable to experience violence and equally responsible for exercising society's violence' (Steihm, 1983, p. 367).

Feminists have also criticized both stereotypes. Sara Ruddick argues that both stereotypes are mythical and that 'women on both sides of the battle lines support the military engagements of their sons, lovers, friends, and mates. . . . [W]omen, like men, are prey to the excitements of violence and the community sacrifice it promises' (1989a, p. 86). Burguieres cites historical examples of instances where women have worked feverishly in support of their men at the battlefront. She notes that feminist rejections of both stereotypes are grounded in analyses of patriarchal structures, both social and institutional, which promote binary conceptual categories that link men with the most desirable social values (objectivity, reason, aggression, etc.), and women with the important but less desirable social values (emotion, nurture, peacefulness, etc.) (Burguieres, 1990, p. 7).

'Productive' power, women and peace

Feminist theorists have called for a reconceptualization of power from what has been labelled the *traditional* sense of 'power over' or 'power as dominance', since the satisfaction of one's will involves the denial of another's will, thereby leading to zero-sum outcomes (see Brock-Utne, 1989a, p. 25). Deborah Kolb and Gloria Coolidge distinguish between 'power over' and 'power with' in the sense of 'mutual empowerment ... which increases understanding and moves participants to joint action' (1988/1995, p. 265). A similar reconceptualization is advocated by Birgit Brock-Utne, who refers to power as 'competence' or 'pleasure' that leads to 'power to' enjoy or perform some action, rather than 'power over' someone (Brock-Utne, 1989a, pp. 25–26). Both reconceptualizations of power move from the conception of power as a zero-sum game involving individuals where some are winners (the powerful) and others are losers (the powerless), to a variable-sum game involving individuals and collectivities where *all* can be winners (empowerment).

The description of 'power over' as the 'traditional' sense in fact simplifies early sociological thought. Max Weber, for example, defined power primarily in the sense of the capacity to exercise one's will and get something done, and attempted to distinguish it from 'domination':

> By *power* is meant that opportunity existing within a social relationship which permits one to carry out one's own will even against resistance and regardless of the basis on which this opportunity rests. By *domination* is meant the opportunity to have a command of a given specified content obeyed by a given group of persons. (Weber, 1980 [1962], p. 117)

Thus the Weberian conception of power sought to distinguish between 'power over' (domination) and 'power to', which was the sense ascribed to the concept of power. This makes the traditional description of power as 'power over' merely a heuristic device to portray more simplistic definitions historically offered by international statesmen and political scientists. The above feminist reconceptualizations of power are consistent with Weberian definitions of power: they do not seem to offer a new paradigm, in so far as power is still viewed in terms of human agents exercising their will, whether individually or collectively. For a reconceptualization that does offer a more radical break with the Weberian conception of power, and that can provide an alternative understanding of human agency and responsibility, let us now turn to Michel Foucault.

Foucault's ideas regarding power and its exercise have proven increasingly influential in social sciences (see Campbell, 1992, p. 4). They provide a radical reappraisal of power that moves away from notions that power is exercised either through human agents (Weberian sense), or political institutions capable of applying coercion (traditional sense), to one where power is embedded in societal processes.[2] Foucault begins his discussion of power and its exercise by distinguishing between the repressive power of the State and the 'power networks' that underpin these:

> The State is superstructural in relation to a whole series of power networks that invest the body, sexuality, the family, kinship, knowledge, technology

and so forth . . . these networks stand in a conditioning–conditioned relationship to a kind of 'meta-power' [the State] which is structured essentially round a certain number of great prohibition functions; but this meta-power with its prohibitions can only take hold and secure its footing where it is rooted in a whole series of multiple and indefinite power relations that supply the necessary basis for the great negative forms of power. (Foucault, 1980, p. 122)

What Foucault is arguing here is that power as traditionally conceptualized in terms of a dominant source (the state institutions),[3] exercising power in terms of repressive or coercive capabilities, in fact is dependent on a nebulous and diffuse set of power networks (or relations) which equates with the exercise of power in a 'productive' sense:

What makes power hold good, what makes it accepted, is simply the fact that it doesn't only weigh on us as a force that says no, but that it traverses and produces things, it induces pleasure, forms knowledge, produces discourse. It needs to be considered as a productive network which runs through the whole social body, much more than as a negative instance whose function is repression. (Foucault, 1980, p. 119)

There is thus a distinction between 'negative power', as something that results in individuals being coerced to do what they otherwise would not do, and power in its 'productive sense'.

The networks of power which are 'multiple and indefinite' are diffused through the social body in a way that does not allow the construction of a systematic theory that can change these networks. Thus, rather than there being fundamental sources for the way power is exercised – state institutions, industrial capitalism – power networks are interconnected in a way that requires an incrementalist approach to change.

The role for theory today seems to me to be just this: not to formulate the global systematic theory which holds everything in place, but to analyse the specificity of mechanisms of power, to locate the connections and extensions, to build little by little a strategic knowledge (or, in Foucault's terms, *savoir* – 1980, p. 145). Thus it is mistaken to privilege some power networks over others as the primary locus for societal change more conducive to peace. For Foucault, this is especially the case for the exercise of power in its negative sense – which, though important, he still sees as subordinate to the more fundamental power networks that undergird 'negative power' (1980, p. 122).

Changes in the exercise of power in any of its specific manifestations – the production of knowledge, identity, etc. – will have an impact on other ways in which power is exercised. Rather than this impact being measured in terms of an overarching explanatory theory, a Foucauldian perspective suggests a 'tool-kit' approach where investigation is 'carried out step by step on the basis of reflection' (Foucault, 1980, p. 145).

Foucault's reconceptualization of power as 'productive' goes significantly beyond the distinction between 'power over' and 'power to', since it does not focus on human agency in the sense of the exercise of will by individuals or collectivities, or on institutional action; rather, it provides the contextual grounding for the way 'power over' and 'power to' manifest themselves. Thus Foucault shifts the understanding of power, away from the analysis of human agency and institutional action; to the underlying networks of power that sustain both. Thereby the analytical spotlight is focused on the wider societal processes and power networks that maintain and support state institutions, and decisions concerning peace and war. This suggests that the creation of a peaceful society begins with changing underlying societal processes that produce what Foucault calls a 'regime of truth', rather than with getting state institutions to pass suitable policies and mobilizing collective action to achieve this (Foucault, 1980, p. 133).

The above might lead to the view that Foucault dismisses the efficacy of human agency, the *sine qua non* of feminist conceptions of power. In other words, just as Derrida (1973, p. 141) explicitly advocated the death of the author in determining the meaning of a text, Foucault is implicitly advocating the death of the human agent in changing power networks. For this reason, Foucault and postmodernism more generally are viewed as leading to 'corrosive and cynical relativism' that supports the status quo (Mason, 1995, p. 130). This is incorrect, as Foucault is merely relocating the central problem confronting the human condition. He writes: 'The problem is not changing people's consciousness – or what's in their heads – but the political, economic, institutional regime of the production of truth' (Foucault, 1980, p. 133). Thus, human agency is directed towards changing 'regimes of truth' – a more difficult task than merely changing institutional policies.

In so far as the 'women and peace' stereotype assumes that the creation of a peaceful society lies in changing the composition of state institutions so as to include a 'critical mass' of female participation or to introduce a conception of power based on cooperative action that empowers, it can be criticized on both counts from a Foucauldian perspective. This stereotype assumes that the male domination of state institutions is the source of the problem, since males exercise the levers of power. This suggests a dichotomy of society into the powerful and powerless, and supports a conception of power in its negative sense. Such a view ignores 'productive' power which underscores negative power, and which thereby invalidates any attempt to dichotomize society into social categories of 'powerful' and 'powerless':

[O]ne should not assume a massive and primal condition of domination, a binary structure with 'dominators' on one side and 'dominated' on the other, but rather a multiform production of relations of domination which are partially susceptible of integration into overall strategies. (Foucault, 1980, p. 142)

What, then, of the idea that women can be agents for the exercise of more collective and empowering forms of power, thereby serving as the instruments of a more peaceful world? For Foucault, this overlooks the fact that there is no conceptual focus for identifying where to start among the 'multiple and indefinite' power networks that exist in a society. Human agency needs to be engaged in an incremental, step-by-step effort to change 'regimes of truth'. Effecting institutional change and subsequent policies by collective action is subordinate to the more fundamental task of changing 'regimes of truth'. This in turn means that women cannot be argued to be the direct or primary instruments for a more peaceful society.

Men and pacifism

Let us now look at the 'women and peace' stereotype in the context of men and pacifism. More specifically, I will examine seminal pacifists in the context of the rejection of the use of force in solving societal and international problems, and the promotion of communitarian values. I will then investigate how this might impact more broadly on the decisionmaking styles of pacifists and women.

Pacifism can be defined as the *principled* rejection of physical force in the resolution of conflict and of war. The rejection is thus based on normative rather than pragmatic or political considerations. A helpful classification of war and peace positions has been developed by Martin Ceadel (1987), who discusses five categories: militarism, crusading, defensism, pacificism and pacifism. He sees 'pacifism' as distinct from 'pacific-ism', which he believes is committed to introducing the political reforms necessary to make war obsolete in terms of cutting defence budgets, building cooperative relationships with other communities and states, 'but accepts the need for military force to defend its political achievements against aggression' (1987, p. 5). This contrasts with 'defensism', which accepts the maxim *si vis pacem para bellum*.

There is a long tradition of pacifism throughout human history. Those we know most of are males who were extensively written about and followed. While many women undoubtedly held similar beliefs, these are not nearly as well known, due to the low social status historically ascribed to women in most cultures. As Ellen Berg explains, throughout history, women have been excluded from 'the great human enterprise of explaining reality' (Berg, 1994, p. 326).

Three men exemplify pacifism for the twentieth century: Leo Tolstoy, Mahatma Gandhi and Martin Luther King. Tolstoy's later thought was dominated by his reading of the New Testament, especially Christ's Sermon on the Mount, which he interpreted as an absolute proscription of physical force (see Tolstoy, 1987). He subsequently became a pacifist and a trenchant critic of all forms of militarism – especially of 'patriotism', which he saw as the incipient cause of all war. Tolstoy's conversion to pacifism arose through his belief that 'the commands of his conscience are more binding . . . than the commands of men' (1987, p. 15). His pacifism led him to hold communitarian beliefs in the brotherhood of humanity and in the sanctity of all life.

Mohandas 'Mahatma' Gandhi was strongly influenced by Tolstoy's writings and likewise abandoned all forms of force in conflict resolution. Gandhi subsequently made non-violence the ethical maxim upon which his life philosophy or 'Search for Truth' was based: '*ahimsa* [non-violence] is the basis of the search for truth. I am realizing every day that the search is vain unless it is founded on *ahimsa* as the basis' (Gandhi, in Hingorani, 1970, p. 255). He argued that to be a potent force, non-violence must *begin* with the mind (non-violence of the strong) and not merely with the rejection of physical force between human beings (non-violence of the weak) (1970, p. 170). Gandhi thus believed that non-violence was synonymous with love, and promoted and practised this principle for most of his life. The means by which Gandhi developed his philosophy of non-violence, as was the case with Tolstoy, was the belief that conscience formed an infallible guide in life. The 'small voice of conscience' underpinned Gandhi's entire political philosophy.

Martin Luther King, influenced both by Gandhi and Tolstoy, held that 'true non-violence is more than the absence of violence' (King, 1964, p. 152). Non-violence corresponded to a 'way of life', rather than solely a useful method in achieving social change. King's reason for rejecting violence was based on his conviction that conscience forbade the use of physical force by individuals against their fellows. Non-violence as a 'commitment to a way of life' entailed communitarian beliefs whereby one acted in a way which showed *agapic* love to others. He used the terms 'Beloved Community' to describe his communitarian vision of an ideal human society characterized by 'love', 'human brotherhood' and 'justice'.[4]

Common to these three seminal pacifists for the twentieth century is that each grounded his non-violent beliefs in *conscience*. Conscience formed an absolute ethical guide for their political philosophy and political behaviour. They also had deeply-held beliefs about the importance of community and of the interdependency of human life. They all valued social relationships, as evidenced by their moral exhortations that mutual love should guide all human interaction. Furthermore, they all operated in a social setting where physical force was readily accepted in the resolution of conflict. Here they demonstrated that they were able to transcend such stereotypes in their own personal lives; and, more significantly, influence a large number of followers to adopt non-violence as a life philosophy. This contributed to a wider reappraisal of the use of non-violence in the resolution of conflict. Importantly, it broke through the 'men and war' stereotype in so far as they succeeded in combating criticisms that pacifism or non-violence was 'unmanly'.

What emerges from the above discussion is that pacifists think and behave very differently from those who are prepared to use force in pursuit of an abstract principle. Earlier it was suggested that relational thinkers value human relationships and emphasize the social consequences of their actions. Since these characteristics are also shared by Tolstoy, Gandhi, King and pacifists more generally, it can be argued that pacifists are relational thinkers. This is consistent with Gilligan's belief that the two modes of thought – relational and abstract thinking – are based on theme rather than gender (Gilligan, 1982, p. 2). As Kolb and Coolidge point out, both relational and abstract forms of thinking are part of healthy adult development, and it is only a question of degree that divides men from women more generally (Kolb & Coolidge, 1988/1995, p. 261).

If we agree that Tolstoy, Gandhi and King did think in relational terms due to their advocacy of non-violence as a way of life that entailed communitarian notions of the interdependence and sanctity of all life, then there appear to be at least to two distinct processes that lead to relational thinking. Conscience is important, as it has been throughout history. For pacifists, their relational thinking emerges as a result of development process based on individuation which leads to decisionmaking being grounded in moral principles, which in turn are grounded in conscience. We should note how this differs from the concept of women as socialized to be relational thinkers whose development process – according to Gilligan's critique of traditional psychological theories that extol individuation, separation and autonomy – is markedly distinct from the course taken by men and pacifists:

> The elusive mystery of women's development lies in its recognition of the continuing importance of attachment in the human life cycle. Woman's place in man's life cycle is to protect this recognition while the development litany intones the celebration of separation, autonomy, individuation, and natural rights. (Gilligan, 1982, p. 23)

Thus there are two different life-cycles taken by relational thinkers: one emerging through socialization, and the other emerging as a result of a normative conversion that culminates in a development process based on individuation. However, while pacifists take a principled position over the use of force in most if not all contexts, this is unlikely to be the case for women in particular, and relational thinkers more generally, since the value ascribed to human relationships makes it likely for women to take decisions to use force in cases where these relationships are under threat. Thus it is *pacific-ism*, rather than *pacifism*, that is arguably 'natural' for relational thinkers.

Gender difference and institutional decisionmaking

I have already pointed out how feminists have challenged, in various ways, the argument posed by Gilligan, Reardon, Brock-Utne and others that women have a special role to play in securing international peace as a result of their being socialized to be relational thinkers. The observation stemming from the discussion of pacifism and relational thinking is that women policy-makers are just as capable as their male peers of making decisions concerning the use of force, and that they resort to a variety of ethical and political justifications for doing so. Thus, it does not seem likely that merely achieving a 'critical mass' of women in institutional decision-making processes will be sufficient to exclude the organized use of force in resolving international conflict.

Another observation emerges from the way power is conceptualized and what this means for human agency in general, and institutional decisionmaking in particular. Power, according to the Foucauldian conception presented earlier, is a set of 'multiple and indefinite' power networks that cannot be analysed in terms of core sources which in turn can act as a locus for reform of social and institutional structures. Rather than being the locus for the exercise of power, as envisaged with the 'traditional' conception of power, institutional structures are dependent on power relations. Because individuals and communities help to shape and give life to these power relations that sustain institutional sources of power, the responsibility for decisions is diffused throughout a society, rather than being concentrated in the hands of those who exercise institutional decision-making.

The analytical focus for introducing peace and eliminating manifestations of violence – physical, structural or cultural – needs to be on how individual and communities interact and produce knowledge, identity and 'regimes of truth'. Foucault's analytical framework does not lend itself to the development of a coherent theory for how human agency is to change or overhaul existing power networks, other than an incrementalist approach to understanding 'the specificity of power relations and the struggles around them' (Foucault, 1980, p. 145). A Foucauldian perspective encourages a more expansive conception of responsibility where societal ills are ascribed to all, rather than being a consequence of mistaken institutional policies. All members of society therefore need to claim responsibility for the task of reforming power networks, and that makes the notion of historic victims problematic. This leads to the view expressed by Gerd Lerner, that women are 'not victims but actors in history' (in Berg, 1994, p. 332). Consequently, women's enhanced participatory role in institutional decisionmaking needs to be explicitly linked to the fundamental, but necessarily incremental, task of reforming power networks so as to eliminate the use of force in resolving conflict. While pacifists are necessarily committed to such a task, this is not necessarily the case with women or 'pacificists' more generally, as our discussion has shown. Unless there is such a transformative focus, simply ensuring a greater participatory role for women in institutional decisionmaking will not serve to advance the cause of global peace.

Notes

1   Kolb & Coolidge, 1988/1995, p. 267. For a study surveying women's attitudes to the use of force in the 1991 Gulf War, see Wilcox, Hewitt & Allsop, 1996.
2   Berg refers to this as 'social construction theory' (Berg, 1994).
3   For discussion of this conception of power, see Sharp, 1973, pp. 8–10.
4   Walter Fluker argues that 'love' is the central concept for King with regard to the idea of the 'Beloved Community' (see Fluker, 1989, p. 109). The concepts of justice and fraternity/brotherhood are implicit, Fluker would argue, in King's concept of love. I believe, however, that King's philosophy becomes clearer if these are analysed as independent concepts that form a basic trichotomy with his concept of love.

5
Gender, Power and Politics:
An Alternative Perspective

Errol Miller

Introduction

In Western liberal democracies, women constitute at least half of the voters. Why, then, are they so under-represented among elected representatives in parliaments? In most of these countries women have had the vote for over 70 years. Surely this is sufficient time for women voters to alter significantly the gender composition of elected representatives in the various parliaments. The puzzle is not relieved by the more recent democracies of newly independent countries: there the same pattern prevails. Yet to suggest that the latter are imitating the former is to fly in the face of the integrity of political process in these countries (Duncan & O'Brien, 1983). To unravel this conundrum we shall have to go beyond empirical reality, and to re-examine and re-conceptualize gender and patriarchy and their relations to power and politics.

Defining patriarchy and gender

While definitions seldom capture the complexity of the phenomena they seek to describe or specify, they are useful in setting the parameters of the discourse and in establishing common meaning between those engaged in dialogue. Given the widely differing approaches that have been adopted towards conceptualizing both patriarchy and gender, we will need to set out as precisely as possible the ways in which these are defined and viewed.

Defining patriarchy

The seminal theoretical contribution of feminist scholarship to social theory has been to place patriarchy firmly as a central category in social theorizing and analysis. But – just what is 'patriarchy'? Max Weber defined patriarchy as *women and younger men being ruled by older men, who were heads of household* (Weber, 1947). A few feminist theorists have followed the Weberian definition, but the more common approach has been to discard the generation difference between men, in Weber's formulation, and to define patriarchy as *that system of social structures and practices in which men dominate, oppress and exploit women* (Dahlerup, 1987; Walby, 1990). Thus feminist scholarship has tended to adopt a narrower and more exclusive definition than the Weberian formulation.

Defining patriarchy solely in terms of men's domination of women means treating both men and women as two separate undifferentiated groups that have sustained their coherence over time and between different cultures. This posture has attracted sharp criticism, especially from black feminists and poststructural and postmodernist theorists. hooks (1984), for example, has argued that while white feminists have traditionally conceptualized the family and the home as major sources of women's oppression, this does not hold true among blacks. Indeed, as more and more black women become heads of households, the family and the home have become the major loci of their liberation from traditional patriarchal roles.

Collins (1990) has extended the line of argument advanced by hooks by observing that race, class and gender constitute three interlocking axes of oppression that are part of an overall matrix of domination. She further makes the point that while most individuals have no difficulty identifying their own victimization, they routinely fail to see how they contribute to the suppression of others. White feminists typically point to their oppression, but resist seeing how much their white skin constitutes a social privilege. Likewise, African-Americans, eloquent in their analysis of racism, often persist in their perception of poor white women as symbols of white power. Failure to see gender as part of the larger matrix of domination inevitably leads to myopia in the approach to and perception of oppression.

Taking a different line, postmodernist theorists have maintained that neither men nor women are unitary categories. They argue that the categories 'men' and 'women' (or 'male' and 'female') actually involve a number of overlapping and cross-cutting discourses of masculinities and femininities which are historically and culturally variable. In their view, the notions of 'women' and 'men' dissolve into shifting and variable social constructs which lack stability and coherence over time. Walby (1990) has offered some rebuttal by her observation that the postmodern feminist theorists draw heavily upon the deconstructionism of Derrida (1976), the discourse analysis of Foucault (1981) and the postmodernism of Lyotard (1978), who are all guilty of not paying serious attention to gender. Indeed, poststructural and postmodernism theorists have been no different from modern or classical theorists in their benign neglect of gender in social analysis. The weakness in the postmodernist conception of gender is that, as Dahlerup (1987) has aptly pointed out, men's domination of society has remained highly uniform across cultures and throughout history.

By contrast, I have approached the definition of patriarchy from the opposite direction of the radical feminists by taking a more inclusive approach (Miller, 1991). The main limitation of Weber's definition of patriarchy lies in its omission of the kinship relations, factual or fictive, that usually exist between the older and younger men and women who constitute the household. In other words, patriarchy needs to be defined as that system of reciprocal social obligations in which final authority rests with the older men of the kinship collective, who exercise that authority over its individual male and female members in the overall interest of the collective.

The differences between these three sets of definitions of patriarchy lie in the choice of the elements to be included. Most feminist scholars have confined their definition of patriarchy solely to gender. Weber's definition included the elements of gender and generation. My definition includes genealogy, gender and generation, and holds that recognition of genealogy is critical to understanding the complexities of patriarchy and gender.

In my view, the gender and generation elements relate mainly to the internal relations of the collective, while the genealogy element defines its external boundaries and relations. From one perspective, genealogy extends kinship outside the immediate circumstances of the household or family, by establishing links with other collectives through common ancestry. At the same time, it defines collectives that are not kin – a critical consideration, both conceptually and empirically.

Conceptually and historically, patriarchy involves not only asymmetry in power between men and women, but also shared identity, group solidarity, common bonds and mutual obligations. These were what differentiated patriarchal collectives from one another. Further, historically, patriarchal collectives had major difficulties with other collectives that fell outside the covenant of kinship, particularly with the men of those collectives. When patriarchal collectives interacted outside boundaries where kinship could be established, whether factual or fictive, then one group had to submit to the hegemony of the other. Failing such compromise, violent confrontation became the means of establishing dominance. In my *Men at Risk* (Miller, 1991) I traced the practices of genocide, where one collective sought the physical elimination of another, the killing of male captives, the castration of male captives and the almost permanent enslavement of men, as historical outcomes of conflict between collectives which did not share the covenant of kinship or where that covenant had been breached. In all of these circumstances, patriarchal collectives found it easier to incorporate women of non-kin groups than the men of such groups. Thus, the external relations with men of hostile collectives is as much an element of patriarchy as are the internal relations with women of the kinship collective.

Within the patriarchal collective generation, age, in addition to genealogy, moderates relations between men: because age is mutable, in time the younger males succeed the older men. Genealogy and generation combine to define the younger males as potential heirs of the older men. Succession dictates male solidarity, manifested in the older men grooming and apprenticing the younger men, who reciprocate by waiting their turn. While genealogy and generation contribute to male solidarity within the collective through the process of succession, gender excludes women, who are left marginalized within the kinship collective by virtue of such exclusion. Within patriarchy, therefore, women are marginalized in the internal relations of the kinship collective. On the other hand, the genealogical relations between men and women of the collective act to ameliorate women's marginalization by virtue of the filial bonds and the men's obligation to protect and provide for them.

Further, I have argued that the genealogy element, defining the external relations of patriarchy, defined non-kin men as potential threats and possible enemies. In these circumstances of relations between unrelated collectives, where the covenant of kinship did not exist, the subordination of one collective relative to the other – voluntarily or by violence – became the only means of establishing the bases of interaction. By definition, therefore, patriarchy must include the marginalization of men of the unrelated collectives, in one way or another.

The essence of patriarchy involves not only the marginalization of women within the kinship collective, but also that of men of unrelated collectives. Two elemental features of patriarchy are (1) the marginalization of women within their kinship collectives; and (2) the marginalization of men of those other collectives over which dominance has been established, by whatever means. This definition of patriarchy implies that gender cannot be understood or interpreted solely in terms of men's domination of women. Gender analysis is not simply about the asymmetry in power between men and women. A gender perspective is not only about women's issues. To understand gender as being synonymous with women, is to misconstrue or misinterpret the concept of patriarchy. Gender analysis cannot assume solidarity between men and women belonging to different groups in society. This is because gender operates in conjunction with the other social criteria according to which societies are organized. These are critical considerations, particularly when competition for political power is the focal point.

Defining gender

In defining gender we must differentiate it from sex. To be sure, the essentialist position holds that sex and gender are almost synonymous. This biological reductionism implies that sex differences between men and women related to size, strength, speed and stamina all determine the gender differences noted in masculinity and femininity. These differences all favour men, and thus determine their leadership in society. To this I would say that not only is there considerable overlap between men and women on these traits, but not even among men are these physical differences the defining features of leaders in society. If anything, they more aptly describe their bodyguards!

The position taken here is that sex is biologically determined while gender is socially constructed. Those who argue that gender is biologically constructed may say that, if gender were totally a social construct, then one should expect to find such wide variations in masculinity in history and contemporary cultures as to defy unifying categorizations. However, there do exist common themes associated with masculinity and femininity across widely different cultures and throughout history. Such common themes, it is claimed, can only be accounted for by biological factors operating through genetics.

In earlier research (see Miller, 1991) I argued that the common themes in masculinity and femininity are not inconsistent with their social construction *if* gender is defined as the sexual division of power related to living-giving and life-taking. It is the universality of these life-giving and life-taking powers – and not genetic determination – that accounts for the commonality observed across history and cultures. My reconstruction of the social construction of patriarchy and gender in antiquity, which incorporates some elements of Lerner (1986), can be summarized as follows:

- Early humans lived in small isolated groups in relatively hostile environments of which they had very limited knowledge. Their primitive technology and shelter made them particularly vulnerable to ecological calamities. Adaptive advantage rested in group living. Hence, the main reason why early humans lived in descent groups was to ensure survival.
- Long life constituted a scarce and treasured resource in pre-literate communities of antiquity, as the aged members of the group represented the resident memory of the group and its reservoir of information and past experiences in dealing with the exigencies of living. Men lived longer than women, largely due to the risks attendant on child-bearing (Lerner, 1986).
- Women were engaged in child-bearing and child-rearing from puberty to the grave, as the average life-span of females at that time was less than 30 years. Fertility and a large number of offspring were another treasured resource of kinship communes attempting to survive the challenges of the time. From early motifs in cave art we can clearly see that the Mother Goddess was highly venerated.
- In addition to dealing with bringing life into existence and preserving it, this small autonomous isolated group also had to deal with the issues of life-taking, as it related to the physical and ritual defence of the group. Since biology determined that women gave birth, and they were perennially involved in this activity and in the preservation of the lives that were brought into bearing, life-taking fell by default to the men, particularly to the older men of the group.
- This separation of life-giving and life-taking powers was the original

sexual division of power that separated masculinity from femininity. Women were socialized principally in relation to all the life-giving and preservation skills and knowledge, while men were socialized with respect to life-taking. Accordingly, the basic definition of femininity and its surviving common themes came to reside in the honing of such traits as caring, nurturing, gentleness, kindness, tenderness, cooperation, accommodation of differences, long-suffering, patience, acquiescence and passivity. Likewise, the basic definition of masculinity and its common themes came to reside in the development of such traits as assertiveness, decisiveness, ruthlessness, courage, valour, confrontation, toughness, conquest and the killer instinct. These latter traits are all related to the capacity to take life with impunity.

- While there was equality, and even a feminine bias, in the initial separation of life-giving and life-taking powers, in group dynamics over the long haul, life-taking proved more powerful than life-giving. While mothers were venerated because of life-giving, this was, after all, a one-shot event. Fathers, however, were feared because they held the power to take life at any time. Thus, fathers exercising the life-taking power became the final authority in all matters pertaining to the descent group. Men and women participated in the separation of the sexual division of power without anticipating its long-term consequences for female marginalization in the kinship commune.
- The sexual division of power was initiated in antiquity. The Druids had a saying that all masters of families were kings in their own households: they had the power of life and death over their wives, children and slaves. The father's power to take the lives of the members of the kinship commune survived well into recorded history. Early Roman law codified this power.

Gender defined as the sexual division of *power* departs from the commonly accepted definition of gender as the sexual division of *labour*, women's work being restricted to the private sphere of the household while men's work extended to occupations in the public sphere (Dex, 1985; Reddock, 1994). This is not to deny that, in the course of history, a sexual division of labour has occurred. However, this has come subsequent to and as a result of the prior sexual division of power. In other words, primacy is accorded to the power relations of gender, and not to labour and work differences.

While the creation of patriarchy and the original construction of gender are shrouded in the mists of antiquity, with only circumstantial evidence to support contemporary speculation about the origination of these phenomena, I would contend that today's unravelling of gender and patriarchy is but a mirror image of the processes involved in their original construction. Here we should note three points with respect to the definition of gender as the sexual division of life-giving and life-taking powers.

First, war is the supreme expression of patriarchy and the warrior the ultimate symbol of masculinity. Unmitigated rage, unbridled fury and unrestrained violence directed at life-taking are the quintessential masculine mode of resolving conflicts. Warriors – men most skilled and successful in taking life with impunity – are the final arbiters and authorities in deciding differences and in determining what will prevail. The universality of war in history and across cultures, and its virtual exclusivity as a male enterprise, testifies to the primacy and pervasive nature of life-taking in defining masculinity and of establishing final authority in societal affairs.

Secondly, at the root of the contemporary controversy on abortion is the question of whether women should have the right to take life with impunity. The right-to-life side of the controversy is basically that women's commitment is to give life without reservation or caveat. It asserts the primacy basis of the definition of femininity and the essence of the ancient social construction of womanhood. The right-to-choose side of the argument fundamentally shifts the ancient foundation of the definition of femininity and womanhood, in that it combines the life-giving and life-taking powers. It thereby not only changes the primary basis of the construction of femininity but also encroaches on and threatens the very essence of the definition of masculinity. By excluding fathers from the choice, women's right to choose fundamentally alters the construction of gender. While the arguments concerning the rights of the unborn child should not be underestimated, the gender definition implications of women's right-to-choose need to be recognized as lying at the core of the controversy. The deep passions evoked testify to the centrality of the issues involved.

Thirdly, in the course of the evolution of society, the father's right to take life became transferred to the king or chief and eventually to the state. Today, the right of the state to take life has been challenged in the movement against capital punishment. In a way this can be interpreted as a tendency towards the reform of masculinity. At the same time, there is increasing escalation of the wanton taking of life by men in gangs, terrorists, enraged loners gunning down unsuspecting victims for reasons hard to identify or rationalize. The move to reform the fundamental life-taking definition of masculinity, by men and groups who have been empowered, is counterpoised, counteracted and even compromised by marginalized men who seem to be seeking to reclaim their manhood through life-taking. Mass murder, terrorism, gangs engaged in savage acts of violence, the escalation of murder, the move to abolish capital punishment and the counter-move to re-institute it where it has been abolished, all stand in screaming contradiction. Reform and reaction to the life-taking in society are yet another example of the fundamental nature of this construction of masculinity and its continuing relevance in contemporary society.

Gender understood as the sexual division of power is the key to understanding many of the great debates in the modern world. It also provides important insights with respect to many complex matters of gender issues and relationships today.

The ethnic origin of nations and the nation-state

Anthony D. Smith (1987) has maintained that the nation-state evolved by encompassing several ethnic communities in a single polity. Unlike the city-states of the ancient world, the modern nation-state encompasses both city and surrounding countryside. Invariably nation-states are made up of several cities, with none having political primacy over the others, such that client relationships are required. Also the nation embodies cities, countryside, diverse ethnic groups and different religions, while claiming autonomy and sovereignty in its relations with other nations. It claims pre-eminence in allegiance and loyalty, over and beyond every other social and political entity.

Invariably nation-states are premised on the utopian values of equality, human rights, social justice and consent as the foundation of government. The fundamental unit of national organization is the individual national, the citizen. Each national, by virtue of his or her nationality, is entitled to equal treatment, enjoys the same rights, is guaranteed the same justice and, after reaching the age of majority, is empowered as an elector in determining the government in the vast majority of nations. These utopian values are invariably enshrined in constitutional law. Further, the state has become the principal mechanism and chief executing agency of the values of nationhood.

By virtue of its construction, the nation-state constitutes a frontal attack on society organized on the basis of patriarchy – that is, on the criteria of genealogy, gender and generation. This assault has focused mainly on genealogy, with tribe, clan, caste, lineage, race and family being officially relegated to social categories devoid of constitutional or legal content. If the ethical vision of the universalist religions rendered these categories 'immoral', then the nation-state has added 'unconstitutional' and 'illegal' to their meaning in the political, economic and social conduct of the nation.

In the nation, the tribe, clan, caste, lineage, race and family are conceded as having only sentimental, nostalgic and cultural meaning. The family itself is reduced to a nurturing unit stripped of the political and economic relationships that once surrounded kinship collectives. On the other hand, non-kin forms of societal organization are now imbued with positive political, economic and social meaning. These include the state, replete with its parliament, courts, military establishment, police force, and civil service bureaucracy, and outside these the political party, the corporation, the trade union, the school and the church. All of these are constitutionally and legally required to practise the utopian values on which the nation-state is predicated.

At the same time, however, civil society within each nation carries the legacy of tribal, clan and lineage society. Kinship allegiance, clan honour, perpetuation of the lineage and patriarchal obligations – these continue to be central values. In several societies the notion of kinship has been transposed to race, with the same assumptions of blood bonds, group solidarity and mutual obligations as in lineage society. In all versions of this type of society the family, organized on patriarchal traditions, remains the fundamental unit of social organization. The social reality of nation-states, therefore, is that of civil society organized on the basis of kinship, clan honour, perpetuation of families, patriarchal authority and filial obligations, and the state predicated on the utopian values of equality, human rights, social justice and representative democracy in which sovereignty rests with the people. Further, civil society sees the family as the basic unit of organization, whereas the state is organized with the individual as the fundamental unit of its constitutional structure.

The national project, by definition, consists of transforming civil society from its ethnic roots, kinship structure and patriarchal traditions into nations in harmony with their constitutions, mandating overarching values espousing equality, justice, rights and consent. Indeed, the mobilization of the nations resides in the implementation of the higher values of nationhood. Finally, the promise of material progress implied in nationhood, particularly to the mass of the dispossessed groups, has added yet another element of meaning to the values on which nationhood is premised.

Here we must bear in mind that the formation of nation-states has not been the inevitable result of social evolution, nor the product of the wholehearted embrace of the high ethical vision of nationhood. Nation-states have all been constructed through the processes of dynamic interaction among groups within nations, where one or two groups become the 'chief nationalists'. While leading the construction of the nation on the overarching values of equality, individual rights and social justice enshrined in constitutional law, these 'chief nationalists' have invariably skewed the construction of the nation in their image and to their benefit, thereby ensuring substantial advantages to their own groups. In this context the state, controlled by the 'chief nationalists', becomes the major instrument of constructing the nation in their image and to their advantage. The greatest promise for the success of the national project resides in the moral conduct of the groups that claim and exercise leadership in implementing the mandate of nationhood. Likewise, the main threat to the realization of the ideals of the national project emanates from lapses in moral conduct on the part of those spearheading its implementation.

Social transformation is being effected in the cross-currents of the tensions that arise when one tries to construct nations founded on utopian values, out of civil society rooted in ethnicity and kinship. These tensions are further heightened and compounded by the acquisition and consolidation of advantage by those groups who lead the construction of the nation in circumstances that should benefit all. The essence of the transformation is from kinship to non-kinship forms of association and organization. According to the national ideal and creed, all persons, all families and all ethnic groups within the nation are entitled to equal rights to participate in the parliamentary affairs of the state, to receive equal justice through its courts, and have equal access to the bureaucracy of the state including the civil service, military establishment, police force, schools and colleges, and statutory bodies. Further, all nationals, irrespective of family or ethnicity, should be free and unencumbered to become members of political parties, religions, corporations, trade unions, clubs and other non-governmental organizations operating in the public sphere.

Practical reality, however, is somewhat different. Not all inequalities of civil society organized on the basis of kinship and ethnicity, and the asymmetry of the power implied in this inequality, are automatically swept away by applying the national creed. Among the factors fuelling resistance to the full implementation of the national project are the following:

- The efforts of those groups that previously held power, commanded considerable resources, were accorded high esteem and whose culture dominated the society, to retain at least some of their former positions within the nation.
- The attempts of the newly empowered groups, not only to lead the construction of the nation, but to consolidate their position in the society and nation. (Indeed, the democratization of political power has invariably brought about more upward social mobility of those controlling and administering the machinery of the state than by the mass of the people themselves.)
- The formation of alliances between the old and the new guard, to their mutual benefit, which are at variance with the overarching values of nationhood.

We should note that nations and societies are almost always organized on the basis of additional criteria to genealogy, gender and generation. Such criteria include class or status group, religion or ideology, region and citizenship. The patriarchal criteria are nested within these other criteria which 'overlay' them, so to speak. The interaction between these several criteria creates the complexities for which social organization and voting behaviour are renown – because groups and segments of the society and nation formed on the basis of the interaction of these criteria invariably establish horizontal and vertical alliances to promote and preserve their interests.

Two additional points need to be noted here. First, gender is by no means primary or pre-eminent as a criterion in the organization of societies or nations. It is embedded within other criteria. Secondly, gender operates in interaction with the other criteria upon which societies and nations are organized. In social and political behaviour in society and nations, the actions of men and women need to be interpreted within the context of the interactions of criteria such as class, race, religion, region, generation and ideology. This is not to say that the actions of men and of women are entirely predicted on the basis of locating them relative to these criteria, since individuals may affirm or oppose or adopt a non-committal stance on any issue. Rather, identification of the criteria, and their interaction, allows the parameters and frameworks of action to be delineated.

The transformation of patriarchy

In the course of constructing the nation-state out of a civil society structured on the basis of kinship and ethnicity, patriarchy becomes transformed, mainly as a result of the operations of two processes. The first process relates to partnership between, on the one hand, men and women of the groups previously holding advantages in the civil society and, on the other, those newly empowered in the nation, in defending and preserving or enhancing and consolidating their groups' interests in the nation. These groups can be termed the dominant groups in the society and nation. The second process relates to the exclusion of men of the subordinate groups in the civil society from much of the opportunities of upward social mobility offered in the nation.

The partnership process

The main features of this partnership process can be listed briefly as follows:

- Easy access to and first choice by members of dominant groups of the most powerful, strategic, prestigious and lucrative opportunities available in the nation.
- Patriarchal rank operative in the dominant groups, so that greatest access and first preference to these opportunities goes to older men while last choice and least preference is accorded to younger women.
- The magnitude of opportunities available to the dominant groups outstripping the supply of men of those groups to meet the demand.
- Women of the dominant groups being recruited when the supply of older and younger men of the groups is insufficient to meet the demand.

This partnership process operates in circumstances where the opportunities available to the dominant group exceed its capacity to meet the demand through its supply of men of that group. In these circumstances women of the group are co-opted and recruited to meet the shortfall or hiatus in supply of men of that group. Failure to recruit the women of the group would result in such opportunities going primarily to the other groups that compete with or challenge the dominant group for position. Thus, women of the dominant group are mobilized to assist the group to maximize its appropriation of available opportunities. In this, men and women of the dominant group can be said to work together to advance or defend the interests or position of their group. Put in the converse, men and women of the dominant groups join forces to exploit the other groups in the nation.

It is the men of the dominant group who retain most of the top positions and most strategic occupations, whereas the women of the dominant group are assigned mainly to the intermediate positions and less strategic levels in the occupational structure. This highlights the demarcation between senior and junior membership of the partnership. The fact that women's marginalization in the dominant group is manifest in this arrangement is secondary to the fact that both men and women of the dominant group are acting collectively in the interest of their group, and against the other groups in the society. This partnership process is first and foremost a mechanism for defending and promoting the interests of the dominant groups, and not that of marginalizing or exploiting the women of the groups.

Put another way, equality of access to opportunity within the dominant group is unlikely to make any material or substantial difference to the establishment, extension or consolidation of the hegemony of the dominant group over the other groups in society. Men and women of the dominant group are united in their intention to advance the interests of their group against those of others. It is the marginalization of the other groups in the society that is the primary mission, not the marginalization of women within the dominant group itself. Men and women of the dominant group are partners in advancing the interests of their group, albeit with the women as junior and men as senior partners. As such the partnership process is neither negative nor demeaning in and of itself, although some women may feel demeaned by it. From the perspective of the dominant group, it is an ennobling enterprise that works to secure the interests and advancement of the group as a whole.

The exclusionary process

The second process involves excluding men of subordinate groups in society from most opportunities for upward social mobility. As a result, most of the opportunities for upward social mobility go instead to the women of the subordinate groups. This process has been described by Miller (1994). The core elements involved in this second process are as follows:

- Conflict between the dominant and other groups in society concerning the basis on which the society is organized and challenges with respect to existing inequalities with respect to access to opportunity within the society.
- The imperative to respond to these challenges by conceding access to opportunities to the subordinate groups in the society. Concessions to such challenges are mandated by the constitutions of nations, required

by the ethical vision of nationhood and usually necessary as a result of elective politics.

- Expansion in opportunities open to the subordinate groups and integration into the mainstream of society.
- Control by the dominant groups of the mechanisms and gateways through which members of the subordinate groups can achieve upward social mobility.
- The willingness of some segments of the subordinate groups to accept the structure of opportunity for upward social mobility as fashioned by the dominant groups.

The exclusionary process operates most successfully in circumstances where the dominant group has control of the mechanisms that govern access to institutions serving the subordinate groups, and where subordinate group access to these institutions is being expanded. In these circumstances, the exclusionary process acts to bias access in favour of subordinate-group females, by excluding most of the males of this group. Expanded opportunities afforded to subordinate groups constitute a strong incentive to their participation, given the limited scope of available opportunities for socio-economic advancement. Acceptance of the opportunities afforded means the advancement of the group by way of their daughters rather than their sons. Many members of the subordinate groups will gladly accept sponsored mobility on these terms.

Here we should note that men of the subordinate group are deliberately excluded from the expanded opportunities offered to their group. And why? Because of the threat they pose to the dominant group for political, social, economic, ideological or cultural reasons. Such exclusion occurs in circumstances of conflict between the groups, or challenge by the subordinate, when the dominant group is constrained to concede some measure of expanded opportunity to the challengers due to the constitutional, legal or political considerations of the imperatives of the nation-state.

Through the exclusion process, men of the dominant groups establish alliances with women of the subordinate groups. The asymmetry of power relations dictates that the latter would be dependent on the former for maintaining their sponsored advancement in the society. Like women of the dominant groups, women of the subordinate groups will occupy middle-level and intermediate positions within the private and public bureaucracies, and in the process operate as lieutenants of the dominant-group men in the top positions. Such alliances will generally earn the resentment of men of the subordinate group.

Implications for the transformation of patriarchy

The partnership process redefines, extends and expands patriarchy within dominant groups to encompass the public as well as the private sphere. This is because their scope of authority and influence is expanded to encompass the subordinate groups. The rule of fathers in the family, lineage, or clan is extended to non-kin groups: political parties, trade unions, colleges, schools, corporations, the civil service etc. Accordingly, it is the men of the dominant groups who become the leaders of political parties, executives of corporations, heads of trade unions, heads of the civil service and top officers in the police force.

The essence of this transformation is that these non-kin associations and organizations within the public sphere of the nation come to have the same structure as that of kinship collectives in the civil society. Patriarchy is transformed: from being a feature of tribal groups and kinship collectives, it takes on new forms within non-kin associations and organizations – as 'fathers' within the groups leading the nationalist charge or holding great economic resources seize or consolidate their places within the nation construct. The end result is the patriarchal state, political patriarchy, corporate patriarchy, trade union patriarchy etc., as men of the dominant groups seize places in these areas within the public sphere in the nation.

The movement away from the rule of fathers in blood-bonded collectives to that of men in political parties, corporations, trade unions, colleges, schools, and other non-kin organizations transforms patriarchy from being the rule of fathers to being the rule of men. In the absence of filial relationships, the rule of fathers becomes the rule of men. Dahlerup (1987) has noted the emergence of the patriarchal state, observing that its defining feature is that it functions in the interest of men. My interpretation diverges slightly from this: I would say that the patriarchal state is commandeered by the men and women of the groups who control its mechanisms, to serve their interests and prerogatives.

As noted, the partnership process extends the patriarchy of the dominant groups from the private to the public sphere and advances or consolidates the hegemony of those groups over subordinate groups, by according some dominant-group women the role of junior partners in advancing group interests in the public sphere. In this process, gender as an organizing principle in society becomes compromised. These junior partners of the dominant group now exercise power over men of the subordinate group. At the same time, their junior position in the partnership raises another question: is it just? This becomes particularly salient in the context of a national creed professing equal rights and justice for all.

The second process, involving male marginalization in the subordinate group, is even more radical in its undermining of patriarchy, since here genealogy, gender and generation are all compromised as organizing principles in society. By sponsoring the mobility of members of the subordinate group to positions previously reserved for the dominant group, it compromises genealogy. By advancing young people over older folk, it calls generation into question. By giving preference to young women over their fathers and brothers, and prospective spouses, it compromises gender.

The net result of such sponsored mobility is that some women of the subordinate groups become even more liberated from traditional patriarchal and feminine roles than their peers in the dominant group. Not only are they accorded roles in the public sphere – they also become heads of households in their own right, not simply substitutes in one generation until male succession can be restored. Patriarchy in the private sphere is reversed in large proportion of the subordinate group as, through the process of male marginalization, many men are without the means and symbols to sustain their traditional masculine and father roles as prescribed by patriarchy.

The exclusionary process undermines patriarchy in the subordinate group. This is accomplished by the following:

- breaching patriarchal rank by promoting women over their fathers, brothers and spouses;
- undermining the material symbols by which the males of the subordinate group reinforce their authority within the group;
- fostering matrifocal forms of socialization in homes and schools, consistent with the structure of opportunity in which girls are most likely to access available socio-economic opportunities for advancement;
- fracturing solidarity in the subordinate group, by differential rates of incorporation of males and females into the mainstream of society, in the long term resulting in the men being blamed for their lack of socio-economic progress, and men resenting the advancement of females of the group ahead of themselves.

These two processes are by no means mutually exclusive. Indeed, they are highly compatible. The first process operates mainly, but not exclusively, within the dominant group and those other groups in society with which it establishes alliances. The second process operates largely within subordinate groups in circumstances of conflict with the dominant group.

Ironically, at the same time that patriarchy is transformed and extended, by both processes, to encompass the private as well as the public spheres in the nation, it is also compromised and weakened. The factors related to this are as follows:

- As the authority and power of the men of the dominant groups are expanded, there comes a corresponding marginalization of large numbers of men of the subordinate groups, resulting in increased polarization between men in the nation. While a few men become increasing powerful, many men become part of a highly marginalized underclass. At the same time, the position of women becomes more equalized, as many women of both the dominant and the subordinate groups come to occupy middle positions in the public and private bureaucracies. While these women are subject to the glass ceiling imposed by the men of the dominant groups, they are still in a much more advantageous position than men of the underclass.

- The masculine bias in the dominant groups and the underclass and the feminization of the middle strata result in a state of flux in relationships previously constructed on the basis of patriarchal norms. Patriarchy becomes compromised as young women exercise authority over fathers, wives become the chief providers of families, mothers become heads of households, women unable to find husbands of comparable social and economic status decide to become single parents, and large numbers of girls out-perform boys in schools.
- The polarized position of men in the nation is marked by the criteria upon which the civil society is organized. If the society is organized on the basis of ethnicity, religion, class, gender and generation, then the men of the dominant group will tend to belong to one ethnic group, the upper class, a different denomination or religion and be older than the men of the underclass, who in turn will tend to be of other ethnic groups, lower class, a different denomination or religion and be younger. These bases of inequality stand officially condemned in the national creed and constitution. Hence the dominant group will find its moral authority undermined and diminished by changes of corruption, patronage, clientelism, nepotism, discrimination and victimization which they cannot successfully defend given the marked disparities.
- Political, corporate, union, school and other non-kin association bonds are relatively weak compared to the blood bonds assumed in kinship collectives. This produces a tendency for non-kin associations and organizations to fracture and disintegrate in the face of sustained resistance or gross failure to fulfil their mandate.

Conflict within the national project

The state-led construction of the nation commences with an assault on the inequalities of civil society organized on the basis of patriarchal norms. It results in both the transformation and extension of patriarchy, while also compromising and weakening it. At the root of this paradoxical situation are the actions of the dominant groups, or chief nationalists, who lead the state in its construction of the nation while also seeking to preserve or promote, defend or consolidate the position of their groups within the nation and society. Such self-serving actions of the dominant groups compromise the overarching values and the high ethical vision of the nation, and bring into question the morality of its chief executing agency, the state.

In the flux which results from patriarchy being transformed and compromised on the one hand, and the moral failure of the state and its leaders to uphold the ethical vision of the nation, conflicts develop: which direction should be taken? One direction is to complete the national project. Related to this are movements focused on the elements of patriarchy: genealogy, gender and generation. These are movements whose mission is to eliminate ethnic, tribe, race, and caste discrimination; movements seeking to promote women's rights and to secure appropriate punishment for crimes of rape and other violence against women; movements promoting children's rights and seeking to eliminate child abuse. The other direction involves returning to civil society organized on patriarchal norms – in other words, abandoning the national project. Here we find movements advocating ethnic cleansing or racial partitioning; maintaining that women's place is in the home, as wife and mother; and asserting the primacy of the family unit in directing and determining the upbringing and discipline of children.

Gender and politics

Gender and patriarchy have always been part and parcel of politics. As kinship communes integrated and amalgamated, usually on the assumptions of common ancestry, the patriarchal principle was extended to the governance of the emergent entities. One clan seized or was granted ownership of the government. On the basis of heredity, royal clans were thus created as kingship (or chiefdom or emperorship) was passed from one generation to the next. While royal clans might be displaced by other clans, who captured ownership of the government, the principle of genealogical descent was kept in place. Within dynasties, patriarchal rank determined that males of the clan should ascend to the throne. If there was a hiatus in male succession then some female of the clan or lineage would be chosen, until a male heir could be found. Through this process of partnership, government was preserved within the dynasty until it was overthrown, usually by violent means. The history of monarchies is replete with its various episodes of queens within the litany of kings. In other words, throughout recorded history, governance has never been about the rule of men, but rather about the rule of *one group* over others. Loyalty to the group has always taken precedence over gender solidarity. Women succeeded to thrones when the interests of the group were at stake. Patriarchal closure was relaxed in the face of a threat to group survival.

The non-Western history of government by consent of the governed still has chapters to be written. For example, the tradition among the Akan peoples of West Africa has been succession of the most able member of the royal clan, and not the eldest. Commoners also had a voice in the succession process within the royal clan, with the Queen Mother acting as intermediary between the royal clan and the commoners.

To return to the Western tradition, let us take the example of the United States of America. This was a republic founded in 1776 on the notion that 'all men are created equal' and therefore had the same rights. Government in this context – as later affirmed by Abraham Lincoln – had to be of the people, by the people and for the people. However, up until 1815, only four states of the Union had granted voting rights to all white males. In all other states, voting rights were qualified by ownership of property and payment of a certain amount of taxes. In fact this meant that voting rights varied with the interactions of race, class and gender. It was the admission of Western states into the Union that prompted change. These states, without old, established estates or large fortunes, wrote universal white male suffrage into their constitutions, making it an issue in the Eastern states as well. By 1825, only Rhode Island was without such a law among Northeastern states, although in both Massachusetts and New York there had been strong resistance to the enfranchisement of the landless, non-taxpaying and largely uneducated mass of white males.

The election of General Andrew Jackson in 1828 marked a turning point in American politics, as a sufficient number of states had enacted white male suffrage to allow the election of a 'man of the people'. With the exception of General Washington, all presidents before Jackson had been college graduates, that is members of the aristocracy of learning and of the families that constituted the colonial elite. They had all come from Massachusetts or Virginia. Andrew Jackson had little formal schooling (although he did study law in a law office and ran a very successful practice for years), and was from the West. He was elected by men who shared his social background and probably had less education, whether formal or non-formal. Jackson won handsomely again in 1832, thereby underscoring the fact that the change – 'Jacksonian democracy' – represented a permanent shift in the nature of power and politics in the Republic. White male citizenship in the Republic was now unqualified. Ironically, it was the social heirs of the Founding Fathers who were the first to feel the full political force of the equality so eloquently articulated in the Declaration of Independence and Federal Constitution.

Male suffrage was broadened to include black men in 1869, during the period of Reconstruction following the Civil War and the emancipation of the slaves. Interestingly, subsequent challenges by states and rulings by the Supreme Court led to limits being imposed on the franchise to black men in several states. By the 1890s, disqualifying conditions were being added to their right to vote and become representatives, a course of action without parallel among whites and in other Western democracies. In effect, qualifications of class were applied to black men, disqualifying large numbers of them.

Female suffrage did not materialize in the USA until the Nineteenth Amendment, proposed in 1919 but not ratified until August 1920. This followed a long campaign that can be traced back to the Seneca Falls convention of 1848. In this matter the American Republic was following and not leading the other Western nations, as several Western states had already granted women full voting rights – for example, New Zealand in 1893, Australia in 1902, Finland in 1906 and Norway in 1913.

Voting is surely the most basic right in a democracy. And yet, in a Republic predicated on the principles of liberty and equality, it took over 50 years for poor white men to gain the franchise, just under 100 years for all black men to be added and then, with some subsequent subtraction, nearly

150 years for it to be extended to all women. Noteworthy here is not only the time-lag between policy and implementation, but the discrepancies between statements of principle and practice based upon those principles, when implementation is dependent on those who stand to be dispossessed by complying with the intent of their noble ideals.

In almost all of the colonies of Western imperial nations, voting in the colonial period was restricted on the basis of ethnicity, class and gender. It was only in the postwar period that adult suffrage was constitutionally granted prior to political independence. Like the US experience, adult suffrage in the colonies and newly independent countries changed the face of politics, particularly its colour, as the newly empowered voted almost *en bloc* to remove the holders of political power in those countries.

Gender solidarity and politics

Let us return to a basic question: why are women so under-represented in parliaments in liberal democracies today? After all, they constitute at least half of the voters. Can we in fact assume that the utopian ideals of equality and social justice, constitutionally decreed in nations, actually exist in reality, and that women are exercising their franchise within this ideal framework?

The stark reality is one of inequality and injustice in the context in which women and men exercise their political franchise. The bases of inequality and injustice become the foci around which men and women of different groups display loyalties and common cause that supersede gender considerations. Put another way, men and women acting individually in elective politics display much in common with the actions of patriarchs acting on behalf of their kinship collectives in councils of elders. In both circumstances, group solidarity – whatever the distinctive and defining characteristics – is accorded greater priority than gender.

In what circumstances, then, is gender equality likely to be accorded priority, so that higher proportions of women will be elected at all levels, including the highest representative bodies of their nations? At least three interlocking and intersecting continua appear to be critical.

- The degree of diversity that marks the civil society that constitutes the nation. At one end of this continuum would be nations with great homogeneity as to race/ethnicity, religion and region, and where the criteria upon which the nation and society are organized are relatively few – probably class, gender and generation. At the other end of the continuum would be nations where all these criteria are fully operative in determining the social structure.
- The depth of the sense of shared identity across groups comprising the nation. At one end of this continuum would be a deeply-held common identity, historically shared between all segments of the society and nation, such that it is almost taken for granted. At the other end would

be a recently constructed common national identity which, although supported by great rhetoric, remains relatively shallow and self-conscious.
- Material resources and their social distribution. At one end of this continuum would be affluent nations with equitable distribution of wealth across social groups, while at the other end would be relatively poor countries with great disparities between social groups.

In the interaction between these three continua we would expect to find equality in the representation of women and men at the highest level of political power in nations characterized by little or no diversity, a deeply-held common identity historically shared among all members of the society, and great affluence in material resources equitably distributed across social groups in society. The voice of gender equality in the political process should be heard loudly in such a setting because the filters of ethnicity/race, religion, region, class and the like would be virtually non-existent and the generation filter sufficiently permeable to allow effective transmission.

Likewise, we would expect women to be least represented in parliaments in nations where there is great diversity in social composition, a recently constructed common identity among formerly disparate groups and limited material resources inequitably distributed in society. Here the voice of gender equity might well be muted to a mere whisper, as the filters of ethnicity/race, religion, region, class, caste etc., would block transmission in the face of inter-group conflicts. We would expect to find patriarchal patterns prevailing at all levels of the political apparatus as group solidarity and loyalty stifle notions of gender equality.

Between these two extremes we could locate all the other nations – in fact, an empirical survey would probably not find any nation at either far pole. Any conclusive such study remains to be done, but this general scenario may explain the relatively high proportion of women in representative politics in the Nordic countries in contrast to the lower proportion in, say, the USA, as well as the very low representation in some Third World nations.

Conclusion

Gender has to be understood as the *sexual division of power*. Furthermore, gender is but one of the several criteria upon which society is organized: it is not the primary one, and is therefore almost always nested within other criteria with which it interacts. This means that we must always qualify gender by the other criteria which define the social structure of the societies of which they are part. For example, if a society were to be organized on the basis of toe length, gender and age, then in studying gender relations in that society it would not be appropriate to address men's and women's issues in aggregate form only – we would also have to disaggregate relations within the framework of interaction between these criteria, beginning with older long-toe men and ending with younger short-toe females, or vice versa.

Thus, in recognizing women's inequality in representation in the political process at the highest level of the exercise of power, we must also recognize the other bases on which inequality exists and operates within the particular context, and we must then examine the interaction of gender with these other criteria. Gender needs to be understood in terms of its dynamic relationships, particularly its interaction with the bases of oppression in the given context. To examine gender disparity in isolation is not only static and naive, but also myopic and misguided, as are policies and interventions that focus entirely on gender without regard for the other bases of injustice and inequality in that society or nation.

Because gender is defined in terms of power, and is nested within the other criteria on which societies and nations are organized, any major shift in power is likely to include corresponding changes in gender relations. Recent developments in Russia illustrate this. In 1985, women constituted 50% of the deputies to the territorial, regional, provincial, district, municipal, village and rural legislative assemblies (soviets). Corresponding figures for the soviets of the autonomous republics were 40%, and for deputies in the Union Republics, 36%. In the Supreme Soviet of the USSR, 33% of the deputies were women. On the other hand, less than 5% of the members of the Central Committee of the Communist Party were women. The all-powerful Politburo was overwhelmingly male: only two women had ever been members of this body (Gray, 1990). Thus, we see that while women had achieved gender equality at the local level and made considerable advances at the intermediate level of the autonomous and union Republics as well as the Supreme Soviet, they were almost absent at the pinnacle of political power in the Soviet Union (Miller, 1991).

In Russia's recent transformation to a market economy with a multiparty representative democracy, the proportion of women has been drastically reduced at all levels of the political apparatus. Not only are women virtually absent from the pinnacle of power, but they are only marginally represented in the Parliament. In the 1993 general elections, women won 13.4% of the seats in the Duma (the lower chamber) and 5.1% of the seats in the Council of the Federation (the upper chamber) (Inter-Parliamentary Union, 1995b). In the 1995 elections, the proportion of the seats won by women fell to 10.2% for the Duma and 0.6% for the Council of the Federation (Inter-Parliamentary Union, 1997). This decline in the proportion of women elected to Parliament has taken place in free and fair elections in which half of those voting were women. It would seem that in this forward move in political economy, Russian women have taken a step backward in the political arena. Clearly this is not a result of any male conspiracy but an outcome achieved with the full participation of women.

Viewed solely from the perspective of gender, these changes in the proportion of women in representative politics in Russia present a conundrum. What if we apply the conceptual tools of the partnership and exclusionary processes? We would then view developments in the Soviet Union after 1917 and the political patriarchal structure of the Communist Party and the state as one of the outcomes of the operation of these processes. The picture becomes even clearer if it is recognized that men and women acted in solidarity to remove the Communist Party from power and to dismantle the structures of the state. These included not only the men who populated the upper echelons, but the women at the intermediate and local levels as well. In this action, gender equality was not the priority issue. The holders of power were removed as a collectivity, by others who were also acting in a collective manner.

The case of the Soviet Union and Russia raises yet another important point: in gender analysis it is foolhardy to adopt conceptual tools based upon the notion of permanent progress. Gender relations are neither linear nor unidirectional nor permanent. Gender operates in dynamic interaction with the other criteria upon which societies and nations are organized. Moreover, in the course of history, the bases of the organization of society are periodically renegotiated. And this applies to gender as well as all other relations.

Once again: why are women under-represented in the parliaments in democracies where women have long had the right to vote? It is probably more important to suggest an approach to finding the answer, rather than attempting to advance one. The critical elements of a fruitful approach appear to be:

- To respect the integrity and rationality of women's choices and actions in these situations. Not to do so is not only to impute blame, but also to imply that the women involved are mindless minions easily manipulated by some kind of masculine conspiracy of which they are totally unaware.
- To recognize that women's marginalization and oppression in society is linked to other forms of marginalization and oppression which invariably involve some men. To ignore this is either an act of great misconception or an unwillingness to take responsibility for confronting these other forms of oppression. Worse, it may mean intervening in the circumstances, knowingly or unknowingly, on the side of one group while using women's issue as a cover.
- To resolve to take account of the complexities of gender relations and not to embrace single-factor and simplistic explanations.

Finally, we need to ask: if women are acting rationally and with integrity in electing men, why raise the question of women's under-representation in political parliaments and other elected bodies? At least three lines of argument could be relevant here.

First, it could be argued that if women vote to elect men, this may be rational and valid, given women's historic exclusion from political arenas until recently, as this would mean that women lack experience in the work of governing. This would indicate a need for compensatory action to redress the deficit, such as quotas constitutionally mandating a minimum proportion of women representatives. The counterpoint to this argument is that, as we have seen in the foregoing, women's under-representation in parliaments and council is related not primarily to any deficit or inexperience on the part of women but instead to the alignment between groups contesting advantage and advancement in society, and the solidarity existing between men and women with respect to these common causes. Without refuting the fact of women's inexperience in the work of governing, and therefore the desire to remedy this situation, quotas and other artificial devices might simply be means by which those holding power could consolidate their position by forming coalitions with women from disadvantaged groups, thus fracturing the solidarity of those groups and further marginalizing the men of those disadvantaged groups. Should the latter succeed in displacing the former, then a backlash against women could be expected.

Secondly, it could be argued that the low representation of women represents a deficit in representation itself because women have special qualities to contribute to political affairs, qualities that are not being tapped. Femininity was originally constructed on the basis of living-giving and life-preservation; this bequeathed to women skills of accommodation, cooperation, conciliation and inclusiveness that are solely needed in today's world. After all, what we need is political and not military solutions in the conduct of human affairs. The culture of peace would be better served by gender equality, or even plurality, in the political apparatus of nations. The empirical basis for testing this hypothesis is admittedly very slender, because gender is socially constructed. All the same, reasonable doubts should be entertained as to whether women holding ultimate power would act differently from men. Faced with the same loyalties, parameters and constraints, women – of whatever group – may very well act in like fashion to their men. Further, the promise that women would make a difference imposes a burden on women that is not imposed on men.

The third and strongest argument is that the under-representation of women in parliaments and other political councils represents inequality even if women themselves have participated in the process that produces this outcome. Equality is the sole ethical and just basis on which to construct and operate society. Hence, unequal representation of men and women in parliaments and councils is a symptom of injustice and unethical practice in the operation and construction of society, states and nations.

The main message of the alternative perspective offered by this chapter is that gross inequality in the representation of women in politics is symptomatic not only of gender inequality but also of gross inequality in the other criteria upon which the society or nation is organized. *Equality is a unified whole.* It cannot be conveniently divided into segments related exclusively to gender, or class, or religion, or region, or generation, or race, or tribe or clan. In assaulting gender inequality we cannot avoid confronting the other inequalities as well. To do otherwise might seem pragmatic, but it is unethical and in the long term reaps it own devastating consequences.

6
Women in Political Decisionmaking:
From Critical Mass to Critical Acts in Scandinavia

Drude Dahlerup

Introduction: four arguments

If more women are involved in political decisionmaking, will that make a difference? Will the political empowerment of women contribute to a more peaceful world? In research as well as in political life, this question has been heavily debated, with no definite answer. And why? Probably because, when put that simply, the question cannot be answered in any meaningful way.

Early in the twentieth century, Georg Simmel had noted the paradox: while women are placed in one general category, this very placement also prevents women from forming a group among themselves and developing solidarity with each other (Simmel, quoted in Cassel, 1977, pp. 17–18). Can women make a difference in politics as *individuals* – through a passive reflection of their being women? Or it is necessary for women to constitute a group *'für sich'*, with an active common platform?

For some two centuries now, feminist movements have sought to create a common platform for all women. The group 'women' is the *raison d'être* of all feminism, but also its Achilles' heel. At times it has been possible to unite relatively large sectors of the female population; at other times it has proven extremely difficult to organize women for feminist aims. Women's suffrage was one such issue that managed to unite large numbers of women in a joint campaign. This was possible only because suffrage had been defined as a goal in itself. After the right to vote had been won, it became clear that there was no general agreement among women about how to use it. Should they prove their political maturity by joining the political parties created before women had any right to participate? Or should they try to enter politics with new and different values? If so, how should that be possible in a world of politics that was defined and controlled by men?

Many leading suffragists have envisaged how women's entry into politics would change both the political culture and the laws. Other parts of the movement, however, rejected that. A vehement debate took place in Denmark and elsewhere, over the idea of a specific political party for women. To those who rejected the idea, women's suffrage was a matter of justice for women, not a means to introduce new values into politics (Dahlerup, 1978).

This discussion has repeated itself ever since women won the vote. Today, there is general agreement in principle that women ought to have their share of the political seats. But various arguments are adduced to support this principle. Here we may identify three basic types of argument – those invoking justice, or different values, or conflicting interests.

A matter of justice. Women constitute half the population; therefore they are entitled to half the seats. If women do not have equal representation, that must show that barriers exist which block women's route to power. This type of argument sees women's equal representation as a goal in itself.

Women and men have different values. In this second type of argument, women's equal representation is a means towards representing the experiences and values of women. It is assumed that women and men have different values because of their different social positions, women's care for children, etc. Biological assumptions may be used, but more often this argument is based on reference to actual differences in the social position of women and of men.

Women and men, to some extent, have conflicting interests. This is the argument used by the feminist movement when arguing that in a patriarchal society women are oppressed, and that consequently men cannot be expected to represent women's interests. This form of argument also sees the equal representation of women as a means rather than a goal in itself.

According to the first argument, it is irrelevant whether women will actually make a difference in politics or not. Equal representation of women and men is seen as a right in itself. By contrast, the two other arguments rest on the assumption – and the hope – that women can change things for the better.

A fourth argument may be identified. It forms part of the value-argument above, but nevertheless deserves a separate heading. *Women have potential for creating change,* because they are not – or at any rate are to a lesser degree than men – incorporated into the industrial-military complex and the government systems of the world. This argument contains the hope that women have unrealized potential for creating change, because they are not part of the present government of the world. However, such an argument is posited on the relative powerlessness of women. How to create a power base to change things, given this status of powerlessness? How to empower women?

Women in minority positions

As a general global trend, women's political representation in elected assemblies has increased over the past two decades, although backlash has also occurred in some countries. From three of the four arguments above, it follows that women should make a difference in politics. Within the male-dominated world of politics, women politicians must prove that it does make a difference when more women are elected. This demand comes from the women's organizations and the feminist movement, which have been asking: why can we not see more of a difference now that there are more women in politics? The demand also derives from people with a generally pessimistic view of the future of our world and who look to women – as the last chance, the final resort – for change. The theory of a 'critical mass' has been used by scholars and women politicians themselves in order to explain why the increasing numbers of women have not made a bigger difference. It is not fair, they say, to expect women to make so much of a difference as long as they still only constitute a minority.

Relative numbers count

In her study of women in a large US corporation, Rosabeth Moss Kanter (1997) makes the point that the *size* of the minority is significant. It is the proportion of social categories – here women and men – that makes an important difference. Kanter identifies four types of group on the basis of different proportional representation of socially different people, be it women/men or blacks/whites:

The *uniform group* or organization has only one significant social group, and its culture dominates the organization.

The *skewed group* (the minority constituting at most 15%) is controlled by the numerically dominant group and its culture. The minority members become token: they are seen as symbols of their entire group, especially if they fumble. 'They are made aware of their differences from the numerical dominants, but then must often pretend that the differences do not exist, or have no implications.' Token members are alone, yet the dynamics of interaction around them 'create a pressure for them to seek advantage by dissociating themselves from others of their category and hence, to remain alone' (Kanter, 1977, p. 239). This implies that token members are unable to form alliances with each other. Situations normally seen as relaxing ones – after-work drinks, sports events – are often most stressful for token members, who lack the protection of defined positions and structured interaction. According to Kanter, organizational, social, and personal ambivalence surrounds people in token situations.

In the *tilted group* (with ratios of 15 to about 40), the minority is becoming strong enough to begin to influence the culture of the group, and alliances between minority group members become a possibility. The 'token members' are now a 'minority'.

In the *balanced group* (from about 60:40 and down to 50:50), culture and interaction reflect this balance, Kanter argues. For the individuals in such a balanced group, the outcome will depend more on other structural and personal factors than their type (gender, race).

The basis of this reasoning is that there are indeed real differences in culture and behaviour between the minority and the majority group. Alongside the similarities between women and men, marked differences also exist – not necessarily from birth, but from their different social positions and their different social experiences.

Kanter does not talk about a 'critical mass', but simply of the gradual change that occurs when the minority within an organization grows larger. The discussion of a 'critical mass' adds to this the question of a possible point of acceleration in the influence of the minority when it reaches a certain size, say 30% (Dahlerup, 1988a). In her important argument that the relative numbers of women are crucial to their performance and efficiency within a corporation, Kanter concludes that the problems of these women derive from their minority position in the organization, not from the fact that they are women. I personally would challenge this part of Kanter's theory, that numbers are the only thing that counts. After all, from this it would follow that men would have the same problem when they were in the minority. Although men no doubt experience many problems in minority positions, the position of men in society in general – what might be labelled their 'majority status' in the general culture – usually compensates for their actual minority position within an organization. No organization or assembly functions in a vacuum.

My counter-argument is based on what Helen Mayer Hacker in her classic article (Hacker, 1952) calls the 'minority status' of women in society in general interacting with their status within the organization. The problems that result tend to be greater than those which white males encounter when they happen to be in a minority position.

Some minorities do well inside an organization if they can get support and resources from outside. Research on the successful careers of male nurses, for example, has shown how having 'majority group status' in society at large may counterbalance an actual minority position inside the organization.

Needless to say, women do not automatically get power simply because they are in the majority. A great many women work in factories or offices where they also constitute a majority, without that enabling them to better their lower pay or monotonous work conditions. They are paid less because they work in positions usually held by women, and they are placed there because they are women. It is true that, despite the relative powerlessness of women, an all-female workplace does have its own workplace culture, within the frameworks set by the company. But does this give women *power*? I would argue that we need to distinguish between different aspects of women's position and possible fields of influence in politics.

Kanter's study dealt with men and women in a large corporation. In democratic assemblies, based on majority voting and on the principle of one man (or woman)–one vote, each member has some value, even the backbenchers. In such a system, the question of the relative number of women assumes specific importance.

A critical mass

In nuclear physics, a 'critical mass' refers to the quantity needed to start a chain reaction, an irreversible take-off into a new situation or process. Here size is crucial. By analogy, the relative number of women is important – the size of the minority in politics is important for the possibility of change. As Kanter has shown, the small minority is subject to marginalization, tokenism, invisibility, even harassment, and over-adaptation to the dominant culture and norms (Kanter, 1977, Ch. 8).

The crucial threshold is often held to be 30%: as long as women constitute less than 30%, they will not be able to change the political scene, the argument goes. There is, however, no solid evidence for this particular figure. This theory has mostly been applied to situations where women do not (yet) constitute a 'critical mass'. Here the theory may even function as an excuse. But today in Scandinavian politics, women do constitute a large minority – and that places the burden of testing and proving the theory on women politicians as well as on researchers! In the following I will make use of Scandinavian research in this area, including my own studies of women in Scandinavian politics.

What might change with more women in decisionmaking?

The discussion of the possible impact of more women in politics needs clarification. What kind of changes are we looking for? There may be questions of efficiency, performance and promotion and drop-out rates for the minority, but fundamentally it is about the *content of policy*. In the following I will operate with five dimensions of possible change: (1) effectiveness of women politicians; (2) reactions to women politicians; (3) political culture; (4) political discourse; and (5) policy changes (Dahlerup, 1988a).

Effectiveness of women politicians

When the size of the minority increases, the general performance of women politicians is expected to improve, because then women are no longer exposed to the many difficult situations that follow from the status of the small minority: high visibility, role conflicts, stereotyping, discomfort, etc. One important indicator of effectiveness is the turnover or 'political lifetime' of women politicians compared to that of men, since the chances of getting elected and achieving higher positions increase with increasing seniority.

Reaction to women politicians

As their numbers increase, women politicians are expected to win political legitimacy. In a patriarchal society, women tend to lack legitimacy as leaders; consequently, the voters as well as the media, the civil servants and the fellow politicians may give women little support and may challenge their authority, thus forcing women into over-accommodation. But such open adaptation to the dominant male culture is a Catch 22 situation, because these women then risk condemnation as 'male women'.

Surveys showing historical changes in voter willingness to be represented by a woman can indicate changes in this dimension. The Eurobarometer surveys for 1975 and 1983 to 1987 show important changes in voter perceptions of women as politicians in Western Europe, although notable differences remain, for example between Germany and Denmark, in this respect (see Eurobarometer, 1987). No doubt, negative attitudes towards women as politicians and in power positions in general still exist in many places. It is an open question whether having *one* woman in a top position can lead to a more positive attitude towards women in politics in general – can we trace a Margaret Thatcher/Benazir Bhutto/Gro Harlem Brundtland-effect?

Of course it is not possible to show empirically that changes in the effectiveness of women politicians and changes in voters' reaction to women as politicians are directly caused by growth of the size of the minority. General changes in the position of women and in the relations between women and men are involved as well, and as a factor behind the increase in women's political representation in itself.

Political culture

Political culture is a complex issue, largely ignored by mainstream political science. Political life is a kind of workplace, with its own social conventions, its tone, its formal and informal rules, its norms of cooperation and conflict. The way of doing politics varies from country to country, from municipality to municipality, and is also subject to changes over time. Politicians themselves are often unaware of these variations.

It is my contention that the relative number of women seems in itself to have a direct impact here. This would support Kanter's theory that numbers count – in this dimension. Surely this is one of the most interesting aspects of the consequences of women's increasing political representation. In a 1984 survey, I asked all national women's organizations, women's committees and equality committees within all political parties in the five Nordic countries the following question: 'Do you believe that having more women in politics will lead to changes in working conditions and social conventions in politics?' All women's organizations and committees except one answered 'yes' or 'certainly'; some added: 'but only if there are many women'. And what changes were envisaged?

- The tone will be softer in politics.
- Meetings will be arranged with more consideration for family obligations – fewer very late meetings, fewer meetings between 4 pm and 7 pm; no more meetings in restaurants!
- Meetings will be less formal and less ceremonious.
- Speeches will be shorter, using less formal language and will be more to the point.

'We believe that fewer women than men look for power in itself. The ways of working and the interaction will become more characterized by cooperation and solidarity, not so much by competition', the women's groups of the Danish Socialist People's Party replied. 'Politics will probably become less formal, but democracy demands certain decisionmaking procedures, which neither women nor man can avoid', the Social Democratic women's organization in Sweden stated. 'Yes, changes towards a more social and less tough climate. . . . But many things, among them the workload, will hardly decrease', wrote the Equality Committee of the Agrarian-Liberal Party in Denmark (Dahlerup, 1988b, p. 254). Most interestingly, several women's organizations responded that women politicians not only will change the political workplace, they already have.

The women's political organizations seem to be in agreement on most of these points. This unity does not necessarily reflect a traditional and uniform women's culture in Nordic society, however. Rather, it is more a reflection of recent criticism of politics and politicians, especially brought forward by women in these countries. A parallel might be drawn between these recent arguments and the arguments used in the suffrage campaign – that women, being more peaceful, could change the hard climate of politics and remove 'the political dirt' (Dahlerup, 1978).

The political culture is in constant flux. In Scandinavia, one considerable change has taken place over the past few decades: the traditional formal style and the authority of politicians has diminished. The increasing number of women in politics is probably part of this development which some will regret and others welcome. Also in many other countries, the political culture is changing, among other things due to the increasing role of mass media in politics.

Even if women politicians as a minority have been forced to and have, to some extent, wanted to adapt to the prevailing political culture, *the presence of women in the assemblies in itself appears to lead to some change in the political culture*. When it comes to the political culture, the size of the minority seems to count more or less automatically. It would appear that the entry of just one woman into an all-male group (and vice versa) changes the discussion and behaviour of that group. We behave differently in front of a woman from the way we behave in front of a man. Recall also the confusion and anger many people feel when confronted with a young person of 'unknown' gender. I would hold that the increasing number of women politicians in itself acts to change some of the social conventions of politics as a workplace, because most of these women will bring into the political institutions traits of women's culture as it manifests itself today, for example taking care of new-comers, showing consideration for the private problems of others, employing a less tough style of debating, having different priorities and partly different criteria for success. The higher the proportion of women in politics, the more social conventions will change. It does not seem possible to identify a special turning point, a critical mass, but numbers *do* count, even if the politicians themselves and the public may not be aware of it.

Political culture, however, is more than the social conventions of politics. The level of conflict is also part of the political culture. A high conflict level in politics seems to bother many women politicians ('politics is a football game to male politicians!'), but this is one of several aspects of political culture that women politicians do not seem to have been able to change. Whereas changes in social conventions may occur without much ado, it takes a conscious effort to alter such fundamental aspects of the political culture at the level of conflict and confrontation. We need more research on this particular point. Politicians themselves are often unaware that while consensus and cooperation may be the norm in one local council, high levels of conflict may prevail in a neighbouring country or municipality. The media preference for reporting on conflicts serves to hide these important differences.

In recent years, several new political parties have tried deliberately to introduce new ways of doing politics. Heavily influenced in their culture by the new social movements from which they are often derived, and especially by the new women's movement, political parties like the Greens and the Left Socialists have emerged with a political culture that seems much more open to women. Here we have seen a conscious attempt to introduce new forms of politics and attempts to avoid being absorbed by the old political culture. It is characteristic that women have played a prominent role in these new or reformed parties. Also some of the old parties have changed.

The most radical attempt to reform the prevailing political culture comes from the various women's parties, notably the Women's Party in Iceland, which fielded candidates in the local elections of 1982 and in the parliamentary election of 1983 with remarkable success. In the 1999 parliamentary elections, however, it merged with another party. Iceland's Women's Party had tried to remain a social movement, arguing that women must form their own party, because the traditional political parties absorb women on male premises (Styrkársdóttir, 1986).

> . . . in the political parties, women are not being listened to, when we speak with our 'women's voices'. Women have to play according to the rules of the

men in order to be heard, and they have to be better and tougher than the men to play the rule of the game to make it in politics.(Dahlerup, 1985, p. 90)

Political discourse

Political discourse may be defined as the language of politics, and the language and meaning attached to political issues. This includes the discussion of what is considered political, and what is suppressed from the political debate, whether by tradition or by direct exclusion. The formation of the dominant political discourse is part of the political struggle. The hegemonic discourse should be considered a part of the overall social structure which influences, directly and indirectly, what is possible in politics.

Until fairly recently, women's position in society has generally not been subject to serious political debate. Politicians have lacked the vocabulary to speak about the position of women, about discrimination, inequality, women's diseases, unpaid labour, division of work between the sexes, sexual harassment or sexual violence against women. Such issues were left to 'nature' or were relegated to the private sphere. With the new wave of feminism since the 1960s, and furthered by the UN Decade for Women and the UN World Conferences on Women, the position of women has entered the political discourse. But the question of what ought to be the goals and the means in policies from a gender perspective remains unsettled.

I will argue that such changes in the political discourse follow not primarily from an increase in the number of women politicians, but from the existence of a strong women's movement outside the formal political institutions. This must be a movement capable of developing new ways of thinking and acting, and of mobilizing around feminist aims.

Policy changes

We cannot isolate the effect of the growing number of women politicians from the effect of what happens outside the formal political arena. But research in Scandinavia has shown that there are differences between the political interests and priorities of male and female politicians, and that issues concerning the position of women in society have been placed on the formal political agenda mostly by women politicians (Skjeie, 1992; Hedlund, 1996; Wangerud, 1998). It is also obvious that women have influenced the way such matters are debated in parliaments and the local councils. On the other hand, an increase in the number of women is not in itself enough to ensure policy changes. Coalition-building is crucial in politics, and here we should note that the most successful policy changes concerning women's position in the Scandinavian countries during the 1970s and 1980s followed from broad feminist coalitions and informal networks across party lines, in which left-wing and Social Democratic women and some men joined forces with right-wing feminists.

There will of course be better chances for women to establish majority coalitions if women constitute 30% of an assembly rather than, say, 5% – this is a question of power. But a crucial point remains: can women politicians develop a common platform they want to fight for? Here we must turn from the question of a critical *mass* of women politicians to the question of critical *acts*.

From critical mass to critical act

The theory of a critical mass does have its weaknesses. Why 30%? Or 25%? If 30–35% of those active in politics are women, is that enough to accelerate the development? Empirically, it is difficult to apply the idea of a turning point, following from a growth in the size of the minority, to the social sciences. Human beings do not act automatically like particles. Only on one point – changes in the social climate – does it seem relevant to talk about a kind of 'automatic' change that occurs when the minority grows in size, as argued above.

Elsewhere I have argued that we should replace the concept of a *critical mass* with a new concept of a *critical act*, better suited to the study of human behaviour (Dahlerup, 1988a). I define a 'critical act' as one which will change the position of the minority considerably and lead to further changes in policies. In the following, we will look at two types of critical act: (1) introducing quotas for women as a means to increase women's representation; and (2) developing a platform for change.

The theory of a critical mass concerns the relative number of women in an organization. When speaking of critical acts, however, we should bear in mind that men as well as women may be actors in attempts to improve the position of women.

Quotas for women

The empowerment of women implies a growth in influence and power – not just that of individual women, but of women in general. Quotas for women constitute one example of a critical act that, by empowering women, might contribute to changing politics. Introducing quotas is in itself no easy matter. It requires that women and supportive men have already acquired a position of power, because there will usually be strong resistance to overcome. But, once in place, quotas for women can serve as an institutional resource for empowering and mobilizing women, a safeguard against women ending up as small minorities in political organizations and assemblies. 'After the introduction of quotas, we do not have to fight again and again for the representation of women', women politicians in one of the three Danish political parties with quotas for women said in 1988 (Dahlerup, 1988a, p. 297).

Are quotas for women a case of *discrimination* or of *compensation*? Their opponents consider quotas discriminatory, and argue that quotas run contrary to the principle that the best qualified should get the job. Advocates, however, consider this a necessary measure – at any rate in a period of transition – in order to compensate for the fact that 'equal opportunity' for women and men does not exist, because of structural as well as direct discrimination against women. Ironically, discussions about measures against discrimination of women soon turn into arguments that it is unfair to discriminate against men – and consequently nothing gets done.

Quotas for women as well as other kinds of affirmative action represent a historical shift away from the simple principle of *equal opportunity* to the principle of *equality of result*. The underlying assumption is that equality of opportunity does not exist in reality.

Quotas for women or gender-neutral quotas?

Most quotas aim at increasing women's representation because the problem to be solved is usually a considerable under-representation of women, seen in relation to the fact that women in most countries constitute 50% of the population. A quota regulation may require, for instance, 'that at least 40% of the members of a committee are women'.

Quota-systems may also be constructed as gender-neutral, which means that they aim at correcting the under-representation of both women and men. In that case, the requirement may read like this: 'that men as well as women should have 40% of the members of the committee', or 'that no sex/gender should occupy more than 60% and no less that 40% of the seats'. Quotas to help men into positions may be applied in sectors with an overwhelming representation of women, as is often the case among teachers for the young, nurses and social workers. In leadership positions, even in the social sector, men make up the majority, so quotas for men usually aim at helping men into a specific education or positions at the lower levels of the labour market. There are some examples of gender-neutral quota systems that have helped some men into politics, for example in the Socialist People's Party in Denmark, which had a man 'quota-ed' to the European Parliament in 1984. In the following, however, the focus will be on quotas particularly for women.

What has been the experience with the introduction of such quotas? It is no doubt easier to introduce quotas for women at the same time as other forms of quotas are formally introduced, such as quotas concerning occupational or ethic criteria. Regional quotas that distribute the seats to various parts of the country, not just according to their share of the population, but giving non-proportional seats to certain regions over others, are in fact used in a great many countries. So quotas are not as rare as people may think.

Experience with quotas so far leads to two conclusions. First, the implementation of quota systems seems easier in a new political system rather than in an older one, where most seats might be 'occupied', and consequently may give rise to a conflict between the new groups and the interests of the incumbents. Secondly, it seems less complicated to implement quotas for appointed posts than for elected posts. At elections the quota system touches the very foundations of the democratic process and may clash with the ideal that it is up to the voters to choose the representatives they want. In most countries, however, it is the political parties, through their control over nominations, who are the real 'gate-keepers' of political office. Thus, quotas act to restrict not the voters' choice, but the prerogatives of the local branches of the political parties which often fight for their right to choose their own candidates without interference from above.

Quotas embodied in the constitution or in national legislation

The core idea behind quotas for women is to recruit women to political positions and to ensure that women are not isolated in political life. Earlier it may have seemed sufficient to reserve seats for only one or, at most, very few women (representing 'woman'), but not today. Modern quota systems aim at making women at least a 'critical minority' of 30–40%. There are various kinds of quota systems in politics today. A distinction can be made between quota systems according to the legal basis. First we will deal with quotas embodied in the constitutional or in national legislation. Later on we will look at quotas established by political parties.

Some examples

In a few countries, quotas for women have been written into the constitution or introduced through national legislation. According to the Constitution of Uganda, one parliamentary seat from each of the 39 districts is to be reserved for a woman. The result has been an increase in women's political representation in Uganda. Other women are elected to parliament in open competition with male candidates. In Argentina, the electoral law establishes a compulsory 30% quota for women candidates for elective posts. This rule has increased women's representation in the Argentine Chamber of Deputies considerably. In Brazil the requirement is 20%. In India, the 74th amendment requires that 33% of the seats in local municipal bodies be reserved for women. Such reservation policies are a well known, and much disputed, measure in Indian politics. Several other countries have introduced such quota systems. Others, for example the former communist countries in Europe, have abolished previous quotas.

Having quotas on paper is one thing: implementation is crucial. We need far more studies of problems around implementing the rules.

Quotas established through the political parties: Scandinavia

Finland, Denmark, Norway and Sweden have the highest political representation of women in the world. This increase mainly took place during the last 30 years. Today women constitute 43% of the members of parliament in Sweden, 37% in Finland, 36% in Norway, 37% in Denmark but only 25% in Iceland. No constitutional clause or any law, however, requires a high representation of women in Scandinavia. In general, the increase may be attributed to the long-term pressure by women's groups and the women's movement to make the political parties increase their number of women candidates – that is, candidates with a fair chance of being elected. This pressure can be identified in all political parties in Scandinavia. Some political parties responded by applying a quota system; these were the large Social Democratic parties, and the parties to the left of the Social Democrats.

The following remarks are limited to the three Scandinavian countries – Denmark, Norway and Sweden – where quotas were introduced by decisions made by the political parties themselves. Quotas were introduced during the 1970s and 1980s in the Social Democratic parties and in those parties that are to the left of them. Most centrist parties and parties on the right have considered quotas 'unliberal'. The pressure came from women's groups within the parties, inspired by the general feminist mobilization of that period.

The Norwegian Labour Party: 'At all elections and nominations both sexes must be represented by at least 40%' (introduced in 1983).

The Danish Social Democratic Party: 'Each sex has the right to a representation of at least 40% of the Social Democratic candidates for local and regional elections. If there are not sufficient candidates of each sex, this right will not fully come into effect' (introduced in 1988, abolished in 1996). The rule also applies to internal party bodies.

The Swedish Social Democratic Party has introduced the principle of 'every second name on the list a woman'. Thus, if the first person on the list of candidates for election is a man, the next one must be a woman, followed by a man, followed by a woman, or vice versa (introduced in 1993, but never labelled 'quotas').

Two important differences can be seen between the regulations of the Norwegian Labour Party and the Danish Social Democrats. First, in the Norwegian party quotas are in force at all elections, in the Danish case only at election to the local councils and to the county councils, not to the national parliament. Secondly, there are no exceptions to the Norwegian clause, whereas the Danish Social Democrats allow for an exception if sufficient numbers of candidates of either sex cannot be found. This exception may endanger achieving the goal of at least 40% of each sex, because it may function as an excuse for the party leadership not to try very hard to recruit more women candidates.

Political parties with quotas for elections will usually have some kind of quota system when electing the party's internal bodies and leadership as well.

Implementation

Rules alone are not enough: implementation is crucial. Unless a specific policy of quota implementation is decided upon, a quota requirement of, say, 30%, 40% or 50% is not likely to be met. The quota must be embedded in the processes of selection and nomination from the very start. If quota requirements are not introduced until the final stages, it is usually very difficult to reach the target, not least because of those who already have the seats in question – the incumbents. Here are some Scandinavian examples of strategies that have been used.

1 The Danish Social Democratic Party When the party introduced a quota of 40% to internal bodies and committees after intense discussions, the number of members of the committees was raised, in order to get women in without having to throw out the men. The party elected two vice-chairmen – one woman and one man. (But only one chairman was elected, and that was a man.)

2 The Norwegian Labour Party The party did not have difficulties in recruiting qualified women candidates. The national party leadership and the party's women's secretariat stressed that the intention of the quota was to have more women elected, not just to have more women on the party's lists of candidates, perhaps without any chance of being elected. In the Norwegian electoral system for parliament, the voters cannot alter the priority given to the candidates by the party, so it is the parties that decide who is elected from their list. In the beginning controversies arose when the top candidates were men who wanted to continue in their positions. Only gradually was it possible to fill the vacant seats with women. The Norwegian experience has shown that in such an electoral system, it takes about three elections to implement a quota system among the elected. Today, when the party is in power, women constitute about half of the parliamentary faction of the party and half of the ministers.

3 The Swedish Social Democratic Party The introduction of the principle of 'every second name on the list a woman' started at the local level in the party. Here is how it started in Järfälla municipality outside Stockholm:

> Before the 1970 election, the party thought that we ought to fill up with women, but we had men with long experience, and we needed that experience. Consequently, the first ten names on the list remained, with their experience, age, representation and knowledge, and then after those names we placed alternately a woman and then a man. At the next election, 1973, we placed a woman and a man alternately from number five on the list.

Before the 1976 election, the local party decided that the whole list for the local council should be made up of women and men, in alternate sequence.

Later the party simply drew up two lists, one with men and one with women, and then combined the two lists before the election.

The only problem that may arise is that of who is to head the list, a woman or a man? Once that decision is made, the rest follows by itself.(Dahlerup, 1985, p. 117)

Later, the government had a public investigation on the matter, followed up by nine million Swedish kronor given to various projects aimed at increasing women's representation, a typically Swedish way of making political change. In one such project, a local chapter of the Social Democratic Party set up a sequence of goals: in 1991, there should be 50% women from number four downwards on the party's electoral lists; in 1994, 50% on the whole list (Eduards & Åström, 1993, pp. 18–19). Today women make up to 43% of the members of the Swedish parliament, and in 1999 for the first time women outnumbered the men in the Swedish government.

To summarize: a successful quota system has led to active recruitment of women by the political parties, in order to have a sufficient number of qualified candidates to fulfil the quota. Once elected or appointed, women are no longer a token few, but constitute a critical mass that will be able to influence the political norms and culture. When they are at least a large minority, women have the possibility to influence the decisionmaking as individuals or, if they so wish, with specific women's or feminist points of view. It is, however, not sufficient to pass rules that ensure women have, say, 30% of the seats. The next step is the rather difficult process of implementing a quota system. The more vague the regulations, the higher the risk that they will not be properly implemented. Pressure from women's organizations and groups is necessary. Moreover, the higher the turnover rate, the easier it will be to implement quotas for the new group.

Finally, contrary to what many supporters of quotas believed and hoped for, conflicts over quotas for women do not seem to be a passing phenomenon. They would appear to be something we have to live with. Quotas for women to *public boards and committees* were introduced in Denmark, Finland, Iceland, Norway and Sweden during the 1980s. Even though the quota requirements are rather weak in most of these countries ('equal representation should be aimed at'), and there are no real sanctions (if, for instance, a minister should appoint a committee with only a few women), these quota laws have been generally successful. In Denmark, for instance, female representation on all public committees and boards increased from 10% in 1981 to 28% by 1995 (Danish Equal Status Council, *Annual Report*). Open information on committee composition is a prerequisite for the public to intervene if the quotas are neglected. In all five countries the law states that any public organization that is entitled to have a representative on a committee or board must name both a man and a woman, so that the appointing minister can select a gender-balanced board. The interest organizations protested, and still protest, strongly against these rules. However, the only answer to excuses like 'but we don't have any qualified women at that level' is 'then start recruiting women to the top levels!'

Quotas for women are clearly one of the most efficient tools for improving women's representation in political decisionmaking, provided such a system can be properly and wisely implemented. All over the world, experiments are taking place. More research is urgently needed into the process of implementing quota systems, and the various strategies used. In the former communist systems, quota systems for women representatives (and for youth, for trade union representatives, etc.) were abolished during the massive changes of the early 1990s. In the new and freely elected parliaments of Eastern Europe and the former Soviet Union, women's political representation has plummeted – now matching the very low level of the USA and of Great Britain.

It is an irony of history that those political parties in Denmark which were at the forefront in adopting quotas for women in recent times – the Social Democrats and the Socialist People's Party – abolished their quota systems in 1996. In both parties, the proposal to abolish the quota system came from the younger generation of women in the party who argued that quotas are discriminatory and no longer necessary. A generation gap has emerged on this issue between the feminist generation of the 1960s and the 1970s and women of the younger generation. Only the future will show whether women in Scandinavia have now actually reached such a high level of real equality that quotas are no longer necessary, or whether in a few years demands for reintroduction of the quota system in the political parties will be raised because women's political representation did not increase further, or perhaps even started falling.

Most important of all is the question of *critical acts* that will influence the political agenda and political decisions, enabling women to use their potential in world politics, potential which until now has not been tapped.

The need for new gender-sensitive platforms

The question of new gender-sensitive platforms involves the crucial question of policy content, of ideas, visions and strategies for change. And although bringing more women into politics does not generally lead to fundamental change in policies, I would still contend that women do have unrealized potential in politics – locally, nationally, and globally.

If women are to make a difference, new policy platforms must be constructed upon which women, and perhaps many men, can act. The prerequisites for developing the potential of women in decisionmaking can be stated as follows:

- The presence of many women in decisionmaking.
- Empowerment of women, so that women may develop potential and self-confidence for changing policies and the political culture, instead of just adapting to traditional politics.
- Strong pressure from women's movements, women's organizations and other grassroots movements.
- The development of gender-sensitive platforms for change, upon which women – and let us hope many men as well – can act.
- The development of strong international feminist movements.

Significant changes in the political system and changes for women as a group have indeed occurred in parallel with women's entry into political institutions. What remains difficult is isolating the effect of the growth in women's political representation from the general social development which has furthered this same increase. The following changes seem to occur in tandem with the move from a small to a large minority:

- The stereotyping of women diminishes, without disappearing totally.
- New role models of women in public life are created.
- The social conventions of politics as a workplace are somewhat changed, even if the main features of the political culture remain untouched.
- Open resistance to women politicians diminishes – now it seems hopeless to try to restrict women to the private sphere.
- Fewer and fewer voters express negative attitudes to being represented by a woman.

Such changes are themselves important, because they serve to increase women's possibility to act politically and to develop their capabilities. Other changes have occurred, such as shifts in the political discourse on women's issues, and the fact that equality between the sexes reached the political agenda in a great many countries in the 1970s, the 1980s and the 1990s. Women politicians and some male politicians as well have clearly played an important role in bringing these new points of view into formal politics.

Since equal opportunity policies are very seldom a salient political issue, and since no clear configuration of interest organizations exists in this field, political decisionmaking remains heavily dependent on pressure from the women's movement and the general discourse on gender.

The 1990s saw a decline in feminist pressure in many countries, especially in the West. By contrast, new waves of feminism might be emerging in the future in the former communist countries, as is the case in several Third World countries today. The lesson from the USA and Western Europe during this period is this: without a strong feminist pressure and widespread feminist grassroots activities, an increasing number of women in political decisionmaking cannot be expected fundamentally to change the content and form of policy-making.

Conclusion: a critical mass?

Does crossing the 30% threshold accelerate the development? We have seen the difficulty in applying the idea of a decisive 'turning point' that is supposed to follow in the wake of growth in the size of the minority. Human beings do not act automatically like particles. What is important is the will to develop new platforms, to develop new ideas and give room for women's potential in political decisionmaking around the globe. Today women have won some influence in political decisionmaking in many countries. At the same time, the globalization of the economy and deregulation seem to have removed power from the national parliaments, and left women as mostly spectators to the many summits of the few ruling men – the new global elite.

We need new efforts and new platforms in order to provide room for women and for women's potential in world politics. It is still too early to say whether the empowerment of women and an increase in women's political representation can lead to fundamental changes.

7
Promoting Peace, Security and Conflict Resolution:
Gender Balance in Decisionmaking

Anuradha Mitra Chenoy and Achin Vanaik

The problem

Can there be a feminization of perspectives pertaining to matters of national security? What does this mean? Is it desirable? And if it is possible, how is it to be done? We would answer that there *can* and *should* be a feminization of national security perspectives. The proposition which we discuss here can be formulated as a question: will altering the gender balance in those decisionmaking structures concerned with peace, security and conflict resolution make a significant difference?

A constraining vision

A strong caveat is in order. The specific formulation is highly problematic and serves to constrain the very perspectives (feminizing national security goals and means) which we should be seeking to promote. The expression 'peace, security and conflict resolution' has become common parlance in the literature on security matters, a seemingly inoffensive way of defining broadly acceptable goals. But to insist on associating the notion of 'security' with notions of 'peace' and 'conflict resolution' means in itself narrowing and restricting the notion of security in ways which greatly diminish any effort to feminize security perspectives.

The context in which the concept of peace is frequently used suggests a very specific reading – the absence of conflict, especially conflict involving physical violence and armed clashes. It might be argued that such a notion of conflict resolution is broad enough to incorporate a wider scope of concerns than the usual preoccupations of 'national security managers'. But it still assumes that security is 'threatened' only or primarily where such conflicts exist – that is, when they have reached that stage of clarity where combatants and forms of confrontation are well defined and visible.

Rethinking notions of national security requires a great deal more than merely accepting the seemingly self-evident virtues of peace and conflict resolution. The *politics of feminization* is an integral part of a wider *politics of democratization and empowerment* which has now decisively altered domestic and international politics alike.

Feminizing the notion of national security presupposes substantial democratization, as traditional conceptions of national security remain elitist, highly state-centric and strongly outward-oriented. State security is often seen as virtually synonymous with national security – or at least as its crucial anchor. For 'security matters' it is the apparatuses of the state that remain the key sites of decisionmaking. To talk of the possibilities of feminizing national security becomes essentially to talk of genderizing the composition of state apparatuses in a more balanced way, thereby genderizing its policies in a positive direction.

Within such a framework, the importance of non-state actors is greatly diminished. Such actors are usually located in civil society outside the state – in the representative institutions (from trade unions to NGOs) of social movements, social classes, segmented groups of various kinds. If state-centrism is one problem with such conceptions of security, the other is its strong outward orientation towards matters of interstate management (including peace and conflict resolution) in the global arena. This is only mildly leavened by references to the importance of preserving internal security, itself understood as something of a law-and-order or a legitimacy problem. With such a conception of internal security, the main issue becomes the actual and potential challenges to the power and authority of the state.

The twentieth-century transformation of the relationship between state elites/state managers and ordinary people has had undeniable effects on the notion of national security. There is no mistaking the direction of this pressure for change: it is pushing for a broadening of the concept of national security, thereby further relativizing the importance of its specifically military dimension. The concept is becoming far more internally oriented, in contrast to the traditional view of what constitutes 'high' security matters, namely interstate behaviour and diplomacy. Increasingly, national security is becoming more society-centred and less state-centred: more and more, it relates to wider and deeper social needs, such as the striving for economic well-being for all, social cohesion, political liberty and egalitarian democratization.

The significance of such democratizing pressures on state security managers has not been adequately acknowledged or dealt with in theoretical work. Most members of the national security establishment remain prisoners of increasingly outmoded perceptions of security, like the Realist paradigm of international relations. The result is a wide gap between motivating perceptions among state decisionmakers and the actual complexity on the ground, with its array of intersecting forces. Rethinking national security should mean rethinking the relationship between state and non-state actors, between state and society, and therefore between the structures of decisionmaking in these two arenas.

A deeper politics of feminizing security perspectives and a thoroughgoing change in the gender composition of decisionmaking structures would be part of this profound reconstruction of notions of security and of its necessary organizational infrastructures. Further intellectual exploration is needed of this difficult and largely unexplored terrain in the project of feminizing security perspectives. It may be wise to begin by operating within a more restricted vision and framework. How might a change in the gender composition of decisionmaking structures (here meant as the various state agencies dealing with security) affect policies and practices? In this chapter we confine ourselves to observations on South Asia, and India in particular.

Even within these constraints, it is still possible to promote a broader conception of internal security than just the usual 'law and order' focus. Problems of internal security must investigate issues concerning not merely explicit challenges to state authority but also the larger terrain of issues relating to the securing and sustenance of social cohesion. Here we will emphasize one dimension crucial to all the countries of South Asia: the issue of communalism/religious fundamentalism/religious nationalism. But first let us look at the external dimensions of national security or, more precisely, *interstate* security in South Asia.

The external dimension

The key axis of interstate security in South Asia is the India–Pakistan relationship, where a mutually *competitive* notion of security has been the hitherto unshakeable norm. After the collapse of East–West rivalry and the decline of Arab–Israeli tensions in older, more intransigent forms, no other part of the world now suffers from as prolonged a Cold War face-off between two rivals. The distinction between hawks and doves in these two countries is only a distinction between perceptions on how best to *manage* this tension-filled relationship, unredeemed by any larger goal or vision of how to *transform* India–Pakistan relations. The terms 'hawks' and 'doves' characterize not different sets of people, but different sets of management perspectives: thus, hawks (or doves) on some issues can be doves (or hawks) on others.

If India and Pakistan could effect the transition from competitive to common security, or even seriously initiate such a process, that would automatically transform the South Asian situation as a whole. It would mean real possibilities of a new era of cooperation at all levels, akin to the breakthrough effected by Western Europe after 1945, when it freed itself from its centuries-long history of state conflicts and began moving towards new forms of trans-state cooperation, like the Common Market and European Community projects.

In both Pakistan and India, institutions dealing with foreign policy/external security are more insulated from domestic pressures than those dealing with domestic policies. Thus, elective and representative bodies, such as Parliament, which have some degree of accountability to a wider populace have scant influence on the conduct of India–Pakistan relations. The fundamental character of this relationship has been one of *strategic hostility*, unchanged and essentially unquestioned since the birth of the two as independent countries.

In such a context, one can reasonably be sceptical about the view that greater female representation in Parliament will in itself make a difference in promoting a rethink over India–Pakistan relations or in 'softening' the conduct of such relations; similarly, that the mere existence of women prime ministers (Indira Gandhi and Benazir Bhutto) would make such a difference to the handling of bilateral ties between the two countries.

This also applies to the larger regional context including Bangladesh and Sri Lanka, where too, there have been women prime ministers – Begum Khaleda Zia and Hasina Wajed in Bangladesh and Shrimavo Bandaranaike and Chandrika Kumaratunga in Sri Lanka. On Kumaratunga's accession to the premiership there was widespread admiration for her initial efforts to defuse the situation in Jaffna and seriously negotiate a peaceful resolution of the struggle with the Liberation Tigers of Tamil Eelam. Factors that might have played a significant part in pushing for such an orientation may well include aspects of her feminine (though not feminist) personality as well as her greater sensitivity to the sentiments of the large constituency of women on both sides who had had enough of war. But the ensuing conduct of the conflict, as well as the subsequent evolution of her own government's policies and practices, clearly indicate that, if these dimensions existed, they were only peripherally pertinent.

A narrow stratum of senior bureaucrats, senior diplomats, senior military personnel and select Cabinet figures provides the principal resources for effective decisionmaking in regard to the India–Pakistan relationship. The respective weights of these components differ in the two countries, given the more militarized character of the state of Pakistan. But even in more civilian-dominated India, it seems unlikely that the existence of more women ministers or top-level women bureaucrats and diplomats would make a qualitative difference to policy, behaviour or routines, unless the paradigm of foreign policy thinking itself could undergo change. Working against this are the social character and ethos of such state apparatuses, as well as the ingrained mechanisms of career selection.

The operative mind-set for the conduct of India–Pakistan relations is Realism, a doctrine that is inappropriate and has an elitist and masculinist bias. This masculinist bias and its gendered effects are closely linked to the strong militarism inherent in Realist thinking, and in the case of India–Pakistan also to the aggressive and insecure nationalisms of both these post-colonial entities. Influential ideologies of nationalism promote a conception of womanhood which sees the family and home as its principal arena, with woman as nurturer, carer and sacrificing supporter for those (mostly males) who are supposedly in the forefront of the bilateral confrontation, whether in directly military or in non-military forms. Any possibilities of a trans-country feminism which can emphasize the common concerns of Indian and Pakistani women, of Indian and Pakistani families, and by extension, of ordinary Indians and Pakistanis, are greatly limited by the existence of such a hostile general environment characterizing relations between the two countries.

Of all group identities in contemporary times, the most powerful has been national identity. Socialist internationalism, Third World-ism, global black solidarity, international feminism, even transnational religious loyalties – all have foundered when pushed to confront nationalism. No wonder reactionary movements which mobilize on the basis of religious identity have generally sought to co-opt nationalist identities or loyalties (religious nationalism) rather than to confront or oppose it in the name of a higher, nation-transcending religious loyalty. Such wariness is a tribute to the ability of nationalism to conjoin culture and politics in a uniquely powerful way; to provide a degree of civic empowerment (the nation-state remains the primary unit of political empowerment for ordinary people through the principle of citizenship) as well as to help the people to locate themselves in a culturally distinct way.

The aggressive and insecure nationalisms that define the mutual security perceptions of India and Pakistan decisively restrict the scope for feminizing such perspectives. Having more women in the senior echelons of the foreign policy apparatuses of the two countries is likely to make little difference. Such women decisionmakers will, in their occupational roles, necessarily be more nationalists than transnational feminists. Indeed, there seems to be a special onus on such women to show that they can be equally aggressive and masculinist in their defence of the 'national interest' – recall the Thatcher–Gandhi syndrome of being 'the only real men' in their respective Cabinets. A more recent Indian example is Arundhati Ghose, India's ambassador to the United Nations in Geneva handling the CTBT (Comprehensive Test Ban Treaty) brief. She has been widely applauded by the media in India for the 'feisty' manner in which she defended Indian national interests. Her diplomatic style was widely recognized as exceptionally aggressive, even within the gallery of senior Indian diplomats. Maleedha Lodhi, the Pakistani ambassador to the USA, was similarly credited with an equally aggressive pursuit of her country's interests, with particular emphasis on strengthening the arms relationship between Washington and Islamabad.

The basic line of causation runs in the other direction. It is only through a *prior* change away from such forms of nationalism that we may expect more positive forms of a feminist politics of 'peace, security and conflict resolution' to emerge. The prospects for feminizing security perspectives presuppose enhanced prospects of a more transformational vision and practice of India–Pakistan relations.

In which areas, then, might this happen? At the official government-to-government level, the two main problems bedevilling India–Pakistan relations are Kashmir and the nuclear question. Significant progress in either area could dramatically accelerate the process of improving, indeed transforming, bilateral relations. Kashmir has been an enduring and intractable problem. For decades the greatest barrier to eliminating nuclear tension in South Asia was India's unwillingness to give up its nuclear option because of its more ambitious self-perceptions. Now, after the Indian tests of May 1998 followed by Pakistan's retaliatory tests, matters on this front have become qualitatively worse. A new dimension – the possibility of a nuclear outbreak between the two countries – has been added to an already conflict-filled situation. The primary responsibility for this must rest on India, since Pakistan would have gone overtly nuclear only if India did so first. The Indian decision was motivated by changing self-perceptions – not by changed or deteriorating threat perceptions. Indeed, India–China relations were steadily improving before the May 1998 decision. The self-perceptions that have led to India taking up the nuclear option have everything to do with the rising popularity of a belligerent and aggressive form of nationalism among a frustrated and increasingly insecure elite. This is embodied in the rise of Hindu communalism and of the various cultural and political forces associated with it. Thus it is no surprise that India carried out nuclear tests when the Hindu exclusivist Bharatiya Janata Party came to power as the dominant party in a coalition government dominated by them.

The best chances for moving towards an undermining of the 'long cold war' between the two countries may lie not at the interstate/intergovernmental level but at the people-to-people level. After all, the East–West Cold War was gradually undermined by the thousands of micro-processes involving the extended interface and communication between all kinds of groups and citizens of both sides in a myriad of ways. This unofficial level of the flow of ideas, people, experiences had as much to do with undermining the Cold War between East and West as did the dramatic official initiatives of Gorbachev.

In South Asia, at this unofficial level of people-to-people contact, women's organizations have played a pioneering role. Here a kind of a feminist transnationalism has thrived and been conducive to the nascent development of feminized security perspectives. Efforts have been made to broaden the concept of respective national security to become part of a wider pan-South Asian notion of *common security*. Moreover, there have been efforts to focus on the impact of Structural Adjustment Programmes on women throughout South Asia, and also to show how women everywhere suffer from the rise of fundamentalist and communal forces and ideologies. In this respect there has been more specific work in regard to the India–Pakistan face-off, aiming to show how an ideology of aggressive nationalism has very definite and powerful gender effects in both countries, effects that help to sustain and reinforce patriarchal ideologies, practices and institutions.

Non-state bodies of all kinds – trade unions, NGOs, professional bodies, business organizations, cultural groups etc. – are an important input into shaping the larger web of India–Pakistan relations. There is a good case to be made for changing the gender composition of such bodies in favour of women as a way of enhancing the tendencies and pressures towards greater democratization and demilitarization of India–Pakistan relations. To the extent that the governments can ease restrictions to facilitate the greater exchange of people, information and commodities, in both societies, this should certainly be demanded. But such easing of restrictions is hardly a single-minded or direct function of changes in the gender composition prevailing in the relevant state apparatuses.

On the whole, then, no convincing case can be made that a mere change in gender composition at senior decisionmaking levels in the state apparatuses will by itself promote a qualitative change in foreign policy orientation. There is some difficulty in justifying such an approach even on the grounds of tokenism. Tokenism, after all, can also have a real, if limited, symbolic-material value. But such a politics of tokenism is able to justify its value only because it presumes that the few women in senior positions somehow embody an alternative perspective to mainstream conceptions and values – in this case, on external security matters.

Where there is no such alternative perspective, merely altering the gender balance of decisionmaking personnel cannot be expected to make a real difference. Nor can such an alternative perspective be brought into existence by short-cuts or by parachuting women into senior positions regardless of how such women relate to the question of a feminized security politics. An alternative politics has first to be articulated and to win adherence on a smaller scale before any attempt is made to transform powerful existing structures.

The development of such an alternative feminization of security perspectives must itself be part of a wider alternative understanding of the necessity to democratize and transform our very notions of security and of their organizational infrastructures. Then the question becomes how to promote the transformation of decisionmaking structures through various methods, of which personnel changes are but one. And it also then matters less whether the carriers of such a feminized and democratized perspective of security are male or female, as long as they are genuine carriers of such perspectives.

It is not in international relations perspectives that such minimum levels of development have shown signs of emerging, but in the dimension of domestic security concerns. It is here that changes in gender composition to favour women today may have significant effects on policies and practices, and here that such rearrangements of personnel can themselves be seen as responses to the presence of real and growing social processes of a pro-democratic and pro-feminist kind. These processes have increasingly empowered women and ordinary citizens, creating a larger space and greater receptivity to a politics of feminization. Personnel changes in such a context tend to reinforce this already existing dynamic.

The internal dimension

Internal security should mean social cohesion. Social cohesion becomes fractured when groups or communities develop adversarial relations with each other or with the state, leading to conflict, violence and war. Conflicts occur when oppressed or exploited groups/communities/classes act to alter these relations, when rising expectations lead to new demands from these groups, when groups see other group(s) as an adversary and build threat perceptions accordingly.

South Asia has been besieged by a wide range of internal conflicts, most often rooted in the colonial past. In recent decades the scale and intensity of these conflicts has only increased and the process of state-building in South Asia has been marked by conflict. The tortuous division of India and Pakistan left the legacy of an unresolved dispute over Kashmir. Religious fratricide communalized the consciousness of vast masses on both sides of the border. In Sri Lanka, Prime Minister Bandaranaike was assassinated – by a Buddhist monk. Bangladesh emerged as a state after a liberation war. Four successive heads of state in South Asia were assassinated between 1975 and 1991.

The processes of state-building are far from complete in South Asia (Uyangoda, 1996). Within each of the states, regional groups are demanding reorganization. Uttarakhand, comprising the hill areas in the large and sprawling northern Indian state of Uttar Pradesh, has after a long time been promised statehood, but the bill for a separate state of Uttarakhand has not been passed. Other demands for regional autonomy and statehood in India include those from Jharkhand, Gorkhaland, Bodoland and Chattisgarh. Regional conflicts flare up from time to time on issues like water sharing, language policy, etc. Separatist movements, as in Mizoram, Manipur, Nagaland and Kashmir, have led to conflicts. Actions or movements which have sought preferential treatment for 'sons of the soil' have often led to ethnic clashes between those to be so favoured and those left out. Resource scarcities and increased inequities in these times of globalization may aggravate regional disputes.

Pakistan has had similar ethnic and regional disputes, with an armed uprising in Baluchistan, tensions in the tightly controlled Northern Territories and Kashmir, and the Mohajir–Sindhi clashes in Sindh (Mumtaz, 1996). In Bangladesh, the Buddhist Chakma tribe in the Chittagong Hills waged a movement for regional autonomy. In Sri Lanka, the Tamil demand for an independent state of Tamil Eelam has led to the prolonged civil war. In Bhutan, 90,000 ethnic Nepalese have been forcibly evicted. There has been no satisfactory resolution of any of these issues, and tension between the conflicting communities and the government continues.

Religious or communal conflicts still divide South Asian societies. In India, communal conflicts were particularly manifest in the anti-Sikh riots of 1984 and the Hindu–Muslim tensions which escalated in the aftermath of the razing of the Babri Mosque in Ayodhya in December 1992. Over 2,000 people were killed in the riots that followed. Not only have several centrist political parties (like the Congress) compromised with religious sectarianism, but communal consciousness among people has increased (Pandey, 1993; Bidwai et al., 1996). Electoral politics reflect the rise of volatile caste and communal politics in India.

This communalization has had an impact on the politics of the entire region. In Bangladesh and Pakistan, fundamental-led rioting against Hindu minorities occurred after the demolition of the Babri Mosque. In Pakistan, the event was viewed as an endorsement of the two-nation theory based on religious divide. However, Pakistan has its own sectarian conflict, manifest in the steady violent outbreaks which mark Shia–Sunni relations, especially in Sindh.

Throughout South Asia, Structural Adjustment Programmes have sharpened the income disparities between classes, cutting into the livelihoods of large numbers of people, especially in the non-organized sectors. This has led to increased social tensions. In India, for instance, the government's decision to allow the entry of foreign, highly mechanized trawlers to carry out deep-sea fishing has led to the sustained agitation of some 8 million indigenous fisher people.

Can such conflicts be resolved through state intervention? What are the institutional mechanisms for conflict resolution? Why have these mechanisms not worked so far? What are the gender implications of these conflicts? Will gendering institutions assist in conflict resolution?

In India, institutional arrangements for a democratic polity were set up after independence. Development, political negotiation and resolution of conflict were to be worked out through consensus or social contract. In most instances of dissent or disagreement, however, these institutional arrangements were by-passed. The state in India, as elsewhere in South Asia, increasingly relied on a host of repressive mechanisms. Demands for autonomy or rights were often perceived by the state as threats to internal security, or as law and order problems.

The police, paramilitary forces or the military itself were, in many instances, used to suppress these demands. The judiciary was by-passed in favour of reliance on extrajudicial mechanisms. In India, the suppression of the Naxalite (Maoist) movement, the Khalistan movement in Punjab, the Naga secessionist movement and the authoritarian internal interlude of Emergency Rule (1975–77) are all instances of this tendency to replace constitutional methods by extra-constitutional measures in resolving conflicts.

In cases of intercommunal conflict or disagreements, the government has often accepted the most conservative elements as representatives or spokespersons and acceded to their sectarian demands, without mobilizing or educating people on the issues in question. An example of this is the Indian government's attempt to accommodate the views of the Muslim fundamentalist leadership through the Muslim Women's Bill of 1986 which endorsed the primacy of the *Sharia*. This method of solving disputes between communities has led to the appeasement of conservative forces and the dilution of secular state practices, thereby laying the ground for renewed conflicts.

The consequences are evident. With the increasing use of police, paramilitary and military forces and extrajudicial methods, there has been a greater militarization of society. Conflicts have been suppressed and anti-democratic methods employed. This has led to the erosion of democratic structures, and a weakening of the institutions of civil society. A key to sustainable conflict resolution is thus the rebuilding and strengthening of the democratic infrastructure of civil society. Whether in situations of conflict or in a militarized society, women, with their multiple identities and thus multiple oppressions, are victims. Rape and humiliation of women have been widespread in all conflicts in South Asia – whether during the partition of the subcontinent, in regional or communal disputes throughout South Asia, or the most recent instance of systematic rape of ethnic Nepalese women in Bhutan.

Militarized societies are more hierarchical and patriarchal than non-militarized ones, and even societies with democratic structures can become increasingly militarized. Militarized societies tend to be most oppressive towards women, in both the public and private spheres. Consciousness and language become militarized. The immediate response to most dissent is coercion, including the use of the military. All this points up the urgent need to bring women into the public sphere in such societies.

Women as key decisionmakers

The women's movement has used protests, consciousness-raising campaigns and increased political participation to express grievances, gain influence and direct public policy. In South Asia, more and more women have become politically engaged and have lobbied for greater representation and influence. Women, however, have been generally under-represented in positions of power (even though there have been women prime ministers in four South Asian states), and in key positions in decisionmaking structures. To what extent have the women in power come to this position on their own strength? Has a gender perspective marked their approach to conflict resolution? Have they acted on behalf of their gender, or as agents of the state/party/class they represent? Has their role been an input into transformation and democratic politics?

In South Asia, those women who have reached the highest levels in politics have done so as daughters (Indira Gandhi, Benazir Bhutto, Chandrika

Kumaratunga, Begum Hasina Wajed), wives (Shrimavo Bandaranaike, Khaleda Zia), or mistresses (Jayalalitha, Chief Minister in the southern state of Tamilnadu in India) of famous political leaders. Sons have had equally privileged positions – because of the importance of hereditary location in political systems where the institutionalization of democratic structures and culture is still weak. In the Lok Sabha (the directly elected central legislative chamber in India), the share of women has never exceeded 10%. (Even during Indira Gandhi's tenure in 1981, the number of women MPs was 20 out of a total of 525 members.) In 1996, 599 women stood for election; in the 1998 elections, 267 women ran for seats in the Lok Sabha. Women have marginally increased their representation in the Lok Sabha: of the now 542-member total, the number of women has risen from 39 in 1996 to 41 in 1998.

Fewer women are joining political parties, and women comprise no more than 10–15% of the membership of most political parties. Very often when women do actively join politics, this is considered 'proxy politics' by male relatives. In India, moreover, the strongest women's groups have been those which are mass fronts of national or regional political parties (e.g., All India Women's Congress, All India Democratic Women's Association, National Federation of Indian Women). Autonomous feminist groups and feminist discourse, originally limited to a small elite, have now spread to encompass much larger sections of urban and rural women. Today the women's movement has established a real and meaningful grassroots presence. The interaction between these groups has led to positive policy positions.

The increasing nexus between criminalization and politics, the continuation of patriarchal values and hierarchical structures in South Asia, the astronomical costs and resources involved in elections, and the belief that politics and policy-making are linked to the powerful, strong, male realist rather than with the archetypal gentle, negotiating woman, cumulatively block women from taking on political/activist roles, especially when there are no guarantees for their physical safety. In India alone, it is calculated that there is one dowry death every 102 minutes, one rape every 54 minutes, and one kidnapping or abduction every 43 minutes (*Indian Express*, 21 September 1994). In the ethnic, communal or regional violence recurrent through South Asia, hatred and violence are directed against the bodies of women. This in turn reinforces the belief that women are to be protected, and that they belong in the home.

Essentialists hold that the female psyche is uniquely given to caring and nurturing. Thus, they say, women would be less corrupt, would assist in bringing about harmony, in seeking negotiation and preventing conflict. Ironically, these arguments have been used to justify excluding women, by claiming that such characteristics have no place in real politics at any level. Against the essentialist view it can also be argued that it is because women have been excluded from power that they have remained more honest and less corrupt. It is thus a combination of features like the gentler aspects of women's nature, their historic location and experience as the oppressed, and their socialization as the other which underlie the belief that women would be able to conduct politics in another way – that there is a feminized perspective of politics worth striving for.

What characteristics have women in power demonstrated? Analyses of the political regimes under various women prime ministers in South Asia show them to be as dictatorial, corrupt, sycophantic as when men have been in power. The policy decisions of all these women leaders in their handling of secessionist, regional, territorial conflicts have been no less militaristic or less violent than those of their male counterparts. Studies of communal violence in India have shown that, in the vicious communal campaigns led by parties like the Bharatiya Janata Party, women cadre have led and incited violence against the other community. Right-wing political organizations are attempting to empower women through the ideology of militant nationalism (Sarkar, 1996). In the 1996 election, it was the conservative parties in India that specifically targeted women voters.

Women, especially those in senior positions in the bureaucracy, act as agents of the state and as representatives of their class. The tougher they are in the masculinist sense, the higher they climb in the echelons of power. When women in politics or bureaucracy do display characteristics defined as feminine, such as gentleness, a pacific or caring temperament, they soon find themselves relegated to the 'soft' areas, like development projects, education, social welfare and health.

Given the structure of power and the patterns of male-oriented social-ization, empowerment and liberation for women are equated with being like men: professionalism means taking the hard masculinist option. In order to survive in male-dominated professions like politics, women act like men – otherwise they risk becoming marginalized. They thus repudi-ate the historic link that women have with the pacific (Elshtain, 1982). The military is almost exclusively male, and its masculinized culture cannot be challenged (Enloe, 1990). When women support war, conflicts or the mili-tary, they do so primarily because of patriarchal socialization. Studies have shown that, compared to men, women kill far fewer people, which also suggests that women are generally less militaristic (Jones, 1991). For these reasons, as well as for the classic egalitarian reasons, conflict-prone soci-eties need to close the gender gap in their distribution of power and authority.

The women's movement continues to demand more representation for women in elected and decisionmaking structures. In India, after pressure from the women's movement Parliament passed a bill in December 1993 to reserve 33% of the seats at the village-level local bodies (*panchayats*) for women. A similar bill was passed for urban local bodies and municipal corporations. With this, about 1 million women entered active political life at the grassroots level.

While this experience for women at grassroots politics is new, prelimi-nary studies (Kaushik, 1995; Mohanty, 1999) have shown that women have influenced the utilization of funds at the local level. For example in some districts in West Bengal and Maharashtra, women have been successful in making changes for their constituencies. For instance, they have used the money allotted to the districts for fixing taps, so that the local people – especially the women – were not burdened with fetching water from wells. Women have demanded schools and better roads, instead of the television/common rooms demanded by men, and have succeeded in persuading the *panchayat* committees to accede to these demands. Women have slowly started intervening in local conflicts. However, women have also participated or encouraged violence against other women who have dissented on caste, religion or even party positions. Closing the gender gap is not enough – the propagation of progressive ideologies is also important.

Bangladesh has reserved 30 out of the 300 seats in its Parliament for women. In the first two assemblies, the role of women within parties and the Parliament was governed by patriarchal norms, and attitudes towards them were essentially paternalistic. After 1991, however, women in Parliament have become more visible and have attained greater status (Chowdhury, 1994). There is growing recognition in Bangladesh that women's concerns must be reflected in party politics for there to be real change in the public position of women.

The women's movement in India has pressed for and received assurances of support from all major political parties for a 33% reservation of seats for women in the Lok Sabha (the lower, more powerful chamber). However, following an attempt to scuttle the bill by various groups of male MPs, it has been referred to a parliamentary select committee. The chances that this bill will get passed will depend on how effective the pressure from the women's movement is in the face of growing unease among male MPs and political activists across party lines. Reserving seats for women in the highest decisionmaking structure of the state is important, because otherwise women are completely marginalized in representative and other bodies. India's public institutions have become self-appointing, patriarchal oligarchies. For example, despite a large number of female law graduates, less than 3% of the judges are women (*Patriot*, 26 November 1993). Put in absolute figures: out of 443 judges in India only 15 are women (Bombay 1:47; Allahabad 1:66; Andhra Pradesh 1:24). The appointments of judges are supposed to be based on merit; candidates must possess high integrity, honesty, skill, emotional stability, legal soundness, judicial temperament, etc. Do women lack all these skills? Or are they less effective in backroom politics?

Reserving 33% of the seats in the Indian Parliament for women will be a pioneering step that will act to increase women's engagement in politics. It will focus attention on life issues like health, literacy, housing, schooling – questions where women have been in the forefront – as well as on specifically women's issues like foeticide, dowry deaths and wife-beating, and the increasing feminization of poverty attendant on globalization. Representation will bring women into the public sphere and will secure a political voice for them, encouraging them to assert their rights and to focus attention on the oppression and plight of women in India.

Women will continue to enter Parliament with their positions grounded in the distinction between parties. Women politicians will generally not be autonomous actors. Patriarchal discrimination has not been renounced in political parties. Though the leftist and socialist parties recognize the exploitation of women and demand equality, in all parties the fight for political power comes before the fight for women's rights, since this would lead to divisions within parties. By reserving a percentage of parliamentary seats for women, the Indian state will highlight the issue of women's political rights and also secure for itself greater international credibility and respect.

Communalism and women

Reactionary religio-political movements – whether labelled as communalism, religious fundamentalism, or religious nationalism – deserve special attention. We find Islamic fundamentalism in Pakistan and Bangladesh, Hindu and Muslim communalism in India, and Buddhist nationalism/ revanchism in Sri Lanka. These reactionary movements feed on each other indirectly: for example, rising Hindu communalism promotes Islamic fundamentalism, and vice versa. The thrust of all religio-political movements is strongly anti-democratic. By their very nature, they have an indissoluble link to the oppression of women and the reinforcement of patriarchy.

These religio-political movements have secular goals – to achieve or influence state power – and they employ a variety of secular means. But all of them are also decisively inspired by religiously-based dogmas and conceptions in two key areas: the organization of family life and of education. That is why all such movements, no matter how vague they might be in their programmatic perspectives pertaining to macro-level entities like the economy and polity, are invariably specific, detailed and insistent when it comes to programmatic injunctions concerning the family, and concerning education.

The organization of family life necessarily means the organization of women in ways which reinforce patriarchy. Not only do all religious systems have no natural thrust towards challenging patriarchy, but such reactionary religio-political movements necessarily interpret complex religious systems in ways which close off the potential for liberating anti-patriarchal impulses. Therefore, women are decisively affected by the rise of such reactionary movements and their ideologies, and have a special role to play in opposing them. Women have an objective interest in promoting more democratic and therefore secular systems of law pertaining to family, personal and civic life; in egalitarian principles for founding marriage relationships, inheritance, custody of children, matrimonial property and a whole range of related issues.

In India, communal politics means the politics of Hindu-ness and Muslim-ness pitted against each other. Such is the immensity and diversity of India that Muslim and Hindu from the same locale are far closer to each other than either will be to a fellow religionist across the multiple divides represented by regional, social, economic and educational distances. Thus, the sole ballasts for stabilizing a politics of Muslim-ness in India are the growing sense of common identity and defencelessness aroused by the rapacity and violence of Hindu communalism; and the uproar over the issue of Muslim Personal Law, with Hindu communalists demanding the forced imposition of secular personal laws overriding the *Sharia*.

The question of community-based personal laws has become deeply communalized, with both Hindus and Muslims uniting behind opposed positions. An issue which above all concerns the oppression of women of *all* communities has instead become an issue of Hindu identity versus Muslim identity. On the one side there is the claim of Hindus that the existence of Muslim Personal Law (when Hindu personal codes have been reformed in a secular direction) constitutes secularist appeasement and favouritism towards Muslims. On the other side there is the view that a collective Muslim identity and the Muslim community is itself under attack. What should be seen as a classic women's issue, a question of their anti-democratic and patriarchal oppression, has been turned into an issue of conflicting group identities. The decisionmaking structures for changing such laws rest at the level of the state as well as within the specific religious communities. Thus it makes sense to demand both changes in the existing state-based legal system and reform within communities. In either case, there is every reason to believe that the greater involvement of women in the structures which discuss, formulate and are prepared to fight for positive changes in personal laws can only be a healthy development. It is one major way of once again de-communalizing the issue of personal laws and of reorienting the focus away from the clash of group identities to where it should be – on the oppression of all women, across groups and communities.

In the more religiously cohesive societies of Pakistan and Bangladesh the issue may not be so much that of inter-religious communal conflict, but here too it is an issue of opposing oppressive patriarchal and anti-democratic laws, values and norms. And here too, the greater presence of women in the structures concerned with discussing, formulating, and legislating such laws will make a major difference. This is one area in which, for example in parliaments, women will be less likely to toe the official party line in voting, if such injunctions are clearly patriarchal and anti-democratic.

Conclusion

The belief that simply add women and stir is enough to solve conflicts is generally erroneous (Zalewski, 1995). Conflict resolution can take place only through such wider-ranging social transformations as greater gender awareness, equity, and the strengthening of democratic and civil institutions. Closing the gender gap will be important for the uplifting of half the population, but in itself it cannot end the kind of economic or social oppression which gives rise to conflicts, nor can it challenge patriarchy in the private sector or workplace, nor put an end to the discrimination against women. Only the strength of an autonomous women's movement in alliance with other democratic movements can ensure this.

Women can be as effective in conflict resolution as they can be in promoting militarism and conflict. While closing the gender gap is important, it cannot in itself be expected to be a solution to conflictual problems. Better gender balance among decisionmaking personnel, unless accompanied by major ideological/social psychological changes, might only displace the pacific characteristics of women by militarist ones, especially if militarism and nationalism are dominant ideologies.

It is the institutionalization of a more humane and feminized worldview that will most effectively lead to the kind of conflict resolution most compatible with the wider agenda of a truly transformational politics. Feminists, progressive women's movements, other democratic movements, as well as gender-sensitive individuals, must become engaged in this overall endeavour. Women have to re-establish their historic links with peace and the peace movement, asserting themselves as the harbingers of a genuine alternative. It is with this perspective in mind that women have to speak to those in public power and when they themselves are in public authority. This is very different from adopting, in the name of the search for equality, the existing masculinist and militarist mentality.

Gender is a constituent of political experience. It is basic to the identity of the state and the structure of the international system. The failure to recognize this has led to artificially neutral constructions of the notion of power. Feminists and progressive movements have begun to challenge this notion of power and political realism, offering a model based on a democratic, transparent and plural alternative. This is a model which can help resolve conflicts in a sustainable manner. Other methods would be short-lived quick fixes with their own inherent long-term contradictions.

In order to devise a gendered vision for conflict resolution, we need a multi-pronged strategy. On the institutional level, gender/feminist perspectives should enter the domain of all decisionmaking structures. From grassroots level to top decisionmaking bodies, all policy-making bodies must move towards having *both* a more adequate gender representation *and* a more feminized perspective. The relationship between the two is complex and fluid. This has its own consequences for operationalization, for the timing and sequencing of changes, especially regarding personnel.

To give political substance to a gendered vision, this must be part of a larger transformative and democratic vision and politics. We will have to move away from political Realism and from the politics of competitive security, so that we may develop an understanding of national and human security more in tune with the needs and pressures of our times. In the case of South Asia, this will mean working towards a politics of common regional security, a politics that can address the collectively shared needs of the majority of the population. It is in this context that a gendered vision is essential and must be situated.

As part of such an institutional strategy, autonomous feminist movements need to be strengthened. Feminist political theory must be discussed, debated and taught in schools and colleges. This will better enable women to deal with political institutions, while also promoting the realization that women's gendered political actions can have different means and goals from those of men. And what this would mean would be nothing less than a paradigm shift in politics itself.

Note

The authors gratefully acknowledge the assistance of Kamal Mitra Chenoy and Pamela Philipose in preparing this chapter.

8
Integrating a Gender Perspective in Conflict Resolution: The Colombian Case

Eva Irene Tuft

Introduction

In recent decades, the major dynamic of armed conflict has shifted from wars *between* states to wars *within* states. Since the 1960s, legal opposition groups in Colombia and throughout Latin America have been the target of counter-insurgency warfare. The enemy of national sovereignty has thus been identified not as an external force, but rather as persons or organizations in civil society wanting to change the dominant structures of power. A constant war has been waged on all levels against this internal enemy: economic, military, political and psychological. The end of the Cold War has brought an end to overtly authoritarian governments and armed conflicts in the region, as seen in the recent peace agreements in Guatemala and El Salvador.

In Colombia, peace talks were initiated on 7 January 1999 between the government of Andres Pastrana (elected president 1998) and Colombia's largest guerrilla organization, the *Fuerzas Armadas Revolucionarias de Colombia* (Revolutionary Armed Forces of Colombia; FARC).[1] The four-decade-long conflict has, in the last ten years alone, killed some 35,000 people and forced a million more to flee their homes. Pastrana's peace initiatives are seen as the most serious since the early 1980s.[2] However, most analysts consider that any formal peace process will be extremely complicated. Some predict it might take as long as ten years to reach a peace agreement.[3] The operations of paramilitary groups and their request for political status and participation in the peace talks constitute a major obstacle to peace. Between 7 and 11 January 1999 the paramilitary coalition *Autodefensas Unidas de Colombia* (United Colombian Self-defence; AUC) massacred 120 civilians. The FARC announced on 19 January the unilateral suspension of any further talks until the government had taken measures to stop the AUC's killings of civilians. The government responded by suspending a meeting on the exchange of captured soldiers and imprisoned guerrillas (*Siglo Veintiuno*, 19 January 1999, p. 2; 20 January 1999, p. 54).

Traditional approaches to conflict resolution are based on some form of settlement between the main protagonists. In the case of Colombia, this would include the government and various armed opposition groups.[4] Here, however, such a traditional approach to conflict resolution is not viable, as it would exclude a significant number of actors who fall outside the official designation. Large sectors of the civilian population have become identified as military targets by virtue of their dissent or the accident of where they happen to live. Broadening the concept of enemy and extending the battlefield to economic, political and psychological realms have made the conflict multidimensional. This in turn means that civilian sectors have become actors and stakeholders in their own right to any peace process.

Efforts at conflict resolution, therefore, must also be multidimensional, reflecting both the modalities of the conflict and the interaction between all the actors involved. This will mean finding alternatives to narrowly constituted official peace negotiations, alternatives that can ensure the inclusion of civilian actors affected by the violence. As long as they are excluded, this can only result in a partial peace that leaves unresolved many issues that are important to the non-official actors.

Integrating a gender perspective in conflict resolution requires recognizing the multidimensional nature of the conflict. Implicit in such an approach is a recognition of the different ways in which men and women are affected by armed conflict. It is of course dangerous to generalize, but reports show that men are the principal victims of the civil and political human rights violations that are directly associated with armed conflict.[5] In contrast, the violations experienced by women occur most often in the sphere of economic, social and cultural rights. The nature of these differences reflects the gender roles assigned to men and women in Colombian society – and the implications of these differences must be taken into consideration in any peace process. Integrating a gender perspective in conflict resolution also requires recognizing that women's choices and opportunities in a conflict situation are not determined solely by their gender, but also by factors of poverty, political culture, ethnicity and geography, as well as their exclusion from political channels within the formal political system and in civil society. This is why any effort at conflict resolution that incorporates a gender-specific approach must be multidimensional and must go beyond an awareness of the structural imbalances in power between women and men.

This chapter begins with an historical analysis of the Colombian conflict and how its multiple dimensions have severely affected the civilian population. The gender-differentiated nature of this impact is included in the analysis. We then proceed to a discussion of the implications of integrating a gender perspective in the resolution of armed conflict. Finally, the chapter concludes with recommendations directed at women's organizations, research institutes and the international community.

Historical context

Bipartisan democracy

On the surface, Colombia would seem to have avoided the political and economic instability chronic to much of Latin America. The country has an elected civilian government; indeed, during this century the military has intervened directly in the political system to take power for only one brief period between 1953 and 1958. However, Colombia is characterized by extreme levels of politically motivated violence. This violence is a direct result of both the closed nature of the Colombian political system and the economic inequalities in society at large.

For almost 150 years the Colombian political system has been dominated by two parties, the Liberals and the Conservatives, ever since their formal consolidation in the 1850s.[6] These two traditional parties have strongly influenced almost every aspect of political life, nation-building and the characteristics of Colombian society itself. 'The Liberal and Conservative parties were the central and inescapable basis of political life ... They were the most fundamental national institutions in society and more significant structurally, culturally, behaviorally than any other social grouping (such as regions or class) or other national institutions (such as the church, the military or even the state itself)' (Wilde, 1978, p. 35). As the dominant structures in the country, the parties possessed the greatest range of 'power capabilities' for organizing civil society behind them. Those capabilities included the ability to mobilize for elections and for violence, which often occurred as an extension of the electoral process, and the distribution of economic rewards to supporters through the use of *clientelismo* (patronage).

Within the emerging bipartisan framework, economic and political elites gradually assumed an identity in the absence of other mechanisms, including autonomous state institutions, to channel, promote and protect their interests. The articulation of those elite interests became indistinguishable from the 'ideology' of the party in question (Hartlyn, 1988, p. 19; Pearce, 1990, pp. 17–22). Party membership itself was hereditary, handed down through generations to the point of assuming the characteristics of political culture. 'One is Liberal or Conservative as one is Catholic, as one is Colombian by birth. One does not even consider *not being* Liberal or Conservative, just as one would never think of not being Catholic or Colombian through a simple act of will' (Buitrago, as quoted in Hartlyn, 1988, p. 18).

The Colombian military has historically been weak. Rather than using the military as an institution of the state, the Liberals and Conservatives have generally bolstered their claims to power through the use of militias associated with the respective parties,[7] leaving only a minimal role to the military. During the nineteenth century, it directly intervened in the political system at the national level on only two occasions, in 1828 and 1854.

Both regimes were short-lived and civilian governance was quickly restored. Subsequently, civilian rule has been interrupted by military rule only once, for the six-year period between 1953 and 1958.

Violence

'Colombia had a heritage of political violence second to none' (Wilde, 1978, p. 29). Historian Gonzalo Sánchez describes Colombia during the nineteenth century as a 'country of permanent and endemic warfare' (Sánchez, as quoted by Bushnell, 1992, p. 12). There were no fewer than 14 national-level civil conflicts and two international wars between 1828 and 1902. Innumerable local and regional conflicts also occurred, including 40 rebellions to seize departmental government during the era of the federal constitution (1863–86) (Pearce, 1990, p. 20), intra-elite wars, land struggles which took on a partisan identity and urban riots in the 1930s and 1940s. 'These wars never ended in decisive victories but there were short breathing spaces before renewed fighting' (Sánchez, as quoted by Pearce, 1990, p. 17).

Political violence occurred primarily in the context of bipartisan competition for control of the state and the power to control the distribution of the resources of the state. The importance of maintaining at least some form of access to political power was a result of the backward economy. In impoverished nineteenth-century Colombia, the ability to award contracts, control political and public service appointments and make policy decisions related to the economy was a critical source of wealth – indeed, sometimes the only one. According to Wilde, 'the state budget was the only industry in a country without industries . . . and the government offered unparalleled opportunities for advancement in the absence of a developed private sector' (Wilde, 1978, p. 26). This was especially the case during times of cyclical economic downturn or recession which increased the inherent value of government resources. For example, the Liberal rebellion which led to the Thousand Day War (1899–1902), in which an estimated 100,000 persons – 2% of the Colombian population – were killed, was initiated by Liberal elites who had been excluded from government positions and had no other economic alternatives (Pearce, 1990, p. 25).[8]

The role of the political parties as catalysts for violence must also be understood in terms of the political culture generated by partisan identification. Hatreds between groups in civil society were fostered as a mechanism for retaining the loyalty of supporters. Restrepo notes that 'beginning in the 19th century [party elites] nourished the sentiment of party loyalty among the subordinate classes, feeding prejudices and mutual hatred . . . in this way they managed to maintain broad-based party loyalty, drawn more from hereditary hatreds then from the ability of the parties to represent and channel the economic and social aspirations of the subordinate minority' (Restrepo, 1992, p. 276).

Conflict resolution through elite pacts

Throughout Colombian history, pacts between elites have been used as a mechanism for conflict resolution to end periods of political violence. The role of elite pacts is also crucial to understanding today's Colombian democracy, characterized by civil conflict and extreme levels of political violence. Dix reports six examples of bipartisan power-sharing arrangements in Colombia before the 1953–58 military rule: the governments of 1854, 1869, 1901, 1930, 1945 and 1949 (Dix, 1980, p. 304). In addition, a period of relatively stable coalition government incorporating both parties existed from 1910 until 1946.

Elite pacts permitted elite accommodation within the context of polarization and political violence and 'undoubtedly contributed to the survival of the two parties into the 20th century' (Dix, 1980, p. 304). They constituted the mechanisms through which the rewards of power could be shared, ensuring that no significant partisan factions capable of destabilizing the political balance were left out. As Dix notes, 'none of the coalitions had a constitutional basis' (1980, p. 306). Rather, the pacts were 'conversations among gentlemen', which tended to be informal, personalistic and narrowly based within the elite elements which were dominant at a given historical moment (Wilde, 1978, p. 58). Such elite pacts fit within the cycle of violence, reconciliation and 'restored democracy', in which 'party leaders launched the people into cycles of civil war that ended in pacts of national reconciliation arranged by the same leaders' (Restrepo, 1992, p. 276).

La Violencia *and the changing axis of conflict*

La Violencia (the Violence, 1946–66) was a *de facto* civil war between the Liberal and Conservative parties that left over 200,000 people killed and an estimated 2 million internally displaced. The conflict has been called the 'greatest mobilization of peasants in the recent history of the Western hemisphere' (Hartlyn, 1988, pp. 43–44). Moreover, the Violence marks the moment in Colombian history when the axis of political conflict shifted from inter-party competition to a new conflict dynamic between the elites of both parties, in alliance with the military and opposition groups in broader society.

The Violence simultaneously integrated two distinct levels of conflict: it had an identity within the old context of bipartisan political competition, but, at the same time, the conflict became 'an incipient revolution' (Sánchez, 1992, p. 80). The old bipartisan hegemony collided with the demands of *new challengers* in civil society who assumed an independent political identity outside the traditional political order. Their origins lay in the *silent revolutions* of profound economic, demographic, social and cultural changes which swept Colombia, and most other Latin American countries, during the first half of the twentieth century.[9] Also critical was the unresolved historical issue of land reform. As the conflict evolved over time, the Violence increasingly assumed an identity within this second level of conflict.

By 1952, Colombia seemed on the 'verge of an irreversible social and political crisis' (Sánchez, 1992, p. 100). The fighting had now escaped the control of the traditional parties, and large areas of the country were devastated as the violence 'followed its own dynamic [of] local and personal agendas of revenge and plunder'. The generalized nature of the conflict made it increasingly difficult for the party leadership to 'use violence selectively for their own purposes' (Peeler, 1992, p. 92). Of particular concern to elites in both parties was the growing independence of the guerrilla groups associated with the Liberal Party. The political discourse of the guerrillas became increasingly radical with the escalation of fighting, threatening elite interests regardless of their partisan affiliation.

As in the civil conflicts and wars prior to the Violence, the parties realized when the destruction 'had gone too far', and they sought a new form of intra-elite/inter-party accommodation. But after years of fighting, inter-party animosity was so deeply entrenched, especially at the rank-and-file level, that a third actor was needed to re-establish stability while the two parties worked out a new governing pact (Pécaut, 1987, p. 560). In this situation civilian elites found themselves 'forced to look for some new form of [temporary] ad hoc consensus' (Wilde, 1978, p. 58). Lacking another alternative, they called on the military to intervene. In 1953, General Rojas Pinilla was essentially 'thrust into power' (Hartlyn, 1988, p. 48). However, conflicts quickly developed between the military government and its civilian supporters when General Rojas Pinilla refused to relinquish power. In 1958, the Liberals and Conservatives managed to put aside their historical animosity and formed a coalition government, the National Front, in order to regain power.

The National Front elite pact

The National Front was a formal 16-year power-sharing agreement between the two traditional political parties. Negotiated in the historical context of 'pacted' solutions to inter-party conflict, the agreement effectively excluded other groups from meaningful participation in the political process. In this regard, it can be seen as a direct response to the dual threat to the hegemony of the two traditional parties. While excluding new challengers from political participation, the pact also sought to restore the historical subordination of the military to civilian rule, as it made General Rojas Pinilla and his new political organization 'supplant the traditional parties by taking away their mass support' (Peeler, 1992, p. 92).

The architects of the National Front pact responded to the first threat by placing restrictions on new challengers' participation in the political process. In particular, no newcomers were involved in the negotiations leading to the National Front agreement, and any parties other than the Liberals and Conservatives were explicitly excluded from participating in the electoral process by new amendments to the Constitution of 1886 which institutionalized the National Front (Sánchez, 1992, p. 113). Any non-traditional candidate would have to run under either a Liberal or Conservative banner (Peeler, 1992, p. 95). Furthermore, the National Front contained no provisions regarding the possibility of expanding political participation. Finally, the agreement was a purely political document with no social content to address historical issues, such as land reform, or changes in society resulting from the 'silent revolutions' (Wilde, 1978, p. 68; Sánchez, 1992, p. 115).

In response to the second threat, the Liberal and Conservative elites managed to remove General Rojas Pinilla from political office, replace him by a temporary military *junta* and regain the loyalty of the military establishment. The military had traditionally played a subordinate role in Colombian politics. Prior to 1953 it had participated in inter-party negotiations as 'the clients of a civilian notable' (Bustamante, 1989, p. 20). It was only with the National Front that the military took part in such negotiations as an actor in its own right. Within the new polity of the National Front, the civilian elites and the military establishment agreed that the military would no longer have a partisan identity. Rather, it would act as the guarantor of the National Front polity, defending the political system from *internal* threats (Bustamante, 1989, pp. 19–20, 31; Trujillo, 1993, pp. 81–83). Importantly, the agreement represented 'a fundamental redefinition of the military establishment's role in Colombian politics' and its relationship to civil society based on a new *civilian elite–military alliance* against perceived threats to common interests (Bustamante, 1989, p. 19). Previously excluded from the political process, the military was now assigned a role.

In exchange for re-submitting to civilian authority, the military was granted three concessions. First, the military received a guarantee that any 'failings or excesses' committed during the period of military rule would be considered the personal responsibility of General Rojas Pinilla (Wilde, 1978, pp. 60–61; Trujillo, 1993, pp. 81–84) – effectively a guarantee of impunity and non-accountability. Secondly, the civilian elites agreed to support the professionalization of the military, in part as a mechanism to ensure its non-partisan character. Professionalization referred to redefining the military's role in national security, modernizing its equipment to enable it to fight an irregular internal war, professional and ideological training abroad (primarily in the USA) and large increases in the military budget (Bustamante, 1989, pp. 17–20). The military was granted relative autonomy over how the process of professionalization would take place. Finally, the military was given a role in the civilian decisionmaking process. For example, regional-level government officials were obliged to consult with their military counterparts on issues related to public order and internal security (Bustamante, 1989, pp. 20–21; Trujillo, 1993, pp. 82–84).

One analyst has noted that the National Front resurrected and institutionalized the pre-1953 polity and 'remarkably represented little more than that' (Wilde, 1978, p. 62). On the one hand the agreement solved the historical problem of providing guarantees that a given party would not be excluded from the rewards of power. However, the National Front included no provisions for addressing the structural changes in society which had led to the breakdown of the old system and the Violence. In explicitly excluding new challengers, establishing a civilian elite–military alliance and redefining the military's role as the guarantors of internal security, the National Front established the context for the contemporary crisis of political violence and human rights violations.

The 'dirty war'

With the realignment of political forces during and after the Violence, the axis of conflict also changed. By the 1970s, both armed opposition groups and social organizations presented a significant challenge to the Liberal/Conservative-controlled state. Representing millions of people by the 1970s, social organizations consisted of unions and associations representing peasants, indigenous communities, the church, women and the urban poor. These organizations were legally constituted and often focused on specific community or sectoral problems, such as schools or other forms of community infrastructure or providing a political voice to sectors of the population that had no representation in the closed formal political process (Ardila & Tuft, 1995, note 11, pp. 133–134).

Legal social organizations attempted to create an opening in the political system for groups other than the Liberal and Conservative parties and to influence the distribution of resources in a manner that would make it more equitable. This generated a sharp response from the sectors of Colombian society threatened by their actions, including the large landowners and the two traditional political parties. At the same time, the guerrillas attempted to take advantage of social organizations to increase their own political influence. Caught between these conflicting forces, actions undertaken by such organizations, including land invasions or civic strikes, were often supported by the guerrillas and condemned as subversive by the government, the military and the Colombian economic elite.

In this context, the main axis of political violence in Colombia shifted. Whereas conflict historically had occurred as a result of inter-party competition, the Liberals and Conservatives, cooperating through the mechanism of the National Front and acting in alliance with the military, now jointly confronted the *new challengers* in Colombian society. During the 1970s, the government used legal mechanisms to suppress opposition. An almost permanent state of emergency rule was invoked and extraordinary laws were used extensively to detain political activists. Between 1970 and

1979 there were 60,325 political prisoners, predominantly from the ranks of legal trade unions, opposition political parties, human rights organizations, social workers, peasant and indigenous organizations.[10]

By the 1980s, however, the use of such extraordinary legal mechanisms appeared to be insufficient to control the opposition, and Colombia moved into a period known as the dirty war. According to the Representative of the UN Secretary-General for Internally Displaced Persons, the dirty war 'denotes the selective extermination of left-wing political activists, such as members of the *Unión Patriótica* [Patriotic Union; UP], trade unionists, members of popular and human rights organizations, teachers etc.'[11] Legal repression was now combined with the use of armed force, including the creation of paramilitary groups. From conventional warfare tactics targeting the guerrillas, the Colombian military also adopted a much broader ideological definition of internal enemy, encompassing both guerrilla combatants and civilians alleged to support or be sympathetic to them. As a result, civilians living in zones of conflict or guerrilla-controlled areas, and who might have had no affiliation with either side in the conflict, were identified by the military as legitimate targets for counter-insurgency operations. The strategy was intended to eliminate the guerrilla's base of support in the civilian population and has been described as 'removing the water from the fish' (Procuraduría General de la Nación, 1994).

In contravention of international humanitarian law, sectors of Colombia's civilian population have, since the 1980s, become the target of military operations. The effect of expanding the concept of the enemy can be seen directly in the number and changing patterns of human rights violations. While the number of political prisoners during the 1980s declined to 21,000, the number of extrajudicial executions increased from 1,053 in the 1970s to almost 13,000 between 1980 and 1989.[12] Of the 14,865 persons reported to have been killed in politically motivated violence in Colombia between 1990 and 1994 only 5,358 died in actual armed confrontations between government and the guerrillas.[13] The remaining 9,507 persons were civilians killed in non-combat situations, almost twice as many as the number of casualties from the actual fighting.[14] Over 2,000 persons were the victims of forced disappearance between 1978 and 1994 and, although torture is forbidden by Colombian law, the UN Special Rapporteur on Torture has called the practice endemic, especially in zones of conflict (Gairdner & Tuft, 1995, pp. 181–183).

Moreover, the United Nations High Commissioner for Refugees reports that almost 1 million persons out of a total population of 35 million have been internally displaced by the fighting (Proenza, 1997, p. 13). The Colombian news magazine *Cambio 16* puts the number of displaced people even higher, at 1.5 million.[15] This is a significant increase over the figure of 627,000 displaced persons used by the Catholic Conference of Bishops of Colombia and reaffirmed by the Special Representative of the Secretary-General of the United Nations, Francis Deng, in 1995.[16] All the same, many observers consider these figures to be conservative, representing the minimum instance of displacement that has been officially recorded. Our 1993 study found that 'there is no national system for registering or counting internally displaced persons and no statistics exist for many regions of the country that have suffered massive displacements' (Ardila & Tuft, 1995, pp. 118–119). Also, many persons flee their homes in secret and try to hide their identity as displaced persons on reaching the community where they take refuge. State human rights officials in Colombia have noted that 'people fled their homes without a word, quietly and almost as if in shame'.[17] The actual number of internally displaced persons, therefore, may be significantly higher than official statistics indicate.

Impact on civil society

Reports on human rights violations indicate that there are two main sectors of the Colombian population affected by political violence.[18] The first are members of legally constituted social organizations and political opposition groups working outside the two traditional parties and their affiliated organizations. As noted, these persons and their organizations have been targeted for repression as a result of their dissent and role as new challengers to the established political order. The second sector consists of persons living in the rural areas that have become zones of conflict. These people often find themselves caught in the conflict between the military, paramilitary groups and the guerrillas. Human rights violations may also occur in the context of counter-insurgency operations that target persons living in rural areas as part of the enemy. Under the strategy of 'removing the water from the fish', the military has attempted to eliminate the base of political support and resources for guerrilla operations within the civilian population. This means that people are often forced to flee their homes and become internally displaced, usually moving to the urban poor areas of Colombia's major cities (Ardila & Tuft, 1995, p. 118).

Measuring the impact of armed conflict requires making a distinction between their direct and indirect nature. A *direct impact* refers to the immediate consequences of military actions. These are often manifest in the more dramatic violations of civil and political human rights associated with armed conflict, including the death and injury of civilian non-combatants and repressive actions taken against legal opposition groups. By this definition, the pattern of human rights violations described above can be understood as the immediate consequences of military actions and, therefore, as the *direct impact* of political violence. This definition may also include the destruction of private property and of the country's economic and social infrastructure.

An *indirect impact* is defined here as the long-term damage caused to economic, political and social infrastructure, institutions and networks as a result of conflict. It is also seen in the general polarization of society (Moreno, 1991, p. 36). Whereas hundreds of thousands of Colombians have been directly affected in the past three decades through their own direct experience with the conflict, many more have been affected indirectly as a result of the damage caused to Colombian society at large. Indeed, the entire population can be said to be touched in some way by the indirect consequences of war. For example, increased military expenditures divert resources from productive uses, including social programmes and the provision of basic services to communities.

In view of the complexity of the indirect and direct nature of the impact on the civilian population, in our 1993 study we found it necessary to distinguish three broad classifications: socio-economic, socio-political and socio-psychological (Ardila & Tuft, 1995). Although listed separately, these three are interrelated and irreducible. Moreover, there is a dynamic interaction between both the direct and indirect consequences of the conflict.

A *socio-economic impact* occurs broadly at the national level through the distorted allocation of resources to maintain the war, including financing military operations and procurements. Such spending often occurs to the detriment of social priorities. At the regional level, a socio-economic impact is the result of the destruction of the economy in a zone of conflict, particularly the infrastructure and productive capacity of the region. For example, military aerial bombardments of rural zones where guerrilla organizations are suspected to be active endanger the civilian inhabitants and result in the destruction of their homes, crops, domestic animals and farm implements. Our 1993 study also found that military operations are often intended to deny guerrilla organizations access to supplies and support from the civilian population. As a result, families in some regions may be permitted to purchase enough food only for a one-week period at a time. Those found to be in possession of foodstocks or medicines risk being accused of belonging to the guerrillas.

The socio-economic consequences of war are also evident in the interruption of education, reduced access to basic services, and an increase in the incidence of infant mortality and disease. The loss or reduced access to basic services is particularly serious, as the majority of those affected belong to the poorest strata of Colombian society. Armed conflict significantly worsens their situation, rendering them more vulnerable to poverty-related disease. In this sense, the conflict causes an increase in the actual demand for basic social services at the same time as it is responsible for further reducing the population's access to precisely those services (Ardila & Tuft, 1995, pp. 109–111).

The *socio-political impact* is related to the denial of fundamental civil and political rights, including freedom of expression, political participation and social organization around issues that affect the well-being of communities. Acts of repression accompanying armed conflict often have the specific objective of preventing the civilian population from organizing itself (Gutierrez, 1993). Fear becomes an important disincentive to community organization or social activism outside the political mainstream, rendering people reluctant to involve themselves in any form of community organization. In this way, the fear generated by political violence is in itself an important mechanism for political control.[19] The long-term consequence is the destruction of both the channels that enable civil society to participate in the political process and the fabric of social solidarity. Thus, political violence is not a problem of individuals: it also has profound social implications (Pérez, 1993, pp. 16–17).

The *socio-psychological impact* refers to the effects of trauma resulting from exposure to or actual participation in combat, including witnessing acts of violence, the violent death of a loved one, the destruction of homes and property or in some way being a target of repression or threats of violence (Macksound, 1993). The resulting trauma is evident in behavioural problems with implications for people's ability to realize their human potential and, therefore, their ability to participate in society. The term 'socio-psychological' also encompasses a recognition of the importance of the general social environment and processes, and the interaction of these factors with the psychological well-being of the individual (Marcellino et al., 1993, pp. 165–166). It is very difficult to make generalizations about the socio-psychological impact of conflict. The effects of trauma and fear are not always immediately visible, and their long-term implications for the individual and society at large are difficult to calculate. In our 1993 study we observed that internal displacement, generally involving an abrupt change from the countryside to urban slums and increased economic insecurity, combined with the fear resulting from political violence, extended the post-violence trauma and undermined the possibility of that person's recovery.

Gender-based differences in human rights violations and their impact

The situation in Colombia demonstrates how men and women are affected differently by the conflict. We can see clear gender-based differences in the type of human rights violations as well as in the impact resulting from those violations.

It is always dangerous to generalize. However, we may safely state that men are the principal victims of civil and political human rights violations associated with armed conflict, including violations of the right to life, the right not to be subjected to torture, the right to freedom of speech and organization and the right to freedom of movement. As a result of the structure of gender relations pre-existing in society at large, men are more likely than women to assume visible leadership roles in a community or in other forms of social organization such as trade unions and left-wing political parties. We have seen how, in Colombia, these forms of dissent have been the principle targets of political repression.[20]

In contrast, the violations of human rights usually experienced by women are most often in the realm of economic, social and cultural rights, falling under the definition of *indirect socio-economic impact*. These forms of violations are perhaps most visible among internally displaced persons, that is those who migrate within the national territory of Colombia because 'their life, physical integrity and liberty have been made vulnerable or are threatened' (Instituto Interamericano de Derechos Humanos, 1992, p. 1). 'The population affected is in large part peasant farmers. Families are large and comprised of [sic] small children or young adolescents. There are usually no adult males and in many cases the father has been killed' (Castaño, 1992, p. 3). The widows and their children are subsequently forced to leave the zone in question under threats to their own safety. In this sense internal displacement is both a *direct* consequence of violations of civil and political human rights at the same time as it produces an *indirect* impact in all three of the sub-categories identified above.

A 1994 study found that 60% of those forced to flee their homes as a result of the armed conflict were women, including 40,000 female heads of households.[21] This means that many families have lost their primary income-earner and women are obliged to assume the traditional roles played by both males and females, including responsibility for the economic and emotional support of the children. Economic hardship is directly related to the circumstances surrounding their displacement. Our study found that in most cases the internally displaced had formerly been able to earn at least a subsistence income as peasant farmers. Any cash income was supplemented by the ability of the family to grow its own food. Once displaced, however, families lose most of their possessions and the source of their livelihood – their homes, farmland and implements, domestic animals and crops. And this in turn means that they also lose access to their primary source of food. Their economic situation declines from subsistence living on the farm to absolute poverty in the city (Ardila & Tuft, 1995, pp. 120–123).

In this new environment, displaced women have few economic opportunities. Not only must they compete for housing and employment with the poor population already living in urban slum areas, they enter into this competition without the support of their extended family or other members of their community, and without economic resources to fall back on. At the same time they must cope with the loss of homes and communities – their very basis of personal, family and cultural identity (Castaño, 1993). Lacking formal education and the work skills to compete in an urban economy, women must turn to the informal sector, where they often find employment as domestic workers. As salaries here are generally below the official minimum level, and insufficient to meet basic needs, many women and women's organizations see the conflict as primarily an economic war against the poor.

Regarding the socio-political and socio-psychological nature of the impact on the internally displaced, this author was told in interviews that men and women suffer differently as a result. Men, especially, often face problems of self-esteem, related to the fact that they formerly exercised political and social leadership in their community of origin. For security reasons, such displaced community leaders are forced to become anonymous and are unable to engage in any meaningful social and political activity. Added to this is the fact that they are no longer able to assume the full economic responsibility for their families that is traditional in Colombian society. The consequences of these dynamics are not well understood in a gender context and merit further research. Research is also needed on why and under what conditions women assume political and social leadership, which in fact makes them targets of politically motivated violence; and why some – both women and men – become politically and socially empowered in the midst of the conflict, whereas others withdraw from all social and political activity.

Integrating a gender perspective in conflict resolution

> Peace includes not only the absence of war, violence and hostilities . . . but also the enjoyment of economic and social justice, equality and the entire range of human rights and fundamental freedoms within society. (United Nations, 1985, paragraph 13)

In the Colombian context, civil conflict arises out of structural imbalances in people's ability to enjoy access to resources and political power and from differences in political culture. Therefore, a gender perspective in conflict resolution cannot be based solely on considerations of the structural imbalances of power between women and men: it must reflect the differences experienced by women and men in how the direct and indirect impacts of conflict affect their lives. Women's choices and opportunities are also shaped by larger issues of class, poverty, political culture, ethnicity and geography, as well as their exclusion from political channels existing within the formal political system and in civil society.

Arguably, the most important precondition for peace in Colombia is the initiation of meaningful negotiations between the government and the guerrilla organizations. In the event that the initial peace talks result in formal negotiations, the dynamics of the conflict imply that a narrowly constituted process of conflict resolution between the government and the guerrillas would be insufficient. Other sectors of society have been involuntarily drawn into the conflict, both as targets of repression and to the extent that they are affected by its direct and indirect impacts. In particular, differences in how the conflict affects men and women dictate that a gender perspective be taken into consideration, in peace negotiations and in post-conflict strategies for rebuilding Colombian society. The larger purpose of integrating a gender perspective into these two processes would be to eliminate the many gender-, class-, regional- and culture-based inequalities in society that are among the original causes of the conflict. Conflict resolution from a gender perspective also implies expanding the concept of conflict resolution to include processes other than the official ones in which the multiple dimensions of the conflict are addressed. These processes must be characterized by the participation of actors other than those directly involved in the conflict.

In this chapter three broad interrelated dimensions of the conflict have been identified as being of central concern: the closed political system, human rights violations, and the exclusive conflict resolution processes.

The closed political system

Colombia's formal democratic institutions remain extremely limited in their ability to serve as a channel for the broader interests and concerns of civil society. Most Colombians are still excluded from meaningful participation; the number of human rights violations indicates that dissent is actively repressed. The political system, therefore, acts as a source of tension rather than as a mechanism through which conflict can be mediated or resolved. The post-Violence civil war, which has lasted for more than 40 years now, created the conditions and broader ideological rationale for human rights violations against civilian non-combatants belonging to legal opposition groups. Despite constitutional guarantees of broad political participation, violence severely limits the real ability for anyone outside the two traditional parties to participate in the political process. To take only one example: over 2,400 members of the political party *Union Patriotica* (Patriotic Union; UP) were assassinated between 1985, when the party was formed, and 1994. Decades of repression have also weakened other non-traditional political parties and social organizations. Observers have noted that the forum for legitimate participation is shrinking (Gairdner & Tuft, 1995, pp. 165–167).

Addressing Colombia's closed political system from a gender perspective implies broadening the overall space for political participation available to actors representing interests in civil society outside the two traditional political parties. This participation must be recognized as legitimate and not condemned as subversive when it is perceived to threaten traditional party interests. Those involved in dissenting political groups must have a guarantee that their constitutionally protected human rights will be respected, including their right to physical security. Within this expanded political space, the participation of women and women's organizations must be promoted. Women need to have a voice inside the formal political system, where both traditional and new political organizations must secure a space for their participation. Equally important, political space must be secured for women's organizations in civil society.

Room for political participation can be secured only if and when the civilian authorities demilitarize social conflict, reducing the armed forces' political influence over the government's policy on public order. An end to the over 130 paramilitary groups is also necessary. Research by human rights organizations and statements by retired military officials have revealed the close working relationship between the Colombian military and these paramilitary groups.[22] Finally, there must be an end to the impunity enjoyed by agents of the state who commit human rights violations. This requires political will on behalf of the civilian authorities to reform the administration of justice and the military penal system.

Human rights violations

The ability of women to enjoy their human rights fully is severely limited by the *indirect socio-economic* consequences of the Colombian conflict. Even though the principle of interdependence between all human rights is stated in the 1990 Constitution, in practice more attention is paid to civil and political rights, to the detriment of economic, social and cultural rights. This may be understandable, given the extreme levels of political violence and violations of civil and political human rights. However, it is precisely the violation of economic, social and cultural rights that affects women, particularly those who are internally displaced. Lack of shelter, drinking water, electricity, adequate food, work, a minimum income or other resources means that women affected by the conflict are likely to suffer from ill health, and are often unable to send their children to school, or to participate in local activities. Until these rights are guaranteed, women will remain excluded from meaningful participation in society.

Addressing the *socio-economic* impact either in peace negotiations or in a post-conflict reconstruction implies analysing possible solutions from the perspective of the gender-based differences in human rights violations. Particular emphasis must be placed on coming to terms with the conflict's economic, social and cultural impact on women. Seen in conjunction with initiatives related to political participation, integrating a gender perspective requires paying attention to the principle of interdependence between *all* human rights by ensuring not only a political space for women's participation but also a minimum level of basic economic, social and cultural rights that can truly enable women to enjoy that participation.

Exclusive conflict resolution processes

Conflict resolution through elite pacts has been used as a mechanism for conflict resolution throughout Colombian history, including during the post-National Front era. Prior to the 1958 agreement, party leaders of the two traditional political parties had launched the country into cycles of civil war that ended in pacts of national reconciliation arranged by the same leaders. The silent revolutions of profound economic, demographic, social and cultural changes which occurred in Colombia between the 1930s and the 1960s created new sources of power and opportunity outside the traditional polity. With these new sources of power came new actors who built their own organizations capable of channelling and satisfying the demands of their affiliates, undercutting the political parties and affecting both the stakes and the exercise of the political process.

In the conflict resolution process that culminated in the National Front of 1958, the traditional elites in alliance with the military effectively excluded the new actors from the procedures as well as from having a voice in determining the substantive agenda of the Front. The result was an exclusive political agreement that contained no provisions regarding the eventual broadening of political participation, and included no social content aimed at addressing substantive issues such as land reform or changes in society resulting from the silent revolutions. The axis of conflict had changed during the Violence, but the scope of the conflict and the scope of the conflict resolution process did not correspond in terms of actors involved and issues addressed. Hence the conflict resolution process itself became a source of conflict in Colombia.

Addressing this dimension of the conflict from a gender perspective means recognizing that the very concept of conflict resolution must be expanded to include and address the conflict's most central dimensions, one of them being the conflict resolution process itself. The sectors of the civilian population most affected by the conflict, and not only its armed actors, must be secured a voice in the process of resolving the conflict. Their demands must be taken into account in every step of a peace process. Even in the absence of official peace negotiations, addressing the direct and indirect consequences of the conflict on the civilian population should be part of the long-term conflict resolution process. A gender awareness needs to be created at all levels, and a gender perspective must feature high on the conflict resolution agenda.

One major challenge for women's organizations will be to address gender-based and other forms of inequality and discrimination simultaneously. This requires working on at least two levels: as members of independent women's organizations and as members of other relevant organizations within civil society as well as relevant agencies and departments of the state. On the first level, the central task is to elaborate a gender-sensitive conflict resolution agenda and gain support for this agenda among the other actors. The second level involves working from within other organizations and agencies in order to create gender awareness among the members. For women, this will mean achieving a position and a voice within the leadership of the traditionally male-dominated political and social organizations. The challenge on both levels is to link a gender profile to the analysis of the main axis of conflict and, on this basis, to elaborate policies and programmes that can contribute to conflict resolution. This in itself is difficult, since most political and social actors see the Colombian conflict as gender-neutral, considering it to be based on factors of class, culture, ideology, ethnicity and geography instead. Moreover, gender is generally not understood as an issue that concerns both women and men: it is understood to be a 'women's issue'. And in turn, the traditional 'machismo' in Colombian culture implies that a 'women's issue' will often be neglected in political and social work.

Lessons from the gender and development trend

Since the beginning of the Decade for Women (1975–85), various strategies have been elaborated to eliminate gender-based inequality and discrimination, and to promote the advancement of women. The feminization of poverty gave rise to the Women in Development (WID) strategy, later complemented or replaced by the Gender and Development (GAD) strategy. The former focused primarily on women, whereas the latter is more concerned with the socially constructed roles of both women and men, and social and power relations between them.

Within the GAD strategy there are differences in focus. Women's organizations tend to focus on substantive policy objectives, such as gender equality and women's empowerment, whereas governments and international and national development agencies tend to emphasize process-focused instrumental objectives, such as women's integration in development, and to give priority to institutional rather than operational strategies. Institutional strategies are the input-side interventions which aim primarily at structural changes within agencies and governments to facilitate the implementation of both WID and GAD policies.[23] Operational strategies are output-oriented measures designed to bring about a change in work programmes of agencies and governments (Jahan, 1995, pp. 12–14).

By the end of the Decade for Women, many women's organizations, agencies and governments had embraced the concept of mainstreaming in their work. Jahan uses two broad categories to explain the approach. The first, an *integrationist methodology*, incorporates gender issues within existing development paradigms. The overall development agenda, with its sectoral and programming priorities, is not transformed. Rather, women's concerns and the larger gender perspective are fitted into predefined sectors and programmes. The second methodology is defined as *agenda-setting*. It implies that a gender perspective provides the foundation on which a transformed development agenda is then constructed. Central to the process is the participation of women as decisionmakers in determining development priorities that can bring about a fundamental change in the existing development paradigm. It is not simply women as individuals but a transformative gender agenda that is recognized by the mainstream. Accordingly, gender concerns not only become a part of the mainstream: women also reorient that mainstream through their interactions with it (Jahan, 1995, pp. 12–13).

By assessing past policies, actions and achievements in relation to women/gender and development as well as the scarce documentation that exists on conflict resolution from a gender perspective, some general as well as Colombia specific recommendations can be elaborated. These come from an agenda-setting rather than integrationist approach.

Conclusion

Women's organizations concerned with integrating a gender perspective in conflict resolution should move the focus towards an *agenda-setting* approach. This requires that a conflict resolution agenda be defined, with a clear distinction between substantive objectives, such as peace as defined by the Nairobi Forward-looking Strategies and the means or instrumental objectives, such as integrating a gender perspective in the mainstream of conflict resolution processes. A distinction should also be made between institutional and operational strategies. One element of an institutional strategy could be the creation of a special gender advisory position or body within a conflict resolution process. Various aspects of the implementation of a gender-sensitive peace agreement would form part of an operational strategy. The analysis of the Colombian case suggests that the indirect socio-economic consequences of the conflict as well as the realization of economic, social and cultural rights must be given special attention in an agenda-setting approach. The feminization of poverty as a general trend worldwide is an indication that this argument might be valid in other conflict situations. However, only further research can prove the validity of the argument.

The long-term success of an agenda-setting approach in conflict resolution depends on a recognition of that agenda among other organizations in civil society. This means that women must work to improve the position of their organizations within civil society and to improve the position of women within other organizations by linking the women's agenda to the agendas of other sectors of the population affected by the conflict. Only with the support of a variety of organizations can a gender-sensitive conflict resolution agenda become part of the dialogue between the armed actors as well as between the non-armed actors of the conflict.

Research institutes should establish cross-national programmes and databases in the following areas: gender-desegregated data on human rights violations and violations of international humanitarian law in conflict situations; gender analysis of the impact of conflict on the civilian population; responses to the impact of conflict originating in civil society; and women's experiences with participating in conflict resolution processes at all levels and the outcome of their participation.

Research institutes should also pay greater attention to the rebuilding of war-torn societies. Documentation and analysis from a gender perspective is needed on the impact of macroeconomic policies as well as other policies on which a long-lasting peace depends. Also required is a gender analysis of women's post-conflict experiences in accessing economic resources and political space. Research findings must be made available to international and national policy-makers and decisionmakers and to the populations affected by conflicts.

The international community, including the United Nations and international development organizations, should support reform to make existing national and international decisionmaking structures related to conflict resolution and peace-building more inclusive. Governments and international bodies can be guided by the Beijing Platform for Action.[24] The international community should also work to ensure that women's organizations have substantive representation at all levels of these structures. It is not sufficient that women *per se* participate: representation must be granted to women's organizations based in those sectors that are most affected by the conflict.

The international community should support initiatives for dialogue at the local, national and international levels. These can be fora or seminars organized in collaboration between state institutions, political parties, and non-governmental and community-based organizations. An agenda-setting gender perspective in conflict resolution should be promoted within these fora.

The work of the international community should be conducted within a multidimensional framework, to ensure that conflict is addressed at the different levels of society where its impact is felt. In the Colombian case, a multidimensional strategy would first require support for political efforts to reach a negotiated settlement between the government and the armed opposition groups. Furthermore, the international community must assist the government in fulfilling peace-related commitments, including social and economic reforms that address the causes of the conflict. It must also work with Colombian actors to ensure respect for international humanitarian law, the *de jure* and *de facto* abolition of the paramilitary groups and an end to impunity for human rights violations committed by agents of the state.

Finally, international support is needed for the elaboration and implementation of gender-sensitive programmes that address the impact of conflict. In the case of Colombia, these should not be restricted to ensuring civil and political rights. Crucial here are conflict resolution and post-conflict programmes that can address the economic, social and cultural dimensions of human rights. Failure to do so will mean that women remain disadvantaged by the impact of violence into the post-conflict period.

Notes

1   The other guerrilla organizations are the *Ejército de Liberación Nacional* (National Liberation Army; ELN) and dissident units of *Ejército Popular de Liberación* (Popular Liberation Army; EPL).

2   Peace talks started in 1982. It was not until 1990, however, that President Gaviria signed peace agreements with the *Movimiento 19 de Abril* (Movement of April 19; M-19), the indigenous, the EPL and the *Partido Revolucionario de los Trabajadores* (Revolutionary Workers Party; PRT). In 1993, Gaviria also signed an agreement with the *Corriente de Renovación Socialista* (Movement of Socialist Renovation; CRS). Negotiations were conducted with the FARC and the ELN between June 1991 and May 1992. However, face-to-face meetings in Venezuela and Mexico failed to produce an agreement. The government formally broke off talks in October 1992. President Gaviria declared 'total war' two weeks later and the guerrillas resumed their military operations. Many blame the failure of the negotiations on a lack of will by both parties. During Ernesto Samper's administration (1994–98), none of the parties to the conflict had the political will, capacity or internal coherence to resolve the conflict through a negotiated settlement. Samper's administration was in particular weakened by allegations that his 1994 electoral campaign received financial support from the Cali drug cartel. The resulting political crisis created the conditions for an increase in the conflict, rather than bringing it closer to resolution.

3   *Prensa Libre*, 17 January 1999, pp. 12–13.

4   The paramilitary groups' request for political status and participation in peace negotiations will not be dealt with in this chapter.

5   A 1995 report shows that women only recently have become increasingly subject to violations of civil and political rights (Amnesty International, 1995, p. 1). Another indication is the fact that the majority of internally displaced persons are women and their children, many of the women recently widowed (United Nations, 1995b, Add. 1, Para. 56; Amnesty International, 1997, p. 35).

6   Uruguay is the only other Latin American country where the parties formed at Independence still retain power. No third political party has ever won power in Colombia at the national level. With the exception of two members of the political party *Alianza Democrática Movimiento 19 de Abril* (Democratic Alliance of April 19; AD M-19) who briefly held minor Cabinet positions during the administration of Cesar Gaviria Trujillo (1990–94), no third party has ever held government office at the national level.

7   The Colombian military has had a closer historical relationship with the Conservative Party than with the Liberals.

8   The Thousand Day War was the largest of Latin America's nineteenth-century civil conflicts (Bushnell, 1992, p. 15).

9   The result of these *silent revolutions* has been to undermine traditional mechanisms for mobilizing political support and weaken party sectarianism (see Uprimny & Vargas Castaño, 1990, p. 144).

10   Liga Internacional por les Derechos y la Liberación de los Pueblos, 1990, p. 16.

11   United Nations, 1995b, Add. 1, para. 25.

12   See note 9.

13   Many of the victims were civilian non-combatants caught in the crossfire.

14   Justicia y Paz, 1994, p. 21.

15   Reported by E.M. Thomas, *International Herald Tribune*, 18 June 1997, p. 9.

16   Conferencia Episcopal de Colombia, 1994, p. 5; United Nations, 1995b, Add. 1.

17   *Guardian Weekly*, 1 June 1997, p. 13.

18   United Nations, 1995b, Add. 1, para. 25.

19   For a full discussion of fear as a tool of social control under repressive governments see Corradi et al., 1992.

20   On the other hand, we should also note that in recent years women have become increasingly subject to violations of civil and political rights. Ironically, that shift reflects the growing trend among Colombian women to assume political and social leadership roles in society (Amnesty International, 1995, p. 1).

21 Conferencia Episcopal de Colombia, 1994, p. 5. A gender breakdown of the latest (1997) figures was not available. As noted above, however, the UN High Commissioner for Refugees recently reported that almost 1 million persons have been internally displaced by political violence, whereas the Colombian news magazine *Cambio 16* has put the number of displaced persons at 1.5 million.

22 Extensive documentation exists on the complicity between the military and paramilitary forces, including reports by the European Union, the United Nations Human Rights Committee, the United Nations Working Group on Enforced or Involuntary Disappearances and the Colombian Prosecutor General's Office.

23 While the women's movement in general has underscored the conceptual differences between different policy goals, approaches and methodologies and has advocated a coherent set, governments and agencies have often applied a combined approach, articulating simultaneously substantive and instrumental objectives, and using both WID and GAD methodologies. Too often, the result has been confusion and contradictory trends (Jahan, 1995, p. 21).

24 The Beijing Platform for Action was adopted at the Fourth World Conference on Women, held in Beijing, China, 4–15 September 1995. Delegates from 189 countries participated in the Conference. The Platform for Action contains strategic objectives and actions for the advancement of women, including sections on women and armed conflict and women in power and decisionmaking. While governments have the primary responsibility for implementing the Platform, civil society organizations are encouraged to participate in the planning as well as in the implementation process (United Nations, 1996a).

9
The Use of Women and the Role of Women in the Yugoslav War

Svetlana Slapsak

We may be forced to agree that women share in the patriotism and commitment to national interest which sustains militarism and condones war. We may even agree that it is feminist rejection, rather than affirmation, of notions of the separate and different nature and greater vulnerability of women which most threatens the morale of men at arms and the motivation for militaristic thinking. We may agree on all these things, and yet we may still appeal to women's values, to maternal values, to save humanity. (Segal, 1987, p. 196)

Introduction

Any serious anthropological attempt at presenting the role of women in the Yugoslav war must take into consideration the anthropological and cultural background of the Balkans (Slapsak, 1997a and b). When it comes to women's anthropology and culture, there are various boundaries – chronological (ancient/modern) as well as national – that must be transcended in order to capture the common, chronologically resistant or recurrent forms of women's behaviour, communication models and cultural production (Herzfeld, 1985). It seems plausible that certain patterns of defining women, ruling women and also reacting to women have produced certain parallel responses on the part of women. The use and the role of women in war are one such action–response complex (Higonnet & Jenson, 1987; Cooke & Woollacott, 1993; Howlett & Mengham, 1994).[1]

Traditional portrayals of women in Yugoslav culture

We may identify at least two features of Balkan women's attitudes towards war that have persisted from the days of antiquity[2] and that are recognizable in a range of Balkan cultures, including modern Greek, Slavic and non-Slavic. These are women's parodies of serious, male matters – such as war – and the position of women in the death cults. I will restrict myself to two examples, both involving the women's peace movements during the war in Yugoslavia.

Kosovo lies at the mythological core of Serbian nationalism. In 1389, the Ottoman army under Sultan Murat met a force of Serbs (and others) under Prince Lazar in the major battle of Kosovo Polje. Historical sources are ambiguous about the outcome, mainly because the Turkish sultan was killed during the battle, supposedly by a brave Serbian knight; but Serbian tradition affirms that the Serbs, having chosen the kingdom of heaven, were defeated, and the subsequent Turkish occupation lasted for almost five centuries. The Kosovo cycle of oral epic poetry, composed well after the events, has been compared to the Homeric epics and has been studied by many authorities, from Goethe to Albert Lord (1960). It forms the main text adduced to support nationalist or indeed any state-forming discourse in the area. This was the case in the late nineteenth and early twentieth century, when intellectuals from future Yugoslav states set about inventing the utopian, republican and democratic South Slavic shelter-state for many oppressed and deprived ethnic groups, not only those of Slavic origin.[3] At the 1911 World Fair in Rome, Ivan Mectrovic (a sample of whose work can be seen today in front of the UN headquarters in New York), then an Austro-Hungarian citizen, constructed a pavilion based on the topic of the Kosovo battle, taken as an example of South Slavic heroism and stoic morality. This utopian and republican Yugoslav movement that gave rise to so much art and scholarship[4] could not, however, incorporate or identify with the monarchy and, in the 1920s, the movement eventually vanished. While Yugoslav-oriented intellectuals interpreted Kosovo in terms of Freudian theory and within various new artistic and literary movements, the state-sponsored culture produced another, conservative and Serb-centred Kosovo ideology, backed up by religious Orthodox thinkers and the Orthodox Church itself.

Vuk Karadzic, a self-educated Serbian philologist who brought traditional epic poetry to light and published it from 1818 onwards, made a primary genre–gender division which still makes much sense. He defined epic poetry as *male heroic poetry*, and all the other genres (like ballads, love poetry, ritual poetry, satiric poetry, riddles and games) as *women's poetry*. In his own manuscripts – collections of oral poetry, published by the Serbian Academy of Arts and Sciences – there are some women's poems which clearly satirize the heroic Kosovo myth: Queen Milica, Lazar's wife, receives a message from her deceased husband via *multi-coloured* birds (as opposed to black ravens in the epic cycle), with a hint that he might be coming back. Milica replies to the messenger birds that there is no need for any such thing, because she has succeeded in marrying off her sons and daughters, and they all live happily.[5] Historic sources affirm that Milica's daughter was married to Murat's son and heir Bayazit, and that she eventually died of sorrow when her husband died as a prisoner of war in Asia Minor. The queen's son was a Turkish vassal, like many other Serbian nobles. The two satiric songs on the same topic date to the seventeenth and eighteenth centuries, which means that they may have been contemporary with some songs of the epic cycle itself. In both cases, we see the women's world of compromises and everyday life as opposed to the male set of values which includes glorious death and an eternal life.

Another example of women's attitudes towards war that can be found throughout the Balkan area is the role played by women in the death cult. This has persisted up to the present. Once a man (a hero, a fighter) is dead, his body belongs to the women, who take care of washing and preparing the body for the funeral. They also hold a wake and perform lamentations during the funeral. In many regions, professional 'lamentors', usually women, are hired to improvise a lamentation which has its epic verses (deeds of the deceased, his glory, his tragic death) but often also includes verses on the family's sorrow, the women's desperation and personal feelings. Later on, especially in Montenegro, this lamentation might form the basis of an epic poem accompanied by the one-stringed *gusle*, but this time performed by a male singer; if the family is rich enough, and if the performer is famous enough, it might be recorded.

As Gail Holst-Warhaft (1992) has shown, this particular women's role, allowing a certain undeniable power over death, goes back to antiquity. Involvement in birth and in death are both *miasma* (see Parker, 1983).[6] Just as men avoid women in childbirth, they also avoid contact with death.[7] Being 'polluted' by their capacity for giving birth, however, women can deal with the 'pollution' of death. Women's relationship with death has been used in pacifist movements in modern times, as in the Israel–Palestinian confrontation: women in black, both Jewish and Palestinian, would appear in public places, warning against death and the perils of war. The model has been taken up by women in Yugoslavia and in many other European countries, as well as in the USA, but Yugoslav women had their own Balkan tradition to play on.

When the first incidents of conflict occurred in 1990–91, many of them staged by Serbian or Croatian nationalists, as their initiators later proudly revealed,[8] urban women were stunned at the sight of peasant women in black around the deceased and at funerals, performing their traditional role, but also stirring up public emotions, directing them towards revenge and against the other side. National television stations made much of such scenes. It was an open manipulation of traditional values and the traditional role of women in order to enhance nationalist feeling and the collective mentality. The subsequent and immediate appearance in the main cities all over the Yugoslav space of groups of urban women dressed in black, silent but with banners proclaiming their anti-war stance, was a logical answer to this misuse of women's traditional behaviour (Zajevic, 1994).

In both these examples, the context gives the main clues for interpretation. It is precisely the lack of knowledge of the context that was to produce many superficial and stereotyped interpretations in the media, foreign as well as domestic, quite a few of them also accepted by uncritical academics. This is why I find it necessary to expand the topic by presenting some broader background and some general explanations of what underlies the women's movement and feminism in Yugoslavia.

Women's struggle for independence

Historically, the first signs of women's economic and social independence in the Balkans appeared in two basic forms after the French Revolution: women (national) freedom fighters and bourgeois women entrepreneurs. The first case can be located in revolutionary Serbia (1804–13), and the second in the rich region of Vojvodina (Panonia), then part of the Austro-Hungarian Empire. During the nineteenth century, feminism in its European varieties appeared in Croatia and Slovenia, both under Austro-Hungarian rule, in Vojvodina within the national–political Serbian movement *Omladina Srpska* ('Serbian Youth') and in Serbia within the socialist movements. Apart from such organizations, which had a pronounced national and/or humanitarian character, women's professional and feminist organizations did not appear until the 1920s and beyond.

In the 1930s women's clubs, societies of academic women, women lawyers and similar groups flourished, along with a ministerial bureau for women's questions in the government. Many women's congresses, especially for Balkan women, marked this epoch. Mention should be made here of two women who have remained largely unknown, even for Yugoslav women. The work of Radmila S. Petrovic (1908–32), was practically unknown until it was published, with an accompanying article by Svetlana Tomin, in the feminist quarterly, *ProFemina* 1997. Although Petrovic died at an early age, she held a PhD in legal sciences and was a brilliant historian of law. She published a great many articles on the legal aspects of the position of women, including research on women judges and women jurors, the state of women's rights in Yugoslavia and related areas of research.

The other, Julka Chlapec-Djordjevic (1882–1969), came from Vojvodina and as well as completing a PhD in philosophy, published two volumes on feminism in the 1930s, many articles and a novel, written in letter-form, on the challenging topic of a love relationship which ends with the man's suicide (Chlapec-Djordjevic, 1932). Chlapec-Djordjevic was well-informed about trends in world feminism of the time, and took up subjects like abortion, sexual ethics, trends in psychoanalysis and gynaecology, women's rights, feminism and fascism, feminism and communism, and feminism and pacifism. She introduced her Yugoslav readership to feminist movements and women's literature of Europe and the USA. She also wrote on women authors and the presentation of women in Yugoslav literature and culture, criticizing several influential authors of the time. Politically, she held similar views as Tomaz G. Masaryk. In fact she married a Czech, learned the language and translated many literary works. She died, completely forgotten, in a village in Czechoslovakia in 1969.

In her double volume on feminism, *Studies and Essays on Feminism* (Chlapec-Djordjevic, 1935), she explored local tradition and presented her feminist predecessors as well as feminism in the international context. She insisted that every feminist must be a sociologist as well, and did not hesitate to criticize the Freudian approach. She also argued that socialist movements enabled feminism to think in big numbers, to organize mass movements and to form the discourse of *us* – women. There is no information on her involvement in the Communist Party, which was illegal in Yugoslavia at that time, but lack of information does not necessarily mean that she was not a member.

Before tackling the topic of socialism and its attitude to feminism, Chlapec-Djordjevic found it necessary to determine the position of feminism in relation to national socialism, nationalism and their adversary – pacifism. In her opinion, German feminist movements did a service to Hitler by presenting some irrational demands, and that the right wing of these movements actually directly helped national socialism. Left-wing feminism consisted mainly of Jewish women, and certainly could not do much to repair the damage. The question of pacifism worsened the situation, both in Germany and Italy. Chlapec-Djordjevic thought that direct pacifist action was far more useful than indirect action, and that feminists should seek to unite with 'feminophile' male pacifists in order to be efficient. The real way to long-term protection against war lay in a low birth rate. When it came to nationalism, Julka Chlapec-Djordjevic argued for respecting the rights of the nations, especially small and new ones, and that feminists can play a positive role in generalizing and socializing national programmes.

Julka Chlapec-Djordjevic started her analysis of socialism and feminism with an unusual example: that of Switzerland. Swiss feminists, deeming feminism unrealistic, identified feminism with socialism, that is Marxism. What followed was quite similar to the later Yugoslav situation: the collision of 'retarded patriarchalism and wild Marxism'. In another admonitory example, the Belgian Parliament proposed in 1921 to give women the right to vote, as a sign of gratitude for their heroic behaviour during World War I. Catholic parties in the Parliament voted *for*, whereas the socialist parties voted *against*, on the grounds that women would tend to vote for the Catholic parties. Chlapec-Djordjevic was especially critical of the work of the Marxist theoretician, Otto Rühle, who was a target of book-burning by the Nazis in the early 1930s. Criticizing Engels for ignoring bio-sexual differences, Rühle proposed that men should be initiated to 'the cult of work' and women to 'the cult of race', because socialism requires large families with lots of children. If this book had not promoted communism, said Chlapec-Djordjevic (1935, p. 52), the *Führer* would not have consigned it to the flames, but would instead have made it recommended reading for youth.

For feminism, the main problem was the Marxist theory of the family. In practice, the welfare state can ensure some basic and important forms of social protection for the family and for working women, and there are many ways to expand the forms of the protection – it does not depend entirely on state ideology. The radical position against the nuclear family only produced more enemies against the socialist project. Thus, the Soviet state immediately abandoned the Marxist position on the family and opted for the classical nuclear family ideal. What happened to other socialist demands for women's rights? Chlapec-Djordjevic praises the rights to vote, work and other socialist legislation that creates equality. However, after reading some direct evidence about the protection of women's health and the practice of abortion in Soviet hospitals, she 'gets goose-pimples with horror'.

Her main criticism of Soviet socialism was the lack of quality in making otherwise good legislation functional, and not the shift towards conservatism in family planning. The other serious criticism, which this time includes the shift towards conservatism, was aimed at the expected model of women's behaviour, with its completely unrealistic demands: women should perform the traditional family and sexual role, plus work, plus political and public activity – all this without any regulated extension of the male role into traditionally feminine tasks. It is a trap for women and, in the words of our author, women would have to be able to do somersaults to perform all these tasks successfully (Chlapec-Djordjevic, 1935, p. 46).

For Chlapec-Djordjevic, equal status for women should be ensured by the birth control system (as practised in many American states), socialist legislation on equality, state endorsement coupled with financial backing, and the flow of tolerant and liberal ideas.

Her analysis of the relations between feminism and socialism remained pertinent to the situation of Yugoslav socialism after World War II. She foresaw the main problems, the traps for women and feminism, and the decadence of socialist ideas when it came to women. Her criticism could have been quite useful, if only it had been read by Yugoslav women some ten years later. Silence covered her work during her lifetime, along with the total exclusion of her ideas in a male-dominated culture, and there was an obvious lack of interest among the next generation of feminists. To be able to recover this same clarity of thought, the evolution of Yugoslav feminism had to endure quite unnecessary defeats, losing too much time and too many lives. It is only now that a reading of Chlapec-Djordjevic reveals the extent of her vision, in the new context of nationalism, war, pacifism and feminism in the post-Yugoslav space.[9]

This modest presentation of perhaps the most important feminist theoretician in Yugoslavia between the wars, aims at a critical revision of both Yugoslav feminist canons and today's feminist presentation of the post-Yugoslav space.

Suddenly strategic: the changed roles of women after World War II

Yugoslav women were among the main targets of the ideological investment in the Communist Party during and immediately after World War II. The Party showed no particular interest in feminism before the war, because its illegal position excluded work with the masses and because its faithful female followers did not explore feminist issues outside Party-imposed limits. As soon as the war started, Yugoslav Communists found themselves faced with the women's question as a major strategic question.[10] For the partisan movement, the presence and the massive collaboration of women were necessary – they needed reliable women in the cities for information networks, and peasant women who could provide food, care, shelter and hideouts. Women soldiers were also necessary in the army which started from nearly nothing. Hence there was an excessive effort on the part of the Communists to please women and to educate them into a feminist way of thinking. In the revolutionary social project which counted on multi-ethnic and multicultural unity in the new Yugoslavia, the position of women was crucial for final success. It was necessary to re-educate partisan warriors, most of them unschooled peasants, and to approach their oppressed womenfolk – all of this during an unequal fight against several different and well-equipped armies. We cannot but admire this high-risk, utopian project, developed under the worst possible conditions, all within the brief period of four years. Communist propagators were working with various ethnic and cultural groups with different behaviour and traditions, some of which were extremely difficult to penetrate, for example the Albanians. Most of the massive re-education effort was undertaken immediately after the war, in a situation in which a victorious group could direct and control consciousness-making through the media and a network of enthusiastic followers. I remember the stories told by my mother and my grandmother, from a former bourgeois family, who joined in the general positive feeling and did a lot of communal work in clearing the ruins, helping the wounded, handicapped and orphans, educating illiterate women and teaching practical courses in civil defence. What the Communist regime needed was not a feminist elite and theory but masses of women ready to work and obey.

A huge organization, the AFZ (Antifascist Women's Front), was established to serve as intermediary between the Party and the common women.[11] This organization was highly instrumental on many occasions – perhaps not so decorative as *tricoteuses* during the French Revolution, but surely impressive in expressing what was assumed to be the people's will. In an interesting twist, the formerly oppressed part of the population was given the role of the real voice of the people.

Voluntary work was the most obvious women's achievement, offered as an example of what the will of the people could do, and it served as a model for later voluntary youth work. Yugoslav Communists, following the Soviet example, immediately abandoned the Marxist utopian family and opted for the nuclear family instead. Lendash also followed the Soviet model, with all rights extended to women, including that of free abortion. The veil was forbidden in Muslim cultural settings. In the early years after World War II, the Yugoslav army propaganda film centre produced several educational movies in favour of education for girls and against the veil and amateur abortions. Women's missions, which taught contraception, modern care for children and women and explained the new legislation, were sent into remote villages, especially in the southern regions of Yugoslavia. It was all done as if nothing of feminism had ever existed in former Yugoslavia except, of course, for the elected heroines and forerunners determined by the Party as the canonical, ideological predecessors. This was the usual Communist mode.

One can hardly exaggerate the positive effects this policy had for Yugoslav women: the acquisition of rights, equality, liberty and self-confidence, being assured basic health and family protection, the possibility and ability to work, the high level of feminine consciousness and the sense of initiative. Although this privileged epoch for women was to prove relatively short, the results in the collective attitude of women remained much longer.[12]

The break with Stalin: recasting feminism in the party's image

The AFZ was instrumental, an ideal weapon, in the various battles that awaited the Communists after victory – for example, the fight against the remaining bourgeois elements, the struggle for nationalization, the search to find war criminals and bring them to trial, and other similar activities in which the mothers of the fallen heroes or other stereotypical models of women could be picked out and promoted. But when the break with Stalin came in 1948, none of the massive para-political organizations was completely secure from suspicion of ideological deviation. What the Party really needed now was a mass of frightened individuals ready to denounce anybody else. In the less stable political situation, the monolithic AFZ represented a constant threat, especially if women were given a certain internal autonomy of expressing the 'people's will'. It was structured to ensure mutual solidarity, which might collide with the twists and turns of daily politics. So the Party gradually diminished the public role of the AFZ which was so large and so much harder to control than other organizations. In the 1950s the AFZ was eventually disbanded, and a small number of *nomenklatura* women were allowed to act as representatives of what had once been perhaps the most important and the most liberal mass movement of women in the entire socialist bloc (see Jancar, 1981; Bozinovic, 1996). By then, however, Yugoslavia itself had moved away from that bloc as well.

Changes were slow in coming and not so visible. The Party never restricted women's rights. In fact, health protection, the distribution of contraceptives and the formalities around abortion were further liberalized (see Bahovec, 1991; Duhacek, 1993; Albanese, 1996; Licht & Draculic, 1996). Politics now became the province of the adepts and the *nomenklatura* so that women should not feel more deprived than other citizens. The national question was solved in a radical way, allowing not only all the ethnic groups to express themselves, but also allowing the legal invention of quite new ethnic groups – as was the case with Muslims in the 1970s, Tito's invention to ensure the ethnic balance between Serbs and Croats in Bosnia. Here we should note that this invention was based not on religious, but on *cultural* identity.

Stressing issues like equality, welfare, social security, job protection and many forms of state policy that were much later to be defined as *affirmative action* in other parts of the world, Yugoslav Communists skipped the crucial point of democracy. Indeed, Yugoslav Communists were quite original in inventing terms and narratives by which people were led to believe that they enjoyed some quite special forms of democracy, like self-government, which was, in fact, an elaborate set of procedures for stopping any real power exchange between the working units and the political centres of power. The special position of Yugoslavia, obtained through deft and constant shifting between great powers, really had quite different features, and quite different narratives from any other socialist country.

By the 1960s, the unique experiment with women was over. Now the Party had to make sure that it would never reappear. Western feminism was therefore presented as something corrupt and decadent, that was not needed by the already emancipated women of Yugoslavia. As the more or less liberal reforms were going on, and a combination of consumerism and ideological monologue was offered as a model of citizen's behaviour, women were gradually given new roles: sex objects, fashion dolls, patriarchal possessions. The somersault predicted by Julka Chlapec-Djordjevic became complete as the 1960s wore on. During the 1968 student uprising in Belgrade, any mention of feminism, among other political issues, was ridiculed by fellow students, who engaged in 'serious' discussions on early Marx, Gramsci, Althusser, Marcuse, Habermas and other revolutionary thinkers.

The new Yugoslav feminism

However, it was the academic commotion which spread all over the world at that time that initiated feminist thinking in academic circles. After many years, the women's elite started to discuss feminist issues, as was the case with the Zagreb (Croatia) group in the 1970s (see Sklevicky, 1980, 1984, 1987; Sklevicky & Papic, 1983). Curiously enough, this was considered politically harmless by the local *nomenklatura*, while feminists in Belgrade

(Serbia) had to meet almost secretly during that same period. In Ljubljana (Slovenia), the situation was quite different: no one seemed to view feminism as a very provocative topic, and quite early the first lesbian groups appeared there. All the three main cultural centres produced collections of feminist writings, usually in the form of special issues of philosophical, sociological or literary periodicals.[13] The tendency was more towards the French theory and not so obviously towards activist feminist writing.

I myself was a dissident at the time, from the 'extremist' (as labelled by the authorities) group of the School of Philosophy in Belgrade. To me, this new Yugoslav feminism seemed too remote from burning political issues, especially freedom of expression and human rights. However, as networks of women developed, feminist discussions became more and more up to date and interesting. A series of international feminist conferences held at the Inter-University Centre in Dubrovnik in the late 1980s opened new horizons and established the international exchange necessary to activate Yugoslav feminism on its own terms. This became increasingly visible in the years preceding the war in Yugoslavia, as feminists from all the Yugoslav republics reacted unanimously against nationalism and against the impending doom of separatism and civil war, producing a number of collective warnings, petitions and other texts aimed at the larger public.

In trying to explain the political developments in Yugoslavia which led to the war, and the position of women in it, we need to trace some of the relationships between feminism and dissidence. After the death of Tito in 1980, there was a huge blossoming in Yugoslav cultural and intellectual production. Even before that, Yugoslavia had been a place in which the first translations, or even the first editions, of dissident literature from the countries of the Eastern bloc were published. This did not mean that the regime had the same attitude toward discovering the recent past in Yugoslavia. Officially, there was no censorship but what happened in effect was that authors, publishers and even readers were at the mercy of communal, regional or federal authorities who judged what was dangerous and therefore punishable by law. An author who revealed his or her experiences from Goli ('naked') island, where pro-Soviet sympathizers were usually sent during the years of the break with Stalin, and a reader of Trotsky's legally published memoirs would have approximately equal chances of finding themselves behind bars.

The question of freedom of expression was therefore crucial for the Yugoslav dissidents, who lived mainly in Belgrade, Ljubljana and Zagreb, and who acted together on many occasions. During the 1970s, about 250 people in Belgrade were deprived of their passports, which gives an idea of the number of individuals involved in dissident activities – writing letters and petitions, signing petitions and, if possible, publishing. The passport petition reached the CSCE conference members in Belgrade in 1975, so most of these people got the right to travel abroad, but the measure was still in use. After getting back my passport, which had been taken in 1968, I was to see it taken away again in 1976 for six months and then, in

1987–89, for more than a year. Importantly, dissident–regime relations were much smoother in Slovenia, where a dialogue was established quite early within the Communist Party. It was in Croatia that nationalist dissidents risked the most.

Tito's death

Everything changed after Tito's death. The 'non-existent' censorship became scarcer but crazier. In a famous night raid on Good Friday 1983 in Belgrade, preventing a lecture by Milovan Djilas at the (secret) Free University, about 30 people were arrested in a Belgrade apartment, as well as another 200 people around the city, and a huge trial was organized. Its main instigator was the City's Communist Party Secretary, Slobodan Milosevic, while Madame Milosevic, as one of the most influential Party functionaries, was the main executor at the Belgrade University, firing professors and expelling students. After a year of protests, hunger strikes and growing public discontent, the trial collapsed.

The next action, against the poet Gojko Djogo, who was manipulated into publishing some of his anti-Tito poetry too early, turned out to be the crucial trial against the ruling ideology. The argument of freedom of expression for poetry was on everybody's lips. Now the old dissident movement, which had been having a very hard time of it since 1968, was no longer alone in standing up for freedom of expression. The cause was also supported by members of the cultural elite who continued to accept Communist ideology, some of whom were even Party members because of the obvious social benefits. However, they cynically refused to mix with the 'crazy leftists' in the dissident movement. Dissidence had become trendy, culturally propulsive and even important in several periodicals, editorial boards and the like.

As the president of the Committee for the Freedom of Expression at the Writers' Association of Serbia in 1986–89, I, together with my ten co-members, wrote and issued over 60 petitions, most of them dealing with various aspects of the so-called 'verbal delinquency' all over Yugoslavia, including that of Alija Izetbegovic. One of the consequences of the interest in his case was the publication of his book on Islam by an independent Belgrade firm in 1988. Most of the petitions and documents were published without any consequences. But when, in 1987, the Committee decided unanimously to ask for the release of Adem Demaqi, the Albanian dissident from Kosovo, then in his twenty-eighth year in jail, the Belgrade Communist Party and media reacted violently against the Committee, and especially against myself as the president. As for Demaqi, he was soon quietly released. I was attacked in the media, fired from my post at the Institute for Literature and Art in Belgrade, my work in the literary periodical was suddenly cancelled by the editor, my passport was again withdrawn and I was arrested and interrogated for more than 16 hours.

But the situation had really changed in the sense that it had now become difficult to stage a political trial, because the judges dared to show their independence, and because some segments of the media sided with the dissidents.

From the first hints from the secret police that I might be charged with high treason, the whole affair ended in a trial against me over the 'misuse of state funds'. In fact, I got a grant for research in France, and asked my institute administration to use it after the Christmas vacations, just as three other colleagues did – only they asked for a longer delay. The process collapsed in the courtroom, especially when the director of my Institute lied as a witness against me. But the majority of my colleagues organized an inside trial at the Institute, very much in the old-fashioned Stalinist style, and I found myself fired before the official trial had ended in acquittal. At the same time, my case was presented in the media and I had the moral support of many intellectuals.

In discussions among the 'old' dissident movement, I was strictly against accepting the new sympathizers, and was rightly accused of intolerance and even 'fundamentalism' by my dissident friends. Their public discourse was a strong one, bringing forward topics like history, historic rights and collective rights as more important than individual human rights, and they captured the public interest and those less involved in 'soft' topics like freedom of expression and human rights. Soon enough, this new dissident majority not only invaded the space of public discourse – protest meetings and dissident committees – but also such public discourse production centres as periodicals and editorial boards.

Writers' Associations and the Academy of Arts and Sciences in Belgrade had tended to be silent in the past or to evince mild solidarity with the dissidents coming mainly from the humanities. Then in the 1980s they began to organize conferences and public debates on hot political topics, above all the historic and national question of Serbs in Yugoslavia. In 1987, Slobodan Milosevic organized a Party mob and staged a coup within the Serbian Communist Party, denouncing the old *nomenklatura* for failing to protect Serbs from Albanians in Kosovo and calling for aggressive measures. The two public discourses met, and the nationalist elite did not hesitate to approach the new winner on the horizon.

It is up to scrupulous historic research to find out if, and then where, how and when, agreement was reached between the *nomenklatura* and the nationalist elite. One thing did become clear for the remaining dissidents and feminists: the only possible politics would be anti-war and pro-Yugoslav. The diversity of Yugoslav cultural and political scenes allowed for certain freedoms that seemed precious under the circumstances. If, for instance, a book or article could not be published in Serbia, it would appear in Slovenia or in Croatia, or vice versa.

But staying 'Yugoslav' in the late 1980s was not an easy decision, judging from several outstanding dissidents who joined the nationalist movement and even became its ideologists – as was the case with *Praxis* editor Mihajlo Markovic and numerous Slovenian dissidents. While in Serbia it was the Communist Party that led the nationalist movement, in Croatia the Party resisted for a while, and in Slovenia the already existing modes of communicating led to a fairly painless melting of all the interests towards a common goal of independence – or rather, towards escaping the Yugoslav catastrophe as soon as possible. On this very shaky ground for any transnational dialogue, with 'Yugoslav' gradually becoming a term of offence, it soon became clear that the population which had the fewest problems with national identities and historical rights were women.

Women were much less powerful in both *nomenklatura* and the dissident circles, so they cared less about the power games in which being Yugoslav could mean exclusion from nationalist circles. In the predominantly patri- archal culture of Yugoslavia, women could defend the rights of the 'mixed' families, at least for a while, before the newly formed states defined their propaganda against mixed families. But the sensitivity of the position of women was also perceived by the nationalist population and the centres of power, so almost all the nationalist groups in Yugoslavia or in the first independent states clearly set out how they planned the future for 'their' women (Milic, 1993).

In Slovenia, the first free elections radically diminished the number of women in the Parliament, which was formerly ensured by a positive seg- regation policy. One of the first constitutional debates brought forward the formulation of the 'sanctity of life', which would have enabled the legal process of destroying the former liberal abortion laws. The response of women in Slovenia was impressive: huge demonstrations, including the siege of the Parliament building, during which conservative women MPs joined the women outside. The formulation was withdrawn. The former peace movement, the strongest of all in former Yugoslavia, col- lapsed with the actions of the Yugoslav army inside Slovenia and during the ten days of war in June 1991. It took several years to repair the damage and to reorganize the peace and the other alternative movements in Slovenia, not least since new issues were emerging such as racism, citizenship, refugee camps and intolerance towards the new 'foreigners' – former Yugoslavs and co-citizens of non-Slovenian origin, Gypsies, non- Catholics, atheists, mixed couples and their children.

The Bosnian case was a good case in point: this was a matter of keeping absolute power by insisting on ethnic equality. Ever since the 1960s, intel- lectuals had been fleeing Sarajevo, heading for Belgrade, Zagreb or Ljubljana. The specific, official Bosnian narrative of the time was affirma- tive action or, in local terms, 'the key', which defined the desired ethnic identity for any available job before the candidate was found. The nation- alist discourse later twisted the argument trying to prove that multiculturalism was *the* reason for repression, and that this was what was causing inequality. When the war in Bosnia and Herzegovina started, this image of idealized multiculturalism was the best way to attract the lib- eral Western media, although the Bosnian government proved to be more multiculturally oriented when addressing the international public than when addressing the local public during the war.

Blurring the issues: the repercussions of the mass rapes in Bosnia

It was the mass rapes in Bosnia that marked the position of women in the Yugoslav war and radically defined worldwide public opinion. The huge media action, followed by an overwhelming response from activist, academic, publishing and generally feminist circles,[14] had noticeable effect, but also blurred the issue. In this process, the role of the Croatian state media and governmental agencies was crucial: the image that was produced presented 'weak' and 'defenceless' Muslim women as being raped by Serbs, with no other perpetrator–victim combinations. Bosnian women were generalized as 'Muslims', even though the majority of the Bosnian population was non-religious before the war. At the beginning of the campaign, Croatian women were also mentioned as victims but they quickly disappeared from the image.

The whole campaign gave rise to some of the most conservative and patriarchal discourses on abortion, openly racist statements and a focus on the alleged differences between the 'Muslim' and the Croat women. At the same time, actions were staged against Croatian feminists, who were publicly accused of 'raping Croatia', proclaimed 'witches' and harassed incessantly (see Tax & Agosin, 1995, p. 39). Their simple statement was that, in the case of mass rapes, *women* are victims, no matter what nationality. That this should provoke such reactions reveals the national politics that were constructed around the rapes and the use of women in the war. This aspect was not noticed, even in Western academic feminist circles. In my opinion, it does not diminish the horrible impact of the mass rapes, nor offend the victims – as the Croatian media also tried to present. On the contrary, this over-emotional twist points up how women are manipulated in the context of war, and reveals the authoritarian ways of 'protecting' women by shutting out their voices and reducing them to a mute collective body, an instrument of the patriarchal invention, while promoting and ensuring the general pro-war state of mind at the same time (Mostov, 1995). Let me exemplify this with one case that did not reach the Western media.

The Serbian media launched a huge action about the alleged rapes of Serbian women by Albanians in 1987. This was presented as a mass, organized action aimed at ethnically cleansing Kosovo so as to make it entirely Albanian. Eventually, Albanians were presented as bestial creatures who raped not only adult females, but also children, the dead, old women and men and animals.[15] Several Western missions and NGOs went to Kosovo in search of the exact data, but this was branded an 'offence' against the victims by local Serb authorities (administration, the Church, national clubs and organizations, etc.). Then, in 1989, one year after the strongest media action about the alleged rapes, the official Serbian Institute of Statistics published a yearly account showing that the number of rapes committed by Serbs against Serbian women had increased, whereas instances of rape committed by Albanians against Serbian women came close to zero.[16] Of course, this annual report had no statistics on how many Albanians or Serbs had raped their own wives, but this could indicate that Albanians, living under strict tribal rules, could proclaim a *taboo* on Serbian women, in order to preserve their collectivity from repression. The example deepens the problem of rapes committed in Bosnia and Croatia, and further indicates the possible uses of rape against the female national collectivity, which is reduced to silence and is totally instrumentalized. The Croatian women's centres and NGOs are still researching the question of these rapes, trying to establish the objective data.

The new nationalism

The rich tradition of feminism in Croatia presented a challenge for the new nationalist government, even before the war. Quite early in the development of the Croatian Democratic Union (HDZ), the ruling party after the two consecutive elections in Croatia, we can note the invention of a 'Croatian mother'. The Catholic Church in Croatia, especially its public discourse makers, filled the media with explanations of why premarital sexual experience should be avoided, along with contraception, and how ethnically mixed marriages could destroy a person and endanger the very future of the nation. New legislation followed the new ideological text by making abortion far less affordable than before. Women were pictured as the silent producers of Croat sons, and even a female culture minister publicly expressed how she felt that she should stand up if a man entered the room. When the war started, women were used to form state-endorsed organizations, like the *Wall of Love*, and to perform a strictly determined role in the patriotic presentation of Croatia abroad and at home. The existing feminist links between Croatia and Serbia never ceased during the war, and the marginal pacifist and women's groups multiplied on both sides. Some of these groups organized international conferences and published some of the reports in English (see Centre for Women's Studies, 1995). Other groups include Women in Black, SOS Hotline for Women and Children, SOS Rape Center, Arkadia, Center for Anti-War Action, Foundation for Human Rights, Belgrade, Center for Women Victims of War, BABA, Zagreb. Here we should note that the growth of independent women's and pacifist groups was also due to international help, most of it from similar marginal, but much better off, groups abroad.

The relation of the Croatian state to women must be seen as a project of diligently constructing the inner feminist enemy. Several Croatian intellectuals, many of them academics, writers and journalists, joined this unlikely campaign, accusing feminist activists of all kinds of crimes against Croatia. In an international action echoing the domestic one, two French intellectuals, Alain Finkielcraut and Annie Le Brun, who had already appeared in France as the defenders of the Croatian cause, gave interviews in Croatia in 1992–93, pointing to the fact that these women were linked to the Communist regime, and expressing surprise that they still had their jobs, ungrateful to Croatia as they were. The fact that *all* Croats had previously lived under the Communist regime and that most of the leading members of the HDZ were members of the Communist Party only a year ago, did not seem to strike Alain Finkielcraut, who was probably the first Western intellectual to denounce the local dissidents in the country while visiting it. All five of these women had to leave Croatia, at least for a while. Dubravka Ugresic, one of the most celebrated young writers in former Yugoslavia, became a wandering academic, with no fixed domicile or job. Alain Finkielcraut, however, became a member of the Croatian Academy of Arts and Sciences. International PEN became involved in the matter through Slobodan Novak, the Croatian PEN president who used his position to denounce the five women even more. Meredith Tax, member of the American PEN, published several pieces on the affair, pointing out the scandalous use that had been made of women (see Tax, 1993).

Again, what we need to take into account here is the cultural context, and not the established collective narratives (i.e., histories, media). As mentioned above, the 1987–89 Serbian media fantasy about the mass rapes of Serbian women by Albanians was stopped, at least at the level of reliable information, by the forms embedded into the traditional behaviour of Albanians, and their strict tribal discipline in effectuating a taboo. When I remarked in 1989 to the poet, Gojko Djogo, a victim of the regime who eventually turned into a rabid nationalist, that Serbs should stop raping Serbian women so that it could be clear who is raping whom, he replied that I no longer belonged to the Serbian culture. In 1990, an author writing under a pseudonym in the Belgrade weekly *Nin* stated that I 'hated pathologically anything Serbian'; and in 1995, the Presidency of the Writers' Association of Serbia issued a document in which I was defined as a national traitor. Such extreme sensitivity to certain almost sacred narratives, up to the point at which the new taboo is established and fiercely protected, reveals some of the techniques that are employed for gaining power and controlling others.

In this complicated cultural context, aggravated by many manipulative uses of the tradition by the local power-bearers, many simplistic Western versions look just like another stereotype – but, thanks to the media, a largely favoured one. It is necessary, at least for feminist academia, to carry out research with criticism and awareness, and especially, not to get enmeshed in the state-sponsored nets and not-always transparent nationalist discourses. Otherwise, they risk not only twisting the facts but also rendering silent the real victims. In the case of Bosnia, the mixture of good

intentions and poor basic knowledge produced a hard cluster of stereotypes.

A clear picture can be produced if we trace how the 1984 Winter
Olympic Games in Sarajevo were perceived. For many outside commentators, footage from the Games, with all the glamour and glory, was the
symbol of Bosnia before, compared with the recent destruction. For many
Yugoslavs, however, the irrational spending on the Olympics, which coincided with a heavy economic crisis in the country, was the symbol of the
unlimited power of the Bosnian *nomenklatura*, at the expense of the
common people. Corruption, bad taste and pressure were the synonyms
for what was going on, although the money that was pouring in did make
life better for some inhabitants of Sarajevo. There were no academic or any
other form of organized feminist groups in Bosnia, but many women from
Sarajevo attended feminist conferences in Dubrovnik and elsewhere, and
Sarajevo periodicals published articles and thematic units on feminism.
Shortly before the war in Bosnia broke out, there were several women's
peace groups, not only in Sarajevo, but also in many cities in eastern
Bosnia, and in the industrial and working-class centres like Zenica and
Tuzla.

Women's organizations: working against war from within

The Serbian case shows that women who oppose war can do the best job in
the country that started the war and that is represented, rightly or wrongly,
as the only, or main, aggressor. In a risky but effective approach, the
women's groups in Serbia started by accusing Serbian nationalists of insti-
gating a war mentality, and Serbian politicians of starting the war. Their
position was affirmed through the specific situation in Serbia and especially in Belgrade. As most of the potential male pacifists, non-nationalists
or simply those unwilling to take part in war actions were not able to
move freely because of fear of the military police and draft documents
that could come at any time in 1991–93, women took over most of the
public and street activities such as protests, demonstrations, 'happenings'
and conferences.[17]

During the crucial war actions in Bosnia in 1993–94, Serbian authorities
allowed the military police of Republika Srpska to draft Bosnian refugees
in Serbia, which was done publicly and by force, on the streets and in the
refugee camps. Here we should note that the number of refugees from
Croatia and Bosnia fluctuated between 700,000 (official figures) and
about 400,000, and that in the course of summer 1995 only, approximately
200,000 additional refugees came to Serbia after the Croatian military
actions in Krajina. State officials claimed that huge costs were involved in
accepting these refugees, but in fact they were stopped from entering
Belgrade and quartered in very bad conditions. There were speculations
about making them live in Kosovo in order to repopulate the region with

Serbs. Finally some of the refugees were forcibly drafted to fight in Bosnia.

Data from independent organizations, such as Radio Beograd 92 (B92), show that much more help for the refugees came from independent sources than from the state. Women's organizations in Serbia took responsibility for caring for the refugee women, for the pacifist politics, dealing with the worsening of women's position of Serbia, and hiding the conscientious objectors and deserters.[18] Of course, many of these categories overlapped or intertwined, or could be defined only temporarily. There were many parents who felt and acted on the side of the nationalist and pro-war politics, but still did not want their children to be drafted. Becoming a deserter was not only an ideological question, it also involved the concrete questions of money, social position or isolation, access to the networks and a host of similar problems.

The Serbian authorities did not do much either way in connection with women's rights. Milosevic used his own wife once again. She founded a 'new left' party (JUL), and in her hyper-production of essays, she always insists on being apart from 'bad' Western feminism. Some bogus women's organizations were retained from the previous system, particularly to cover up the lack of activity around refugees, and in the nationalist discourse they often drew a parallel to the revival of some old nationalist women's organizations.

The Serbian Orthodox Church (SPC), especially its militant clergy, expressed quite aggressive views on the role of women in bringing more Serbs into the world, echoed by the excessive views of some nationalist intellectuals. In 1997, the SPC left the World Council of Churches, protesting about the introduction of women priests to some Western Churches. The term used by the SPC in the public statement is 'polluted', referring to Churches 'polluted' by the presence of female priests.

Scarcely any of these public outbursts went unchallenged by public reaction from women's organizations. The legislation was not radically changed, but when the small group of non-nationalist MPs in the Parliament began working on legislation against family violence in 1994, the majority did not even allow it to come to an initial vote, but laughed openly at the idea that any law could stop them from beating their own wives and children. Interestingly, research done by several SOS women's phone services and women's centres in Belgrade showed that most family violence against women happened after the television evening news at 17.30 pm. This result gives a very specific insight into the forms of victimization of women during war.

Women's peace activities featured a new visualization of women, like *Women in Black* and street happenings like lighting candles, exposing babies in front of Milocevic's office window, or symbolically wrapping the centre of Belgrade in black cloth. All of these manifestations included men. Writing about women's problems and experiences, even in the independent media, was a more serious problem, except for Radio Beograd 92, which supported a feminist periodical *ProFemina*. Until women started their own publications, and eventually two periodicals, *ProFemina* and *Zenske sveske* in 1995, the independent media in Serbia remained impenetrable to any regular cooperation on women's problems and politics. In fact, *ProFemina* got more media responses in Vojvodina, traditionally feminist-oriented, and in Montenegro, traditionally a very patriarchal region, than in Belgrade itself.

In Kosovo, the scarce data indicate that the position of women, utterly silenced in the Albanian community, changed slightly through the forms of peaceful resistance to the Serbian police and administration oppression from 1987 to 1996. Unfortunately, no anthropological or sociological research has been carried out on this, nor has the topic itself yet penetrated the Albanian resistance media and organizations. The question is how to conclude anything from the almost total silence that surrounds women's issues among Albanians, with the exception of the few visible Albanian women who represent the cause at international conferences. One might venture to hypothesize that the case follows the pattern often found concerning the role of women in national liberation movements: women are urged 'to serve the cause' and to forget their demands until this higher goal has been achieved. Other Balkan examples of this policy in the past show that such demands were forgotten as soon as the older patriarchal rules emerged with even greater force from the national liberation movement.

In Macedonia, the very sensitive national question and the fact that the state never joined the Yugoslav war led to a certain closure of the question of women. Legislation did not touch on women's rights. Their social position generally worsened because of economic problems, and the need for peace failed to motivate large masses of women. Faced with the same old combination of socialist-patriarchal attitudes towards women and feminism, Macedonian women would have to invent new ways to promote their ideas and new spaces to develop activities. Cultural activities, artistic production and ecology seem to be neutral and large enough for such initiatives.

While visiting Macedonia in November 1996, I had a chance to speak with several feminists in Skopje, who showed me the examples of public reactions to feminism, which were defined as bad in media, political parties and even cultural spaces. The fact that women's rights from the previous regime were not abandoned in the new socio-legal system makes it more difficult to bring up the question of women in the new society. The new social tendencies which include less state support in many domains of public and intellectual work, the rise of the influence of the Church, the nationalist discourse in the media and the reinforcement of the old patriarchal structures certainly do not promise a bright future for women and feminism in Macedonia.

Conclusion: what could be done?

This fragmented review of the range of women's use and women's roles in the Yugoslav war should, above all, open new questions about this problem. The specific overall Yugoslav aspects and the specific regional aspects might also have some universal implications. They have been unfolding in full view of a media-oriented world, a world that is becoming culturally unified, but at the same time they open up the way for reflection on the use of the local Balkan tradition. All of these aspects can be focused upon in different ways. In conclusion here, I will look at one kind of focus, pointing to the relation between women's use of tradition and the innovations which mark the Yugoslav war.

Preparations for the Yugoslav war were made in the media and in the public discourse. Due to the traditional authority of the intellectuals in the Balkans, they were instrumental in propagating war politics, historic and collective rights, and traditional gender patterns of behaviour. The only possible way to react to this was to oppose it in the public discourse. The growth of independent women's social centres, groups for solidarity and mutual help, research groups, women's academic institutions outside the traditional academic settings and finally women's media all came as an obvious response to the challenge. Many of these new institutions, especially in Croatia and Serbia, would not have been possible without international help. Giving a voice to women on all the levels of public discourse, from media to academia, therefore became the immediate aim of feminists. Here we need to note that in an extraordinary situation like war, with the almost revolutionary social changes, feminism and women's movements have extraordinary chances to move fast and to ensure changes on their own terms, especially when they link their politics to pacifism. This, at least, was the case with the societies which cherished *revolution* as a positive connotation in historiography, the school system and political jargon.

During the Yugoslav war, the cases of rape or mass rapes have been reported in media practically while they were happening. This helped women to define rape as a war crime and to urge world organizations to act immediately, and not decades later when most of the victims are already dead, as was the case with the Korean or German victims of rape during World War II. Despite all the undoubted exaggerations, mistakes, ignorance and backing up of the nationalist state politics, the media's echo of rapes, along with research on types of violence in the war regions, make clear the arbitrary violence towards women in unstable situations. This might reflect patriarchal patterns of behaviour, but it also might point to the process of brutalization, comparable to similar processes found in regions with the death penalty and no wars at all.

The role of women in the Yugoslav war shows that stereotyped causes of conflict proposed by many analysts, political commentators and historians – like differences in religion, history, collective memory, cultural incompatibility and the like – were not important, at least not for just over half of the population in question. This can be explained by the position of women and the defence of mixed marriages and children of mixed origin, but also by the Balkan tradition whereby women take over communication with other ethnic groups on the everyday level. Women's general lack of interest in high politics also had its good consequences: for one thing, women simply disregarded the demands of the state, as in the case of draft.

In the Yugoslav war, women's use of models from traditional culture was twofold. Urban women experimented with the ritual fear of death, copying rural women's behaviour, but changing the sense and universalizing the meaning, and exploited the already existing ironical treatment of traditional male values. The second procedure can be interpreted as a carnival procedure (in the sense of Mikhail Bakhtin's theory) taking models from antiquity, medieval urban culture and student culture from 1968. Judging from the success of the two months of non-violent street rallies in Belgrade in the winter of 1996–97, the model practised by peace and feminist activists during the Yugoslav war was a good choice.

Women's sensitivity to regional differences and the refusal of the offered stereotypes on collectivities made communication between women on the warring sides not only possible but in many cases the only existing channel of communication. Very early in the war, almost all Yugoslavia was covered with e-mail networks, allowing women to communicate and to spread information. Coming mostly from the Western NGOs, this was a great benefit. Women were the main travellers between the cut-off regions and the new frontiers because it was slightly easier for them to cross the new borders. Again, the patriarchal mentality offered unexpected possibilities to women who were considered less capable in politics, missions, or even smuggling. Inside the new states, women were more motivated to communicate with the refugees, trying to get and exchange information on relatives and friends and to establish new networks of solidarity. This is not an idealistic picture, but more a spontaneous creation of a kind of women's market of information and services. Such networks were crucial in transferring money and goods, exchanging homes, sheltering deserters and other fugitives, combining individual interests, providing jobs, medicaments and all kinds of services – a vital role which indeed they still fulfil.

The main strategy, which covers all the cases mentioned, involves turning handicaps into advantages. This is the main strategy of all the marginal groups, and it can be compared, imitated or reinvented by any other group that is marginalized on the basis of race, religion, origin, language, culture, customs, behaviour or age. As the potentially biggest marginal group in the world, women can and should make a difference in preventing, stopping and healing the damage from war. The long history of women's culture, even the vernacular and oral forms, can be seen as a huge encyclopedia, open to anybody, full of devices, strategies and patterns of thought against war and violence. One of these available narratives, ready to use, is the narrative of the *peaceful nature* of women.

Notes

1   For many revealing parallels, see Davis, 1983; Holloway, 1992.
2   The earliest and probably the best example for any research on women's 'car-nivalization' of war and the attitudes of male citizens is Aristophanes' *Lysistrata*. Curiously enough, this aspect of ancient women's studies is still less developed than other fine analyses of gender roles in Aristophanes's come-dies. See, for instance, Zeitlin, 1996. For an elaborate study of the ancient Greek's (both men and women) relationship with death, see Loraux, 1989. A rare example of the research which follows an ancient phenomenon down to the modern times is Gail Holst-Warhaft's (1992) study on women's lamenta-tions in Greece.
3   Young intellectuals and artists, many of them studying in Vienna, Paris or Prague, invested their newly acquired knowledge of anthropology, psycho-analysis, expressionist and futurist ideas and even theory of relativity, to provide the argumentation for the new South Slav state (the literal meaning of the word Yugo-Slavia). Among them, classicist Milan Budimir, who excelled in paleobalkanology (linguistics), argued for a special place for the Albanian language inside the basic Indo-European division. He also founded a short-lived party in Sarajevo, just after World War I, to which he gathered Orthodox, Catholic, Jewish and Muslim intellectuals. His colleague, classicist Anica Savic Rebac, who inspired Thomas Mann's definition of love in *The Legend of Joseph*, and some of the finest pages in Rebecca West's *Black Lamb, Grey Falcon*, coined a term for her own research, *erotology* (the study of the philosophy of love). She married a Bosnian Muslim and tried to promote an English-style socialism (along the lines of Shelley and Fabianism) even after World War II. They both taught at the University of Belgrade.
4   During World War I, many young academics who had been transferred from the Balkan battlefields to Paris or London by the Allies published overviews on the necessity of Yugoslavia, on history, geography, linguistic mapping and politics of this region – among them future pillars of Yugoslav scholarly endeavour like Jovan Cvijic, anthropologist, or Aleksandar Belic, linguist. Many of these enthusiastic Yugoslav intellectuals were disappointed by the monarchic constitution of the new state and, after World War I, retreated into academe. The most radical, democratic and multicultural ideas did remain in some circles during the inter-war period. *Revue Internationale des Etudes Balkaniques*, a journal issued in the 1930s by Milan Budimir and his Croat col-league Petar Skok in Belgrade, is one such example: published in English, French and German, this review gathered the most avant-garde researchers in ancient studies, balkanology, anthropology and history of that time, and dis-played an openly anti-fascist position.
5   Karadzic, 1818.
6   *Miasma* is a Greek term, translated into Latin as *pollutio*.
7   Information about taboos on women during childbirth and the period after-wards can be found in Vuk Karadzic' *Dictionary* (1818), which can be read as a kind of popular encyclopaedia. There is a special term in Serbo-Croat to denote the period in a woman's life after a child is born, *babinje*, which involves very specific rituals, taboos, rules of behaviour for the mother, for other women, and for male members of the family and the society. All these rituals can be compared with the death rituals when it comes to the level of exclusion/seclusion of women.
8   Milan Martic, former Minister of Police in Republika Krajina, gave several interviews in Serbian media in 1993–94, explaining how many incidents between Serbs and Croatian authorities in Krajina before the war had been staged by him and his friends in order to provoke tension and eventually

armed conflict. The plan was obviously a success. This throws a special light on the role of the media in Serbia. Did the journalists reporting the events know about this and consent? Or did they show a stunning level of professional incompetence?

9   Again, Julka Chlapec-Djordjevic was rediscovered and published in *ProFemina*, with the accompanying articles by Svetlana Tomin and Svetlana Slapsak.

10   Lydia Sklevicky (1952–90) was a feminist and a sociologist from Zagreb (Croatia) who did extensive research on this topic. See Rihtman, 1996.

11   'The Movement and the Order', in Rihtman, 1996, pp. 107–115.

12   Rihtman, 1996, pp. 50–63.

13   Among such special issues, indispensable for any local research because they functioned as opinion-makers, I quote: *Student*, Belgrade, 24 March 1976, no. 9, pp. 7–8; *Vidici*, journal for culture, literature and social questions, Belgrade, November–December 1977, no. 5–6, pp. 9–24; *Marxist Thinking*, Belgrade, 1991, no. 4, pp. 3–80; *Delo*, monthly for theory, criticism, poetry and new ideas, Belgrade, 1981, no. 4, pp. 1–134; *Marxism in the World*, Belgrade, 1981, nos 8–9, 500pp.; *Vidici*, Belgrade, 1984, nos 1–2, pp. 7–84; *Knjizevnost* (Literature), Belgrade, 1986, nos 8–9, pp. 1386–1490; *Review for Sociology*, 'Women and the Society', Book 4, Zagreb, 1987. Various publications have been issued by different political organizations linked to the Communist Party or to international organizations (see Dojcinovic-Necic, 1996).

14   A seminal publication is Roy Gutman's Pulitzer Prize winning *A Witness to Genocide* (1993); see also Stiglmayer, 1996.

15   Nebojsa Popov and the group of authors, *Kosovo Knot: To Unravel Or To Cut. Report of the Independent Commission*, Titograd, 1990 (in Serbo-Croatian); Svetlana Slapsak, forthcoming.

16   Ibid.

17   Pecic, 1991, Table 1, p. 31; Papic, 1999. Also the documents, information and personal experiences in the series of publications *Feminist Notebooks* and *Women for Peace*, Belgrade, 1991–96.

18   Several handbooks, leaflets, posters and similar material have been published by Belgrade women's groups, dealing with such themes as working with refugees, victims of rape, violence and war-induced mental states. See Dojcinovic-Necic, 1996.

10
Gender Difference in Conflict Resolution:
The Case of Sri Lanka

Kumudini Samuel

Introduction

This chapter explores the role of women in conflict resolution within the context of ongoing ethnic conflict. It is based on the author's personal experience within the human rights and women's rights movement since 1980 and focuses on the activism of women and women's groups in Sri Lanka's predominantly Sinhala south and in its Tamil northeast.

Forms of socialization and identity construction have been the basis for continued differences in power relations between men and women, in the family and in society. For most Sri Lankan women, this gendered identity construct has been defined around the role of mother and wife. A woman's status – social, economic, political – has been dependent on that of her husband, father, brother or son: always dependent on men, and subordinate to them (see Molyneux, 1985).

In recent years, the women of Sri Lanka have been assuming new gender roles, due to the ethnic conflict which has been accompanied by widespread state repression and human rights violations, and due to market-driven changes in macroeconomic policy. There are an increasing number of female-headed households and women who are primary breadwinners, whether on the plantations, in the free trade zones or as migrant workers (Coomaraswamy, 1994, pp. 39–57). However, this has not served to change the overall situation of Sri Lankan women in society, which still values a married woman over a single women, and a wife over a widow.

In terms of political participation,[1] particularly in the context of armed struggle, more and more women have been recruited into the armed movements of national liberation as active combatants. But they remain bound by patriarchal control, subordinate to male political leadership and removed from high-level political decisionmaking.

Within the parameters of political activism, the women of Sri Lanka have been able to appropriate their 'motherhood' as a political force to bring about significant changes in the political power balance. But they have not been able to sustain this activism or use it as a means of achieving genuine empowerment. Nor have women's aspirations for peace, and their activism within the peace movement, been translated into a force that can determine the content or the direction of the peace process.

At the grassroots level, women's activism has been appropriated by both traditional party politicians and the armed movement. They have used women's contributions at critical moments in time, but have never invested them with any power within the political process. Neither, with the exception of the Sri Lankan presidency, have women had a significant presence at the highest level of participation and decisionmaking during peace negotiations, even though women's activism calling for peace was a key catalyst in bringing about these peace initiatives.

Background to the ethnic conflict

Colonized by three European powers, Sri Lanka (known as Ceylon until 1972) won independence from the British in 1948. It has a parliamentary form of government and an executive presidency created in 1978. Sri Lanka is home to an ethnically diverse population of about 17.5 million, of whom an estimated 74.6% are Sinhalese, 12.6% Sri Lankan Tamil, 7.4% Muslim, and 5.5% are Indian Tamil (Tamils of more recent Indian origin, living primarily in the central hill country.) The remainder are a mix of Burghers (Eurasians, primarily descended from Portuguese and Dutch colonizers), Moors, Malays and descendants of other trading peoples from the Middle East and East Asia. There is also a small indigenous population, the Vaddahs.

The Sinhalese are predominantly Buddhist; Tamils predominantly Hindu; a small percentage of each ethnic group are Christians. The Muslims speak the language of the regions in which they are located – in the northeast and the central hill country, most Muslims speak Tamil whereas in the rest of the country they are predominantly Sinhalese-speaking.

Traditionally, Sri Lankan Tamils have lived mostly in the northern and eastern provinces; however, a significant number have settled in the south, particularly in the capital. Many are temporarily resident in the south for reasons of employment, education, or because they have been displaced from the areas of conflict in the northeast. Tamils of fairly recent Indian origin, also known as hill country or Indian Tamils, were brought to Sri Lanka primarily as indentured labour in the mid-nineteenth century, to work on British-owned plantations in the central hills. A small percentage lives in Colombo; some have moved to the north and east.

The Sinhalese make up the majority population in all of the provinces outside the north and east. As a result of the war, there are virtually no Sinhalese living in the northern peninsula today; in the eastern province they make up about one-third of the population. The Muslims too are no longer present in the north, due to forced evictions and ethnic violence, but constitute one-third of the population of the eastern province. The remaining third is made up of Tamils.

Since independence, the primary conflict has been between the Sinhalese and Tamils, although other ethnic groups, particularly Muslims and Tamils of recent Indian origin, have also been drawn in. Sri Lanka's ethnic conflict encompasses a complexity of issues ranging from identity to socio-economic and political grievances and discrimination. It is, however, predominantly a reaction to the failure of post-independence governments to establish a political framework that is able to reflect the ethnic plurality of Sri Lankan society and to ensure respect for the democratic rights of all citizens.

The following are among the key factors behind the current ethnic conflict and political crisis:

- The Buddhist Revivalist movement in the late nineteenth century which started off as an anti-imperialist movement but ended in the reconstruction of a Sinhala–Buddhist identity with claims to political and ideological hegemony.
- The disenfranchisement of hill country Tamils as a result of new citizenship laws passed in 1949, after independence, and the entrenchment of notions of majoritarian democracy.
- The declaration of Sinhala as the sole official language to replace English in 1956, which led to a serious reduction of opportunities for Tamils in state services.
- The enactment of the 1972 Constitution which removed minority safeguards and gave Buddhism the 'foremost place'.
- State-aided settlement schemes in predominantly Tamil regions which altered the demographic patterns in these areas.

These acts of discrimination led Tamil political parties to voice demands for some degree of regional autonomy and power-sharing, demands which were ignored. Continuing acts of discrimination by the Sinhala majority state brought an escalation of demands – for a federal state in the late 1960s, and for an independent, separate state in the 1970s. The Tamils' sense of alienation was heightened by anti-Tamil riots in 1958, 1977, 1981, 1982 and 1983, involving attacks on Tamils living outside the north and on their properties. The lack of a political response and the attacks on Tamils combined to give rise to a Tamil militant movement and the launching of an armed struggle for a separate state, which continues to this day. The Liberation Tigers of Tamil Eelam (LTTE) soon emerged as the dominant militant group, through a process that included the liquidation of rival groupings. The war has resulted in LTTE domination over large areas of the northern and eastern provinces and the displacement of nearly one million people as a result of state and LTTE confrontation. It has spread to other parts of the country through sporadic attacks by the LTTE. The various governments in power have sought to counter this struggle through emergency regulations and special laws such as the Prevention of Terrorism Act.

Emergence of armed conflict

The emergence of armed militant confrontation with the state goes back to 1974, when the Mayor of Jaffna, Alfred Duraiappah, was assassinated by Tamil militants. The conflict has since escalated, with only brief periods of respite. In addition to state confrontations in the Tamil majority areas of the north and east, the LTTE have also launched sporadic attacks in the predominantly Sinhala south, and have been responsible for a series of assassinations of military and political leaders. The state's response has not been limited solely to armed confrontation, but has included widespread search-and-cordon operations, arbitrary arrests, incommunicado detentions, disappearances and extrajudicial executions in Tamil areas.

The conflict intensified after the state-sponsored ethnic pogrom against Tamils in 1983. The years since then, however, have seen changes in the dynamics of both Sinhala and Tamil politics. An important shift occurred with the signing of the Indo–Sri Lanka Accord in 1987. Since then there has been a growing acceptance that Sri Lanka is a multi-ethnic society and that a solution can be worked out within the framework of a united Sri Lanka, accepting the concept of devolution of power. This has led to the strengthening of arguments for a politically negotiated resolution of the conflict. The last large-scale ethnic pogrom against Tamil civilians was in 1983. Noteworthy is the absence of civilian-led retaliatory violence against the Tamil people in the south, though civilian militias called 'home guards' have, on occasion, engaged in retaliatory killings of Tamils where ethnic communities live in close proximity.

Shifts are also evident in the emergence of a genuine aspiration for peace among members of all ethnic communities, which manifested itself in the election victory of President Chandrika Kumaratunge in November 1994. A multi-ethnic electorate extended its support for the peace platform she proposed, and President Kumaratunge won an unprecedented 62% of the vote. Her election victory was forged on the activism and struggles of women's groups, particularly the Mothers' Fronts of both the north and the south, the human rights movement and the peace movement that emerged in the 1990s, linking the issue of conflict resolution to the protection of human rights and democracy.

Attempts at conflict resolution

As the ethnic conflict escalated in the post-1983 period, various attempts were made to negotiate a settlement. An All-Party Conference was held in 1984. In 1986, Indian-sponsored talks between the Tamil militant groups and the Sri Lankan government were held in the Bhutanese capital, Thimpu. In 1987, the Prime Minister of India imposed a Peace Accord on the Sri Lankan government and the LTTE. In 1990, the then Sri Lankan President and leader of the United National Party (UNP), Ranasinghe Premadasa, brokered a ceasefire between the LTTE and the state, and held talks with the LTTE leadership in Colombo. The most recent venture at peacemaking was initiated by Kumaratunge, the current President and head of the People's Alliance (PA) government, following the signing of a cessation of hostilities agreement with the LTTE in January 1995.

None of these initiatives was destined to succeed, even to the extent of de-escalating the conflict, although they did result in periodic 'ceasefire' agreements and welcome breaks in the fighting. After the breakdown of each initiative, however, the conflict re-erupted more fiercely, setting back political resolution even further.

The work of the human rights community

Efforts to promote human rights and establish monitoring and advocacy organizations for their protection in Sri Lanka date from the early 1970s. The first systematic effort was initiated by the civil rights movement in response to state repression of the 1971 youth insurrection led by the Janatha Vimukthi Peramuna (JVP) in the south of the country.[2] By the late 1970s human rights work also began to cover rights violations in the context of the ethnic conflict, concentrating mainly on state violations of civil and political rights. Broader human and democratic rights work gradually gained ground in the 1980s with the establishment of organizations working on a wide range of civil and political rights issues, as well as women's rights issues.[3] These groups helped to spearhead campaigns to re-establish democratic institutions and practice, calling for a resolution of the ethnic conflict and the return to peace. Sri Lanka's human rights movement has been an active and important part of the movements for peace, freedom of expression and free and fair elections.

Through their unflagging work, human rights groups helped in mobilizing support for a peace platform at the 1994 presidential and parliamentary elections, as well as keeping the government's peace initiative alive through negotiations with the LTTE in 1994, and establishing the basis for a political solution to the conflict.[4] The efforts of human rights groups have also contributed towards significant changes in perception: many Sri Lankans now realize that the ethnic conflict cannot be won by military means, but needs to be resolved politically. Particularly among the Sinhalese, perceptions of civilian Tamils and their involvement in the conflict have also changed, thereby preventing retaliatory ethnic violence.

A significant facet of the human rights movement has been the involvement of women. Female lawyers, academics, educators, activists, journalists, writers and politicians have played an important role in the direction of its work. Among the activists have been workers, women from the peasantry, students, church workers and trade unionists. An appreciable number of women also hold leadership positions within human rights organizations and interact closely with male colleagues. Thus, the human rights movement serves as a springboard from which women can make a significant contribution to conflict resolution.

The contribution of women's groups to conflict resolution

The Women's Action Committee (WAC)

Since the early 1980s women's groups in Sri Lanka have been increasingly challenged by issues of human rights, ethnic politics and the armed conflict, in particular their impact on women. The first significant formation of progressive women's groups was within the Women's Action Committee, established in 1982. Based predominantly in the Sinhala south, these groups were organized among women workers, peasant women, students and church denominations. They also had contact with Tamil women's groups in the northern city of Jaffna and among Tamil plantation workers in the central hill country. The work of the Committee included documentation and dissemination of information, consciousness-raising, networking, campaigning, lobbying and advocacy. Its national-level public activities were centred around International Women's Day, International Human Rights Day and International Labour Day. The WAC sought to link women's rights with human rights and to establish a democratic culture that respected human and democratic rights. In the context of the ethnic conflict, it consistently and systematically called for political negotiation as opposed to military confrontation. At the micro-level, the work focused on awareness-raising. At the national level, the ethnic conflict was discussed at WAC National Conventions and was taken up in public campaigns – demonstrations, marches, public appeals and pickets.

In July 1983, Tamil militants ambushed a group of soldiers near Jaffna, sparking a backlash of violence against Tamil civilians living in the predominantly Sinhala south. Thousands were forced to take refuge in makeshift camps in the south; many ultimately fled the country to become part of an ever-increasing Tamil diaspora living in Western countries and in India. The ultimate horror of July 1983 was the massacre of thousands of Tamil civilians who had taken no part in the armed hostilities between the state and the Tamil militant groups. Individuals and organizations belonging to the WAC actively assisted, sheltered and worked among the displaced Tamil population.

In the aftermath of July and into 1984, sentiments on both sides of the ethnic divide began hardening. The state and the Tamil militants, predominantly the LTTE, were engaged in armed combat. The Prevention of Terrorism Act and Emergency Regulations were invoked by the state to crush the Tamil movement, and widespread cordon-and-search operations, detentions and extrajudicial assassinations became commonplace in the Tamil areas of the northeast.

Throughout the 1980s, the WAC continued its call for a solution to the ethnic conflict, joining with other women's groups. It sought to speak of the consequences of war; the right to self-determination of the Tamil people; and the need to redress Tamil grievances, highlighting in particular human rights violations perpetrated against the Tamil people, the institution of non-democratic structures and the abuse of state power. It also linked the ethnic conflict and the politics of violence to the deterioration of democracy, with its consequences for all ethnic communities of Sri Lanka.

'Women for Peace'

In the climate of fear, intimidation and insecurity fostered by increasing ethnic chauvinism on the part of the executive and the state, warmongering was the preferred policy. It was in this climate that the WAC joined forces with a group of women academics and professional women to call for peace. Realizing that they needed to forge the broadest possible support for the call, and at the same time harness the voice of influential women, the group began canvassing support for an appeal published in December in the Sinhalese-, Tamil- and English-language national newspapers. The petition, signed by 100 women, called for an end to the war and the commencement of talks that could lead to a politically negotiated settlement to the conflict. The women were among leading professionals – doctors, lawyers, writers, administrators, teachers, theatre and media people, journalists, religious people, women's rights and human rights activists, trade unionists and politicians. The appeal was issued in the name of a new formation called 'Women for Peace' and was extended for signature to all women. Within 30 days, more than 10,000 signatures had been collected. Together with this call for peace came the first round of political negotiations between the government and the Tamil militant leadership: this was the All-Party Conference, held in late 1984. Significantly, however, not one woman participated in these negotiations.

Throughout the second half of the 1980s, Women for Peace organized marches, vigils and protests, calling for peace and denouncing the anti-Tamil and undemocratic practices of the state. This campaign involved calls for the repeal of the draconian Prevention of Terrorism Act, the freeing of political detainees, the dismantling of security zones in the north, humanitarian assistance for the displaced and protests against illegal detention and disappearances.

Mothers and Daughters of Lanka (MDSL)

In the aftermath of the Indo–Sri Lanka Accord and the advent of the Indian Peacekeeping Force, politics in the south too underwent a violent transformation. The period 1988–89 was marked by unprecedented violence on the part of government forces and the JVP alike. The JVP, now reorganized into an extremist political group, had adopted a position violently antagonistic to the Indo–Sri Lanka Accord and had established itself as a militant patriotic movement. It engaged in a campaign of unmitigated violence that included widespread assassinations of not only members of the security forces, MPs, and leading members of the ruling party, but also those belonging to opposition parties. Through a sustained campaign of enforced work stoppages, arson and political assassinations, the JVP was seeking to bring the administration of the country to a complete halt.

The state responded with counter-violence and repression against anyone suspected of belonging to the JVP or sympathizing with its politics. Using the same repressive mechanisms used to curb the Tamil struggle, the Prevention of Terrorism Act and Emergency Regulations, together with death squads, the state apparatus brutally suppressed the JVP rebellion with unprecedented detentions, summary executions and disappearances. Many of the victims were in fact totally unaffiliated with the JVP. A considerable number were members of the main opposition party, the Sri Lanka Freedom Party (SLFP).

As in the north, women's political activism in the south shifted to respond to immediate human rights violations – disappearances and summary executions. Initially, the WAC had welcomed the Indo–Sri Lanka Accord as a first step towards a political settlement to the ethnic conflict; now many of its members had to cease activity due to violent threats from the JVP. Many women activists living outside urban centres were forced to seek shelter in the relative safety and anonymity of the cities. The WAC was disbanded in 1989. However, the women's groups reconstituted themselves, with broader participation, to form the Mothers and Daughters of Sri Lanka (MDSL) in December that year. As with the formation of Women for Peace at a critical juncture in the ethnic crisis, in response to state terror and armed conflict, the MDSL mobilized among women and went public with an appeal, this time calling for a 'Stop to All Killings'.[5]

The Southern Mothers' Front

In another significant mobilization of 'motherhood', the Southern Mothers' Front was born in Matara in 1990. This formation, according to its conveners, was inspired by the Mothers' Front established by Tamil women in the north of Sri Lanka in 1984 as well as the Mothers of the Plaza del Mayo in Argentina. (The formation of the Northern Front is dealt with later in this chapter.) In response to continuing abuses of human rights, especially disappearances in the district, over 1,500 women attended an inaugural meeting; soon the Front spread throughout the Sinhala-majority southern districts.[6] However, it was organized under the auspices of the main opposition party, the Sri Lanka Freedom Party, and its conveners were two male

MPs. As the Front grew in strength it began to be used as a political weapon against the ruling United National Party. Its first national meeting and rally were held in Colombo in 1991, amidst heavy military presence, threats and malicious diatribe in the state-owned national press. The Front itself was a powerful presence. Admittedly, many of its members were members of the SLFP, but there were also women with no party affiliation, mothers and wives of police and military personnel who had been killed, and even a few Tamil women who had lost family members in the ethnic war.

One woman who came to symbolize the Front was Dr Manorani Saravanamuttu, the mother of assassinated journalist Richard de Zoysa. Middle-class and Tamil in ethnicity, Dr Saravanamuttu strove to keep the movement non-partisan and aimed at seeking peace. She emphasized, 'Make no mistake: our aim is peace, our method is peaceful. We have wept alone and have come together for comfort. From this has arisen our desire to collectively seek peace in our country.' Stressing that the Mothers' Front was in no way 'anti-government', she said it would act as a peaceful watchdog on whatever government was in power. As to its political linkage: 'The most important facet of this political linkage at the start, is that it gives the mothers some measure of protection in the initial stages of their campaign.' She pointed out that 'as the women learn to fend for themselves, and develop their organization, they become independent.'[7]

Another speaker at the rally was Chandrika Kumaratunge, then on the fringes of her mother's party the SLFP, and herself the recent widow of an assassinated politician. Only three years later she was to be elected president of the country. In a powerful speech delivered amid total silence Chandrika spoke to the Mothers of their needs, asking them not to let themselves be taken over by politicians or political parties but to 'take the struggle into their own hands and make it their struggle'.[8] However, this exhortation was to no avail – neither she, the SLFP or any other independent representation within the Front was able to divorce the Mothers' needs from the exigencies of party politics.

The Mothers had a single demand: calling for justice and accountability, they demanded the return of their children. The SLFP clearly exploited this demand, not for the reinstatement of democracy and to see justice done, but more to overthrow the incumbent government and secure political power. This appropriation had positive and negative sides. The women were able to use their gendered role of motherhood in a positive expression of anger and emotional outrage in a situation where traditionally male forms of struggle were either ineffective or impossible due to political violence and terror. The methods of struggle adopted by the Front were clearly innovative and accessible to the women. Marches and demonstrations were interspersed with ritual invocations to the Gods, in the form of *Kannaluwas*, both for the return their children and to wreak vengeance on the guilty.[9] While the issue of democracy and human rights – and in particular disappearances, extrajudicial executions and accountability –

became political slogans in the campaign to overthrow the UNP, the Mothers' invocations to the Gods became the psychological weapon that was to prove most disturbing to the incumbent president. At the same time, the use of *Kannaluwas* restricted the women to seeking refuge in the irrational. It reinforced, both for themselves and for society at large, the notion that irrational power use was the preserve of women. It failed to give them any independent or sustainable political strength.

The presence of the Mothers' Front was without doubt a powerful catalyst in shifting the political balance of power. The political issues rooted in questions of democracy and peace were epitomized by the presence of the Front. Many politicians – both women and men – were to take on the issues of peace and democracy in their political campaigning. Several women politicians of the SLFP came to espouse the cause of the Mothers.[10] Chandrika Kumaratunge herself made peace, the resolution of the ethnic conflict, the re-institution of democracy and the protection of human rights the main planks of her election platform. However, the Southern Mothers' Front disintegrated with the 1994 electoral victory of the PA (People's Alliance) government. Female party activists put their faith in the newly elected president for the delivery of justice, while male coordinators of the Front became ministers in the new Cabinet. When three geographically-determined Commissions of Inquiry were established in 1995 to look into the issue of disappearances, this appeared to obviate the need for the Mothers' Front. Never having been politically independent from the SLFP, and relying on it for leadership, the Front could not become the watchdog body envisaged by Manorani Saravanamuttu. As with the Northern Mothers' Front, its mobilization was around women's role as mothers and their duty and moral obligation to protect their children, so the Front never challenged disempowering or limiting gendered roles. The Southern Mothers' Front may well have served as an important catalyst in pushing the process of democratization forward, but it was unable to translate that gain into the political empowering of its members. Its members exerted influence on the political process, but never managed to acquire positions of power that would allow them to participate in decisionmaking.

The protest movements

The Mothers' Front also made possible the creation of other spaces for protest. The human rights movement and the alternative press, spearheaded by both Sinhala and Tamil activists, mobilized in 1992 around the 'Campaign for Freedom from Fear', taking on the objectives of challenging the undemocratic practices of both the ruling UNP and the LTTE. The alternative media became bolder and critical and helped to break the fear psychosis that had gripped the country since 1989. The Mothers' Front, together with Mothers and Daughters of Lanka, was also actively involved in the series of elections that led to the change of government in 1994.

Commencing with provincial council elections to the southern and western councils in 1993, through to parliamentary and presidential elections in 1994, members of the Front campaigned around issues of human rights and democracy. At the local level they also supported the Movement for Free and Fair Elections that monitored the conduct of the parliamentary and presidential elections and organized against electoral malpractice and political intimidation.

The peace movements

Another formation in which women played an active role was the Movement for Peace with Democracy, established in 1994. It sought a political resolution to the ethnic conflict, calling for the democratic and peaceful transformation of political and social structures to serve as the basis for a plural democratic polity with full equality for all ethnic groups. Involving activists from all ethnic groups, the movement organized workshops, discussions, seminars, meetings and rallies throughout the southern districts and in the eastern province. Its work met with tremendous support. Immediately after the parliamentary and presidential elections of 1994, celebrating International Human Rights Day, the Campaign for Peace with Democracy attracted over 10,000 people to a march and major rally in Colombo. The event culminated in an appeal to the newly elected president and the LTTE to carry the peace process forward.[11]

In January 1995 the appeal to the LTTE was taken to their stronghold in Jaffna by a peace delegation made up of human rights activists, politicians and representatives from Women for Peace and Mothers and Daughters of Lanka. This was the first predominantly Sinhala delegation of peace activists to make an independent visit to the LTTE-controlled northern province in four years. It also marked the culmination of the first stage of the Campaign for Peace with Democracy which organized its final rally in Vavuniya, the northernmost town under state control. Predominantly Tamil in population, and under tight military control, Vavuniya was flooded by thousands of (mainly Sinhala) peace activists who arrived on a specially chartered 'peace train', calling for an end to the ethnic conflict and for the re-establishment of peace. In Jaffna, the delegation was given an overwhelming welcome by the people of the northern peninsula. Whatever the political agendas of the newly elected People's Alliance or the LTTE may have been, the hope and expectations of the people were for *peace*.[12]

Activism by women in the north and east

In the early 1960s, Tamil resistance to ethnic discrimination perpetrated by a Sinhala majority state was led by the Federal Party, mainly within the context of parliamentary politics and non-violent peaceful agitation outside parliament. During this early phase, women were among those participating in *satyagraha*[13] and protest marches. In the north and east, Tamil women were used as speakers and crowd-drawers at political meetings. However, their role was perceived within patriarchal social constructions – first as wife, then as mother. The women who formed the vanguard of this activism were also mainly wives of male politicians, and their role was viewed as nurturing and supporting both their husbands and the struggle (see Maunaguru, 1995).

Although non-violent in content, these actions were spurred by rhetoric filled with violent battle imagery. Here women were constructed either as victims of the Sinhala state or as those who would nurture valour in their sons, who in turn would fight to regain lost dignity and the pride of the Tamil community.

When the peaceful agitation of the 1960s gave way to the militant armed struggle of the 1980s, women were again drawn into the struggle, and many of them joined Tamil nationalist organizations. Used first as propagandists and service providers, recruiters and fundraisers, women were gradually trained as fighters and used in combat. The LTTE was in the forefront of using women both in traditional units of combat and later on in the exclusive units as suicide bombers. Women who could not be recruited to active fighting were exhorted to make the supreme sacrifice of their children – their sons in particular – to the struggle. Women's roles were extended: now they were wives, mothers and nurturers both of men and of the struggle. They were also bearers of sons and daughters, reproducers for and of the struggle and, ultimately, they were also warriors in the struggle.

Women were thus made to perform their traditional reproductive and nurturing duties as wives, mothers and liberation fighters. It is widely held that the LTTE's women cadres make up 50% or more of its fighting force today. All the same, no woman was allowed into the patriarchal male echelons of political decisionmaking of the LTTE, which had now emerged as the main Tamil separatist group battling for a separate state of Tamil Eelam. As Maunaguru (1995) observes, in the early 1980s all the major Tamil nationalist groups, except the LTTE, addressed the women's question as part of their political agendas. This was seen as a means of eliminating barriers to women's participation in the national liberation struggle, promising women equal status with men in the liberated society that would eventually emerge out of the conflict. Women's sections of the various militant groups as well as autonomous women's organizations tried to use this opportunity to discuss the concepts relating to the subordination of women. Since this issue was personal as well as political for them, they extended the discussion beyond the boundaries of ethnic repression. The literature emerging from this period reflects the debates among and within women's groups on feminism, emancipation and the national liberation struggle. Importantly, within this ideological space emerged a new categorical formulation – *puthumai pen* ('new woman'). Feminist activists now challenged notions of the traditional feminine qualities of passivity and submissiveness, and questioned the patriarchal aspects of Tamil cultural ideology (see Maunaguru, 1995, pp. 165–168).

Rejecting traditional notions of femininity were also those women who committed themselves single-mindedly to the armed expression of Tamil nationalism. Some of these were the women who joined the LTTE to become part of elite battalions such as the Black Tigers (suicide killers: one of whom was responsible for the assassination of former Indian Prime Minister, Rajiv Gandhi; another assassinated the incumbent Sri Lankan President, Ranasinghe Premadasa). For them the national liberation struggle is the paramount issue; women's subordination within it is not a question.

The decade of the 1980s was also to witness the use of yet another construction of 'womanhood'. In response to increasing state repression that took the form of arbitrary arrest, detention, torture, disappearances and extrajudicial executions, women began to organize, almost spontaneously, using their roles as mothers. Women who were active in the 1980s assert that this was a necessary form of protection in a climate where state repression was at its height and open opposition to military presence and military activity was fraught with danger. It was also well suited as a space within which women could assert what they perceived to be their legitimate and moral duty and right to protect their children, especially their sons, from danger.

The Northern Mothers' Front

In a response to the round-up in the Jaffna peninsula of a large number of Tamil youths in 1984, who were then transported to the south, Tamil mothers spontaneously organized to demand the release of their sons. They marched to the office of the Government Agent (GA) in Jaffna, the representative of state authority, and there, in the teeth of armed military presence, they staged a peaceful protest until the GA successfully communicated with the central government and secured the release of most of the young men. Calling themselves the Mothers' Front, the women continued to mobilize and call for a political settlement to the ethnic conflict, condemning human rights violations perpetrated against their community.

In a situation where the Tamil political parties represented in Parliament were outlawed and the only articulation of Tamil aspirations had been through violent militant struggle, this mobilization of Tamil women in non-violent peaceful protest was a significant move indeed. It was also the mobilization of motherhood in an attempt to safeguard life, in a climate where civil protest was difficult and dangerous to organize. Motherhood was invoked as a protection against reprisals, as well as being used as implying a moral duty and the obligation to safeguard life.

Responding to an immediate experience as opposed to an abstract political goal, women mobilized to form an autonomous organization, seeking to protect their children from the human rights violations of the state. Importantly, this formation was not linked to the LTTE, which held political authority throughout the Jaffna peninsula and was opposed to any form of dissent or independent organization. Between the mid- and late 1980s, the LTTE went on to annihilate all other militant formations in political opposition to itself within the northeast. That the Mothers' Front emerged in this period was a significant factor. It also enabled women to articulate political positions independent of the LTTE, linking its political work with humanitarian assistance and work among the displaced.[14]

With the breakdown of the Indo–Sri Lanka Accord, imposed on the LTTE by the Indian government and flouted by it in 1987, the people of the peninsula had to contend with the occupation of an Indian army. Originally welcomed as a peacekeeping force, the Indian military was actively engaged in armed combat by the LTTE, which went underground and resorted to effective guerrilla warfare. The LTTE next set about eliminating all opposition, emerging as a ruthless, dictatorial force. Unable to survive with any significant independence, the Mothers' Front disintegrated in 1987/88 into a welfare organization with no political voice. Many of its leading activists were forced to flee the peninsula or drop out of active political work.

The use of motherhood as a political means of mobilization could not be sustained as a means of genuine empowerment to women. When it was first formed, the Mothers' Front was obviously considered expeditious by the LTTE and allowed to survive. Later, however, as the LTTE gained physical control of the peninsula, the need for the existence of a women's movement within the dictates of patriarchal nationalist politics evaporated. The women themselves were unable to transform the organization into a more positive, effective and political force, not least because it had been founded around the notion of motherhood, which did not fundamentally challenge gendered roles.

While Tamil nationalist ideology perceived women as objects to be controlled in its own interests, Tamil women attempted to formulate constructions, such as the 'new woman', which could express gender interests and thereby empower women. Even though these attempts and visions failed to materialize into positive changes, they must not be forgotten. Imperative to the concept of the 'new woman' is the challenge to the patriarchal control exercised over her personal and political being by Tamil nationalism (see also Maunaguru, 1995).

A woman president and the peace process

President Kumaratunge, elected in 1994 with an overwhelming majority of the vote across all ethnic groups, was entrusted with a mandate to seek a political solution to the ethnic conflict and re-establish peace. She herself had been the victim of political violence, losing first her father and then her husband in politically motivated assassinations. The murder of her father was widely believed to be the result of his attempts at political accommodation with the Tamil political leadership. Her husband, the leader of the Sri Lanka People's Party, was a popular proponent of a peaceful settlement to the ethnic conflict. A widow with two young children, living in a climate of political insecurity and threat of personal assassination, the President campaigned for a mandate to seek an end to the ethnic conflict. Assuming office on the wave of unprecedented popular support, she then successfully negotiated a cessation of hostilities with the LTTE.

As Radhika Coomaraswamy observes (1994, p. 46), South Asia has the greatest concentration of women heads of state. There is ideological acceptance of women in the public realm, but this is because the women have appropriated the discourse of motherhood. Kumaratunge's ascent to political power can be seen as an example of this. It came in the wake of her husband's assassination. She was seen as the courageous widow and mother figure that could lead the nation out of its political crisis, taking forward the vision of her husband, and also avenging the brutal human rights violations of the period from 1987 into the early 1990s. In addition, Kumaratunge articulated a political vision: she called for an end to the ethnic conflict, distancing herself from Sinhala chauvinism and promising radical constitutional reform that would enable substantial devolution of power to the minorities. It was in these aspirations that she differed from her predecessors. While her motherhood, womanhood and personal experience of political violence may have informed her decision, it was also a politically courageous move that went beyond any articulated by a previous Sinhala head of state.

The long-desired political solution to the ethnic conflict seemed an achievable reality in the spring of 1994. Soon, however, it became apparent that the government and the LTTE had fundamentally different agendas that ran parallel to each other, instead of converging. By April 1995, the LTTE had unilaterally ended the ceasefire and recommenced hostilities. Various explanations have been offered for the breakdown of the peace process: that the Kumaratunge government was not serious about restoring normalcy to the civilians living in the northeast; that both the LTTE and the military used the ceasefire to recuperate, regroup and rearm; that the LTTE leadership was unwilling to accept the possibility of entering the mainstream political process.

The President's peace initiative, begun in the face of military scepticism, was in shambles. Extremist nationalists of both sides were justifying a return to war and the peace constituency was effectively silenced. In an attempt to keep the notion of a political solution alive, Kumaratunge put forward a set of political proposals in August 1995, tempered with a caveat that the LTTE had to be weakened militarily and dislodged from its northern stronghold in the city of Jaffna. In the face of politico-military pressure and Sinhala chauvinist upsurge, particularly among the Buddhist clergy, the President yielded and launched a 'war for peace'. Jaffna was 'captured' in November 1995 and its entire population displaced. The LTTE retaliated by massacring Sinhala civilians living in border villages, launching attacks on military camps and bombing the capital. The political proposals of August 1995 became substantially watered down to a legal draft which has remained in limbo before a Parliamentary Select Committee on Constitutional Reform ever since January 1996.

However genuine Kumaratunge's aspirations for seeking a permanent settlement to the conflict may have been and however far she was willing to go with a blueprint for a solution, her peace initiative failed. Pressure on her as head of state was obviously what informed her decisions: political and military considerations had to overcome her reluctance to recommence the war. The military's initial successes, such as the capture of Jaffna, gave chauvinistic forces a new lease of life and made the discussion of an extensive political package difficult. Subsequent military reverses have only meant a further drive to re-establish military superiority – and so the cycle of conflict has continued.

The President has been criticized repeatedly for not establishing an inclusive process and for having alienated her opposition and her supporters. Many of her confidants were not from her ruling coalition, the People's Alliance. This also compounded her isolation once the peace process failed and left her with no assistance to push through the more unpopular set of political reforms.

Other women party members and parliamentarians were not involved in the peace process – even though some of them were themselves victims of political violence under the previous regime, and had been actively involved with human rights work, particularly with issues of disappearances and extrajudicial executions. There was simply no women's political participation in conflict resolution at the highest level of government. In addition, Kumaratunge did not appear to consider the possibility of involving non-party women professionals – the many academics, lawyers and human rights activists who had played a key role in the peace movement and who were, in fact, largely responsible for her earlier political success.

Women in civil society: implications for political participation and conflict resolution

The recommencement of hostilities in 1995 meant the resumption of the cycle of violence, terror, insecurity and distrust. This pattern of events indicates that a sustainable solution to Sri Lanka's ethnic conflict cannot be implemented without serious political commitment and without a spirit of accommodation on the part of the government, the LTTE, the opposition and nationalists on both sides of the ethnic divide. It will also require the continued participation of the vast majority of civil society, whose aspirations for peace bolstered the efforts of Sri Lanka's first woman president to put chauvinistic and opportunist politics behind her and make resolution of the ethnic conflict her priority goal.

Belief in a peace process or the viability of negotiations becomes difficult in the face of such repeated setbacks. However, the continuation of violent conflict as an alternative cannot be sustained or justified. Political solutions that address the fundamental core of conflict are necessary; in the interim, civil society can play a significant role in mitigating, reducing and perhaps eventually achieving an end to conflict. Processes that may help lead towards conflict resolution should begin at the local level, involving those hardest hit by the conflict – the civilian populations living in conflict zones, women in particular. Perhaps it is the lack of such participation that has so far doomed to failure all political initiatives for resolving Sri Lanka's ethnic conflict.

While it is noteworthy that no peace initiative to date has had the participation of women at any level of negotiation or decisionmaking except for the President herself,[15] actions by women have contributed to the positive shifts in political thinking. They have played a significant role in forging a change of perceptions in the need for democratization and respect for human rights. And women have – both by the use of the ballot in the presidential and parliamentary elections of 1994 and by participation in the peace movements – made clear their aspirations for a peaceful settlement.

Women's role in de-escalating the conflict

At the local level, women have played a major role in de-escalating the conflict and mitigating its effects. Fundamental in this process is the protection and promotion of human rights, and here women's groups have been particularly involved. Their actions were instrumental in the establishment of Sri Lanka's Commissions of Investigation into involuntary removal or disappearances of persons.

The formation of autonomous women's groups and citizens' organizations to monitor human rights and continue to act as watchdogs to prevent violations is crucial to this process. The continued importance of this work is borne out by recent actions in the form of protests, vigils, demonstrations and pickets. This commenced in 1996 and continued in 1997 to push the state into investigating the rape and murder of schoolgirl Krishanthi Kumaraswamy in Jaffna by armed forces personnel in September 1996. The perpetrators were brought to trial in 1997; the case was concluded in 1998 with the sentencing of one policeman and five soldiers to death and concurrent 20-year sentences for abduction, rape and murder.

Women can help to strengthen civil intervention in the conflict by campaigning for demilitarized zones, for humanitarian access to conflict areas and for safe evacuation and resettlement of civilian populations. The ongoing nature of the conflict and the continuous displacement of civilian populations, the vast majority of whom are women, necessitate greater attention to these areas of intervention from a specifically gendered perspective. Women and civil organizations must continue to demand that international humanitarian law and norms be obeyed by all parties to the conflict. Women must also actively seek to become involved in humanitarian assistance at the levels of decisionmaking and implementation alike. Their involvement could serve the twin goals of more responsible decisionmaking and of informing better decisions on how to assist affected populations.

Confidence-building and reconciliation are further key factors in the process of conflict de-escalation and resolution. This points up the importance of continuing to build interactions between ethnic and religious groups towards establishing an understanding of diversity and respect for plurality.

These are some of the ways in which women can begin to assert their presence in the process of conflict mitigation. If it can be accepted that women have had to supersede their traditionally gendered roles to survive in hostile and repressive environments produced by conflict, women can indeed play a proactive role in determining how that conflict affects their lives and how it can be resolved.

Women's role in civil society

For the north and east of Sri Lanka, the immediate reality of the war for women has been the loss of men, of physical safety and economic survival. This has brought about a significant shift in the gendered roles of women. Men have died in the fighting as active combatants or as victims caught in crossfire. They have been detained by the state or disappeared, sometimes extrajudicially executed. They have also fled the conflict areas to live in safer locations or have left the country. Women have also joined the combatants; they have died in the conflict or fled to safety. However, a far greater number have had to remain, experiencing continual armed conflict, fearful for the security and safety of themselves and their families. They are repeatedly displaced from their homes and relocated to unfamiliar surroundings. In their constant battle to keep themselves and their families fed and sheltered, they are trapped in gendered roles that demand that women assume sole responsibility for the care of families, children and elders, left behind to hold together the fabric of society.

These women of Sri Lanka are survivors. Sheer necessity has made them forge creative and innovative survival strategies. Women socialized into belief that their role in society is linked to their biological functions of reproduction have also seen their socially constructed functions as nurturers and caregivers restricted to the private spaces of family and home. As a consequence of the conflict, these women have had to become the breadwinners and protectors of immediate as well as extended families. They have crossed the barriers into public space. Today they are dealing with economic survival, competing in the marketplace, contending with political and military authority. In short, they have assumed roles traditionally thought to be the preserve of men.

In response, many women have begun to organize among themselves, into women's collectives or cooperatives – mainly for economic survival, sometimes for protection. Others have joined existing civil organizations or are employed by non-governmental organizations as service providers, social mobilizers, activists or the like. Some have initiated self-employment projects, venturing into non-traditional fields of work and income generation. These are some of the many non-formal organizations within which Sri Lankan women now play a role in public life. Such changing circumstances and gender roles reflect women's experiences of coping with ongoing conflict, and their aspirations for peace: they need to be better harnessed in the efforts to resolve the conflict.

Women's participation in civil society should be extended to a more political plane. The resolution of conflict needs to look at the root causes as well as the consequences of conflict. Root causes are often political in nature and require a political solution brokered by all parties actively involved in the conflict. For Sri Lanka, this is primarily the state and the LTTE. Women can be instrumental in bringing about such a process of brokering or mediation by identifying and by influencing key actors.

Women and humanitarian assistance

Women are also major recipients of humanitarian assistance, a necessary intervention in the context of dealing with ongoing conflict. Sri Lanka has a large community of humanitarian aid agencies, both local and international, present in the conflict areas and responding to the humanitarian crises engendered by the conflict. To date, women have been largely absent from the work and decisionmaking of these agencies. There is a need for more active participation of women, both in delivering humanitarian assistance and in determining what that assistance should be and how and to whom that assistance should be delivered.

Women and peace initiatives

Women's participation in the peace movement and in the movement for democratization are valuable examples of innovative approaches to conflict resolution. In addition, activism in the 'Mothers' Fronts' challenged the state to end human rights violations and begin a process of investigation and to establish accountability. By virtue of the fact that they are the buttress of civil society in war zones, women are also challenging the continuation of conflict. They should increase their participation in the monitoring and documentation of violations of human rights and humanitarian norms.[16] They should also call for the protection of human rights and humanitarian norms by aligning themselves with human rights and women's rights organizations.

There can be no doubt that many women have been active participants in opposing the conflict and the violations of human rights in Sri Lanka. The challenge now is to effectively increase women's participation, at both the local and the national level, in a process that can bring about a permanent solution to the conflict.

Political participation at the national level in terms of representation in Parliament is obviously a long-term goal. Women's concerns arising from the conflict and aimed at influencing political reforms to assist conflict resolution can also be reflected in other spaces more immediately accessible to women. One possibility is by means of the media. Sri Lanka has a vibrant alternative press with wide public circulation and significant influence. Women can use this space to make their concerns heard.

These interventions can help increase the participation of women in the push for political negotiations and in determining the contours of a political solution to the ethnic conflict in Sri Lanka. Ultimately, such a solution will also need to incorporate the gendered aspirations of women in broader civil society, and not merely the rhetoric of political opportunism or desires for absolutist political power.

Notes

1   Political participation is defined here to include political representation in Parliament, local government, membership in political parties or groups as well as participation in civic groups and civic actions to bring about political change.

2   The JVP or the People's Liberation Front was formed in May 1965. Composed mainly of southern Sinhala youth, it launched an insurrection against the state in April 1971, aimed at establishing a socialist state. The insurrection was defeated within a few months. In a second phase of militant uprisings the JVP took on the state during the period 1987–89. For studies of the two JVP uprisings in Sri Lanka, see Alles (1976, 1990), Chandraprema (1991) and Gunaratne (1990).

3   Specific women's rights issues have included violence against women, reproductive rights, equal pay for equal work, migrant labour, law reforms in relation to rape laws, and abortion laws.

4   The peace initiative ended in April 1995 with the resumption of hostilities.

5   The MDSL appeal, in the form of a poem, was published in the mainstream Sri Lankan newspapers of all three languages on 1 October 1989.

6   Letter of invitation dated 6 February 1991, titled 'National Convention and Public Rally 19 February 1991', signed by Mangala Samaraweera, MP and Coordinator, Mothers' Front. The Mothers' Front was jointly coordinated by two SLFP MPs, Mangala Samaraweera and Mahinda Rajapakse. The Front was created in response to the many demands received, in particular by these two MPs from the southern constituencies of Matara and Hambantota, from mothers and family members of the disappeared. Although coordinated by the MPs, it was never an official party organization.

7   'Statement of Dr. (Mrs) Manorani Saravanamuttu on the Convening of the Mothers' Front in Sri Lanka on 19 February 1991', issued as a press release by the Mothers' Front on 19 February 1991. The statement was delivered by Dr Saravanamuttu at the National Convention of the Mothers' Front held at the New Town Hall in Colombo on 19 February 1991.

8   Informal notes on the Mothers' Front Convention held at the New Town Hall,
     Colombo on 19 February 1991, made by INFORM, a Human Rights organiza-
     tion based in Colombo.
9   *Kannaluwa* is an invocation to the Gods, in the form of an appeal or lamenta-
     tion, where the Gods are implored to give succour in times of need.
10   Among them were Pavitra Wanniarachchi, Priyangani Abeyweera, Sumedha
     Jayasena and Hema Ratnayake.
11   'The Campaign for Peace with Democracy: An Appeal to the Government of
     Sri Lanka and the Liberation Tigers of Tamil Eelam', read at the Rally on 9
     December 1994 at the Vihara Maha Devi Park, open-air auditorium, Colombo
     and subsequently published in the mainstream Sinhala-, Tamil- and English-
     language newspapers in Sri Lanka.
12   See the editorial and centre-spread article, 'We Want Peace: Notes on an
     Unfinished Journey . . . in Jaffna . . .' by C. Dodawatte in *Yukthiya*, 26 February
     1995, vol. 3, issue 8. *Yukthiya* (Justice) is a weekly Sinhala-language newspaper
     published in Colombo.
13   *Satyagraha* is essentially a form of non-violent protest, first used in the Indian
     Independence struggle by Mahatma Gandhi.
14   The Front assisted people displaced within the peninsula, both as a result of
     ongoing armed confrontation between the LTTE and the state, and where
     sources of livelihood were inaccessible due to state imposition of 'no go' or
     security zones. Particularly affected by these decrees was the fishing commu-
     nity which was prohibited from putting to sea beyond a limited range. The
     Front also engaged in rehabilitation work among released detainees and dis-
     placed persons.
15   The only woman reported to have been present at some of the negotiations
     was Adel Balasingham, the Australian-born wife of LTTE theoretician, Anton
     Balasingham, widely seen as mentor to the LTTE's women's wing.
16   This information can be used for advocacy and change – for example, to estab-
     lish principles of limit to force, government accountability, independence of
     the judiciary and obligations to protect bodily integrity. Established interna-
     tional mechanisms and machinery can be lobbied. National mechanisms such
     as the courts, Commissions of Inquiry, the Human Rights Commission and the
     Human Rights Task Force can also be used.

Notes on Contributors

Anuradha Mitra Chenoy is Associate Professor at the School of International Studies, Jawaharlal Nehru University, New Delhi. She has written extensively on gender and international relations and is currently working on a book to be entitled *Russia in Transition* (Macmillan, forthcoming).

Drude Dahlerup is Professor at Statsvetenskapliga institutionen, University of Stockholm. She is Vice-Chair of the Danish Government's Council for European Politics and a board member of the Danish Center for Information on Women and Gender. Her most recent publication is *The Redstockings. The Rise and Fall, the Ideas and the Impact of the Danish Redstockings Movement, 1970–85*, vols I–II (Gyldendal, 1998).

Dorota Gierycz is Chief, Gender Analysis Section, Division for the Advancement of Women, Department of Economic and Social Affairs, United Nations Secretariat, New York. Her recent publications include 'Education on the Human Rights of Women as a Vehicle for Change' in *Human Rights Education for the Twenty-first Century*, George J. Andreopoulos & Richard Pierre Claude, eds (University of Pennsylvania Press, 1997) and 'Women in Decision-making: Can We Change the Status Quo?' in *Towards A Women's Agenda for a Culture of Peace*, Ingeborg Breines, Dorota Gierycz & Betty Reardon, eds (Cultures of Peace Series, UNESCO, 1999).

Errol Miller is Professor of Teacher Education at the Institute of Education, University of the West Indies. He is Editor of *Education Reform in the Commonwealth Carribbean* and his recent publications include 'Gender and the Family: Some Theoretical Considerations' in *Gender and the Family in the Caribbean*, Wilma Bailey, ed. (Institute of Social and Economic Research, University of the West Indies Mona, 1998) and *Jamaican Primary Education: Policy Relevant Studies* (Green Lizard Press, 1997).

Michael Emin Salla is Assistant Professor in the Peace and Conflict Resolution Program, School of International Service at the Australian National University. He has conducted research and fieldwork in the ethnic conflicts in East Timor, Kosovo, Macedonia and Sri Lanka. He is the author of *America's Seventh Hero's Journey and the Second American Century* (forthcoming 2000).

Kumudini Samuel is Joint Coordinator, The Women and Media Collective, Sri Lanka, and Editor of *Women's Rights Watch*. Her most recent publications include *Women's Rights Watch Year Report 1999* (The Women and Media Collective, Colombo, Sri Lanka, 1999), *Women's Rights Watch Quarterly Report 1997/1998/1999* (The Women and Media Collective, Colombo, Sri Lanka) and 'Straining Consensus: Government Strategies for War and Peace in Sri Lanka 1994–1998' in *Demanding Sacrifice: War and Negotiation in Sri Lanka*, Jeremy Armon & Liz Philipson, eds, *Accord: An International Review of Peace Initiatives*, Issue 4, August 1998, London.

Inger Skjelsbæk is a researcher at the International Peace Research Institute, Oslo (PRIO). Her most recent publication is *Sexual Violence in Times of War: An Annotated Bibliography* (PRIO Report 4/99).

Svetlana Slapsak is Professor of Anthropology of Ancient Worlds and Anthropology of Gender at Institutum Studiorum Humanitatis, Ljubljana Graduate School of Humanities, Slovenia, and is presently a Fellow at the Netherlands Institute for Advanced Study in the Humanities and Social Sciences. Her most recent publications include *For the Anthropology of the Ancient Worlds* (ISH, 2000) and *Women Icons of the 20th Century* (Urad za zensko politiko, 2000).

Dan Smith is Director of the International Peace Research Institute, Oslo (PRIO). His most recent publication is *The State of War and Peace Atlas*, 6th edition (Penguin, 1999).

Eva Irene Tuft is Resident Representative, Save the Children Norway, Guatemala Office. Her most recent publications include 'Monitoring the Human Rights of Women' in *Manual on Human Rights Monitoring: An Introduction for Human Rights Field Officers*, Araldsen & Thiis, eds (NORDEM, 1997) and *Democracy and Violence – The Colombian Paradox* (Christian Michelsen Institute Report R., 1996).

Achin Vanaik holds the Honorary Academic Chair in Geo-politics and International Relations at the Naval War College, Mumbai. His most recent publication [with Praful Bidwai] is *South Asia on a Short Fuse: Nuclear Politics and the Future of Global Disarmament* (Oxford University Press, India, 1999).

Bibliography

Adelman, Howard & Astri Suhrke (with contributions by Bruce Jones) 1996. *The International Response to Conflict and Genocide: Lessons from the Rwanda Experience. Early Warning and Conflict Management*, Volume 2. Copenhagen: Joint Evaluation of Emergency Assistance to Rwanda.

Ahlström, Christer, 1991. *Casualties of Conflict: Report for the World Campaign for the Protection of Victims of War*. With contributions by Kjell-Åke Nordquist. Uppsala: Uppsala University, Department of Peace & Conflict Research.

Ajami, Fouad, 1993. 'The Summoning', *Foreign Affairs*, vol. 72, no. 4, pp. 2–9.

Albanese, Patricia, 1996. 'Leaders and Breeders: The Archaization of Gender Relations in Croatia', pp. 185–201 in Barbara Weiner, Metta Spencer & Slobodan Drakulic, eds, *Women in Post-Communism*, vol. 2. London: JAI Press.

Alles, Anthony Christopher, 1976. *Insurgency 1971*. Colombo: Apothecaries Co. Ltd.

Alles, A.C., 1990. *Insurgency 1971*. Colombo: Apothecaries Co. Ltd.

Amnesty International, 1993. *Bosnia Herzegovina: Rape and Sexual Abuse by Armed Forces*. London: Amnesty International.

Amnesty International, 1995. *Women in Colombia: Breaking the Silence* (AMR/23/41/95). London: Amnesty International.

Amnesty International, 1997. *'Just what do we have to do to stay alive?' – Colombia's Internally Displaced: Dispossessed and Exiled in Their Own Land* (AMR 23/48/97). London: Amnesty International.

An-Na'im, Abdullahi Ahmed, 1995. 'State Responsibility under International Human Rights Laws to Change Religious and Customary Laws', in Rebecca J. Cook, ed., *Human Rights of Women: National and International Perspectives*. Philadelphia, PA: University of Pennsylvania Press.

Anderson, Benedict, 1983. *Imagined Communities*. London: Verso.

Ardila, Edgar & Eva Irene Tuft, 1995. 'Children and Armed Conflict in Colombia', *Iberomericana: Nordic Journal of Latin American Studies*, vol. 25, nos 1 & 2, pp. 99–139.

Ardila, Ruben, 1996. 'Political Psychology: The Latin American Perspective', *Political Psychology*, vol. 17, no. 2, pp. 339–351.

Arendt, Hannah, 1963. *On Revolution*. New York: Viking.

Arendt, Hannah, 1969. *On Violence*. New York: Harcourt Brace.

Atkinson, Paul & Martyn Hammersley, 1994. 'Ethnography and Participant Observation,' pp. 248–261 in Norman K. Denzin & Yvonna S. Lincoln, eds, *Handbook of Qualitative Research*. London: Sage.

Bahovec, Eva Dolar, ed., 1991. *Splav: Pravica do izbora?* [*Abortion: Right to Choose?*], Ljubljana: Urad za zensko politiko [The Women's Group for Politics].

Bennett, Olivia, Jo Bexley & Kitty Warnock, 1995. *Arms to Fight, Arms to Protect: Women Speak Out about Conflict*. London: Panos.

Berg, Ellen Ziskind, 1994. 'Gendering Conflict Resolution', *Peace and Change*, vol. 19, no. 4, pp. 325–348.

Berger, Peter L. & Thomas Luckmann, 1966. *The Social Construction of Reality*. New York: Doubleday.

Bergman, Arlene Eiser, 1975. *Women of Vietnam*. San Francisco, CA: Peoples Press.

Bidwai, Praful, Harbans Mukhia & Achin Vanaik, eds, 1996. *Religion, Religiosity and Communalism*. New Delhi: Manohar.

Bohan, J.S., 1993. 'Regarding Gender: Essentialism, Constructionism and Feminist Psychology', *Psychology of Women Quarterly*, vol. 17, pp. 5–21.

Boman, Ann, 1987. *Varannan damernas: Slutbetänkande från Utredningen om kvin- norepresentation* (SOU 1987:19) [Every Other Slot to the Ladies: Final Report from the Secretary of Labour's Project on Women's Representation]. Stockholm: Allmänna förlag.

Boulding, Elise, 1976. *The Underside of History: A View of Women through Time*. Boulder, CO: Westview Press.

Boulding, Elise, 1981. 'Perspectives of Women Researchers on Disarmament, National Security, and World Order', *Women's Studies International Quarterly*, vol. 4, no. 1, pp. 27–40.

Boulding, Kenneth, 1989. *Three Faces of Power*. Newbury Park, CA: Sage.

Bourne, Jenny, 1987. 'Homelands of the Mind: Jewish Feminism and Identity Politics', *Race and Class*, vol. 19, no. 1, pp. 1–24.

Boutros-Ghali, Boutros, 1995. *An Agenda for Peace* (DPI/1623/PKO) (second edi- tion). New York: United Nations.

Bozinovic, Neda, 1996. *Zensko pitanje u Srbiji u 19. i 20. veku* [*The Women's Question in Serbia in the 19th and 20th Centuries*]. Belgrade: 94' – Zene u crnom.

Brock-Utne, Birgit, 1989a. *Feminine Perspectives on Peace and Peace Education*. New York: Pergamon Press.

Brock-Utne, Birgit, 1989b. 'Gender and Cooperation in the Laboratory', *Journal of Peace Research*, vol. 26, no. 1, pp. 47–56.

Brownmiller, Susan, 1975. *Against Our Will: Men, Women and Rape*. New York: Simon & Schuster.

Budimir, Milan, 1969. *Sa balkanskih istocnika* [*From Balkan Sources*]. Belgrade: SKZ.

Burguieres, Mary, 1990. 'Feminist Approaches to Peace: Another Step for Peace Studies', *Millennium*, vol. 19, no. 1, pp. 1–18.

Burr, Vivien, 1995. *An Introduction to Social Constructionism*. London: Routledge.

Bushnell, David, 1992. 'Politics and Violence in 19th Century Colombia', pp. 11–30 in Charles Bergquist, Ricardo Penaranda & Gonzalo Sanchez, eds, *Violence in Colombia: The Contemporary Crisis in Historical Perspective*. Washington, DC: SR Books.

Bustamante, Fernando, 1989. 'The Armed Forces of Colombia and Ecuador in Comparative Perspective', pp. 17–33 in Augusto Varas, ed., *Democracy under Siege: New Military Power in Latin America*. Westport, CT: Greenwood Press.

Butler, Judith, 1993. *Bodies That Matter*. London: Routledge.

Calhoun, Craig, 1991. 'The Problem of Identity in Collective Action', pp. 51–75 in Joan Huber, ed., *Macro-Micro Linkages in Sociology*. London: Sage.

Campbell, David, 1992. *Writing Security: United States Foreign Policy and the Politics of Identity*. Minneapolis, MN: University of Minnesota Press.

Carroll, Berenice, 1987. 'Feminism and Pacifism: Historical and Theoretical Connections', pp. 2–28 in Roach Pearson, ed., *Women and Peace*. London: Croom Helm.

Cassel, Joan, 1977. *A Group Called Women: Sisterhood and Symbolism in the Feminist Movement*. New York: McKay.

Castaño, Berta Lucia, 1992. *Alteraciones psicopatologicas observadas en victimas de la violencia sociopolitica en Colombia* [*Psychopathological Alterations Observed in Victims of Sociopolitical Violence in Colombia*]. Bogota: Universidad Nacional.

Castaño, Berta Lucia, 1993. 'El desplazamiento y sus consecuencias psicosociales' ['Displacement and its Psychosocial Consequences'], paper presented at 'Seminario sobre desplazamiento interno' [Seminar on Internal Displacement]. Lima.

Ceadel, Michael, 1987. *Thinking about Peace and War*. Oxford: Oxford University Press.

Centre for Women's Studies, 1995. *What Can We Do for Ourselves? East European Feminist Conference, Belgrade, June 1994*. Belgrade: Centre for Women's Studies.

Chandraprema, C.A., 1991. *Sri Lanka: The Years of Terror: The JVP Insurrection 1987–1989*. Colombo: Lake House Bookshop.

Chlapec-Djordjevic, Julka, 1932. *Jedno dopisivanje* [*A Correspondence*]. Belgrade: Zivot i rad.

Chlapec-Djordjevic, Julka, 1935. *Studije i eseji o feminizmu* [*Studies and Essays on Feminism*], vols 1 & 2. Belgrade: Zivot i rad.

Chowdhury, Najma, 1994. 'Bangladesh: Gender Issues and Politics in a Patriarchy', pp. 94–113 in Barbara J. Nelson & Najma Chowdhury, eds, *Women and Politics Worldwide*. New Haven, CT: Yale University Press.

Chowdhury, Neerja, 1996. *Indian Express*, 17 September, p. 4.

Coleman, Christopher C., 1993. *The Salvadoran Peace Process: A Preliminary Inquiry*, NUPI Research Report no. 173. Oslo: Norwegian Institute of International Affairs.

Collins, Patricia Hill, 1990. *Black Feminist Thought*. New York: Routledge.

Conferencia Episcopal de Colombia, 1994. *Estadisticas del desplazamiento interno* [*Statistics of Internal Displacement*]. Bogota: Unpublished report.

Connell, Robert William, 1995. *Masculinities*. Berkeley, CA: University of California Press.

Cooke, Miriam & Angela Woollacott, eds, 1993. *Gendering War Talk*. Princeton, NJ: Princeton University Press.

Coomaraswamy, Radhika, 1994. 'To Bellow Like a Cow: Women, Ethnicity, and the Discourse of Rights', pp. 39–57 in Rebecca J. Cook, ed., *Human Rights of Women: National and International Perspectives*. Philadelphia, PA: University of Pennsylvania Press.

Corporacion Maria Cano y ORFEDEC, 1993. *Mujer y desplazamiento en Cordoba* [*Woman and Displacement in Cordoba*]. Monteria: Unpublished working paper.

Corradi, Juan E., Patricia Weiss Fagan & Manuel Antonio Garreton, 1992. *Fear at the Edge: State Terror and Resistance in Latin America*. Berkeley, CA: University of California Press.

Dahlerup, Drude, 1978. 'Women's Entry into Politics: The Experience of the Danish Local and General Elections 1908–20', *Scandinavian Political Studies*, vol. 1, new series, nos 2 & 3, pp. 139–162.

Dahlerup, Drude, 1985. *Blomster og spark: Samtaler med kvindelige politikere i Norden om deres historiske rolle – og deres dagligdag* [*Flowers and Kicks: Conversations with Women Politicians in Nordic Countries*]. Copenhagen: Nordic Council of Ministers.

Dahlerup, Drude, 1987. 'Confusing Concepts – Confusing Reality: A Theoretical Discussion of the Patriarchal State', pp. 93–127 in Anne Showstack Sassoon, ed., *Women and the State: The Shifting Boundaries of Public and Private*. London: Hutchinson.

Dahlerup, Drude, 1988a. 'From a Small to a Large Minority: Women in Scandinavian Politics', *Scandinavian Political Studies*, vol. 11, no. 4, pp. 275–298.

Dahlerup, Drude, 1988b. '*Vi har ventet længe nok: Håndbog i kvinderepræsentation*' [*We Have Waited Long Enough: A Handbook for Women's Political Representation*]. Copenhagen: Nordic Council of Ministers.

Danner, Mark, 1998. 'The Killing Fields of Bosnia', *The New York Review of Books*, vol. 45, no. 14, pp. 63–77.

Davies, Bronwyn, 1990. 'The Problem of Desire', *Social Problems,* vol. 37, no. 4, pp. 501–516.

Davis, Angela Y., 1983. *Women, Race & Class.* New York: Vintage Books.

Derrida, Jacques, 1973. *Speech and Phenomena, and Other Essays on Husserl's Theory of Signs.* Evanston, IL: Northwestern University Press.

Derrida, Jacques, 1976. *Of Grammatology.* Baltimore, MD: Johns Hopkins University Press.

Dex, Shirley, 1985. *The Sexual Division of Work: Conceptual Revolutions in the Social Sciences.* Brighton: Wheatsheaf Books/Harvester Press.

Dix, Robert, 1980. 'Consociational Democracy: The Case of Colombia', *Comparative Politics,* vol. 12, April, pp. 303–321.

Dojcinovic-Necic, Biljana, 1996. 'Od zenskog pitanja do pisanja tela i dalje' ['From Women's Issues to Writing the Body and Beyond'], introduction to Biljana Dojcinovic-Necic, ed., *Izabrana dela iz feministicke teorije/feministicke studije 1974–1996* [*Selected Bibliography of Works in Feminist Theory/Feminist Studies 1974–1996*] (in Serbo-Croat and partly in English). Belgrade: Zenske Studije.

Duhacek, Daca, 1993. 'Women's Time in the Former Yugoslavia', pp. 131–138 in Nanette Funk & Magda Mueller, eds, *Gender, Politics and Post-Communism.* New York & London: Routledge.

Duncan, N. & K. O'Brien, 1983. *Women and Politics in Barbados, 1948–1981.* Cave Hill, Barbados: Institute of Social and Economic Research, Eastern Caribbean, University of the West Indies.

Eduards, Maud Landby & Gertrud Åström, 1993. *Många kände sig manade, men få blevo kallade: En granskning av arbetet för ökad kvinnorepresentation* [*Many Were Called, But Few Were Chosen: An Analysis of the Attempts to Increase Women's Representation*]. Stockholm: Ministry of Social Affairs.

Elshtain, Jean Bethke, 1982. 'Women as Mirror and Other: Towards a Theory of Women, War, and Feminism', *Humanities in Society,* vol. 5, nos 1 & 2, pp. 29–44.

Elshtain, Jean Bethke, 1987. *Women and War.* New York: Basic Books.

Enloe, Cynthia, 1983. *Does Khaki Become You? The Militarization of Women's Lives.* London: Pluto Press.

Enloe, Cynthia, 1990. *Bananas, Beaches and Bases: Making Feminist Sense of International Politics.* London: Pandora Press.

Enloe, Cynthia, 1993. *The Morning After: Sexual Politics at the End of the Cold War.* Berkeley, CA: University of California Press.

Fischer, Kurt W. & Arlyne Lazerson, 1984. *Human Development: From Conception through Adolescence.* New York: W. H. Freeman.

Fluker, Walter, 1989. *They Look for a City.* New York: University Press of America.

Foucault, Michel, 1980. 'Truth and Power', pp. 109–133 in Colin Gordon, ed., *Power/Knowledge: Selected Interviews and Other Writings 1972–1977.* New York: Pantheon.

Foucault, Michel, 1981. *The History of Sexuality.* Harmondsworth: Pelican.

Gairdner, David & Eva Irene Tuft, 1995. 'Human Rights in Colombia', pp. 153–202 in Peter Baehr, Hilde Hey, Jacqueline Smith & Theresa Swinehart, eds, *Human Rights in Developing Countries: Yearbook 1995.* The Hague: Kluwer Law International.

Garreton, Manuel Antonio, 1995. 'Redemocratization in Chile', *Journal of Democracy,* vol. 6, no. 1, pp. 146–158.

Geertz, Cifford, 1973. *The Interpretation of Cultures.* New York: Harper Collins.

Gellner, Ernest, 1983. *Nations and Nationalism.* Oxford: Blackwell.

Gergen, Kenneth J., 1994. *Realities and Relationships: Soundings in Social Construction.* Cambridge, MA: Harvard University Press.

Giddens, Anthony, 1991. *Modernity and Self-Identity.* Stanford, CA: Stanford University Press.

Gierycz, Dorota, 1996. 'Frieden durch Gleichberechtigung? Zur Demokratisierung durch Gleichberechtigung der Geschlechter' ['Peace through Equal Rights? On Democratization through Gender Equality'], pp. 369–383 in Wolfgang R. Vogt, ed., *Frieden durch Zivilisierung? [Peace through Civilization?]*, vol. 1. Munster: Agenda Verlag.

Gilligan, Carol, 1982. *In a Different Voice: Psychological Theory and Women's Development*. Cambridge, MA: Harvard University Press.

Gray, Francine du Plessix, 1990. *Soviet Women: Walking the Tightrope*. New York: Doubleday.

Greenfeld, Liah, 1992. *Nationalism: Five Roads to Modernity*. Cambridge, MA: Harvard University Press.

Gunaratne, Rohan, 1990. *Sri Lanka: A Lost Revolution? The Inside Story of the JVP*. Kandy: Institute of Fundamental Studies.

Gurr, Ted Robert, 1995. *Minorities at risk: A Global View of Ethnopolitical Conflicts*. Washington, DC: United States Institute of Peace Press.

Gutierrez, Diana, 1993. *Acerca de la violencia politica en los ninos desplazados [On the Political Violence against Displaced Children]*. Bogota: Unpublished working paper.

Gutman, Roy, 1993. *A Witness to Genocide: The 1993 Pulitzer Prize-winning Dispatches on the 'Ethnic Cleansing' of Bosnia*. New York: Macmillan.

Hacker, Helen Mayer, 1952. 'Women as a Minority Group', *Social Forces*, vol. 30, no. 1, pp. 60–69.

Halvorsen, Marit, 1992. 'The Role of Women in Building Democracy in Europe: Theory and Practice', pp. 29–44 in *The Democratic Principle of Equal Representation: Forty Years of Council of Europe Activity: Proceedings of the Seminar, Strasbourg, 6 and 7 November 1989*. Strasbourg: Council of Europe.

Hare-Mustin, Rachel T. & Jeanne Marececk, 1988. 'The Meaning of Difference', *American Psychologist*, vol. 43, no. 6, pp. 455–464.

Harris, Adrienne, 1989. 'Bringing Artemis to Life: A Plea for Militancy and Aggression in Feminist Peace Politics', pp. 93–113 in Adrienne Harris & Ynestra King, eds, *Rocking the Ship of State: Towards a Feminist Peace Politics*. Boulder, CO: Westview Press.

Harris, Adrienne & Ynestra King, eds, 1989. *Rocking the Ship of State: Towards a Feminist Peace Politics*. Boulder, CO: Westview Press.

Hartlyn, Jonathan, 1988. *The Politics of Coalition Rule in Colombia*. New York: Cambridge University Press.

Hartsock, Nancy, 1989. 'Masculinity, Heroism, and the Making of War', pp. 133–152 in Adrienne Harris & Ynestra King, eds, *Rocking the Ship of State: Towards a Feminist Peace Politics*. Boulder, CO: Westview Press.

Hedlund, Gun, 1996. *'Det handlar om prioriteringer': kvinnors villkor och interessen i lokal politik*. Göteborg Studies in Politics 35, Ørebro Studies 14, Göteborgs universitet, Göteborg.

Herman, Judith Lewis, 1992. *Trauma and Recovery*. New York: Basic Books.

Hernes, Helga Marie, 1984. *The Situation of Women in the Political Process in Europe, Part III: The Role of Women in Voluntary Associations and Organisations*. Strasbourg: Council of Europe.

Herzfeld, Michael, 1985. *Ours Once More: The Making of Modern Greece*. Austin, TX: University of Texas Press.

Higonnet, Margaret Randolph & Jane Jenson, eds, 1987. *Behind the Lines: Gender and the Two World Wars*. New Haven, CT: Yale University Press.

Hingorani, Anand, ed., 1970. *The Selected Writings of Mahatma Gandhi*. Bombay: Bharatiya Vidya Bhavan.

Hobsbawm, Eric & Terence Ranger, eds, 1983. *The Invention of Tradition*. Cambridge: Cambridge University Press.

Hogg, Michael A. & Dominic Abrams, 1988. *Social Identifications*. London & New York: Routledge.

Holloway, Karla C., 1992. *Moorings and Metaphors: Figures of Culture and Gender in Black Women's Literature*. New Brunswick, NJ: Rutgers University Press.

Holst-Warhaft, Gail, 1992. *Dangerous Voices: Women's Laments and Greek Literature*. New York: Routledge.

hooks, bell, 1984. *Feminist Theory: From Margin to Center*. Boston, MA: South End Press.

Horowitz, David, 1985. *Ethnic Groups in Conflict*. Berkeley, CA: University of California Press.

Howlett, Jana & Rod Mengham, eds, 1994. *The Violent Muse: Violence and the Artistic Imagination in Europe, 1910–1939*. Manchester: Manchester University Press.

Human Rights Watch, 1996. *Shattered Lives: Sexual Violence during the Rwandan Genocide and its Aftermath*. New York: Human Rights Watch.

Huntington, Samuel, 1993. 'The Clash of Civilizations?', *Foreign Affairs*, vol. 72, no. 3, pp. 22–49.

Huntington, Samuel, 1997. *The Clash of Civilizations and the Remaking of World Order*. New York: Simon & Schuster.

Instituto Interamericano de Derechos Humanos [Inter-American Institute of Human Rights], 1992. *La Migracion en Centroamerica, 1980–1990* [*Migration in Central America, 1980–1990*]. Series: *Exodos en America Latina* [*Emigration in Latin America*], no. 7. San José: Instituto Interamericano de Derechos Humanos.

Inter-Parliamentary Union, 1994. *Plan of Action to Correct Present Imbalances in the Participation of Men and Women in Political Life*. Series: *Reports and Documents*, no. 22. Geneva: International Centre for Parliamentary Documentation.

Inter-Parliamentary Union, 1995a. 'Number of Women Decreases in World Parliaments despite 50 Year Upward Trend', 27 August 1995, no. 50.

Inter-Parliamentary Union, 1995b. *Women in Parliaments 1945–1988: A World Statistical Survey*. Series: *Reports and Documents*, no. 23. Geneva: International Centre for Parliamentary Documentation.

Inter-Parliamentary Union, 1996. *Women in Parliaments, as of October 1996: Worldwide Projections*. Geneva: Inter-Parliamentary Union.

Inter-Parliamentary Union, 1997. *Men and Women in Politics: Democracy Still in the Making: A World Comparative Study*. Series: *Reports and Documents*, no. 28. Geneva: International Centre for Parliamentary Documentation.

Jahan, Rounaq, 1995. *The Elusive Agenda: Mainstreaming Women in Development*. London: Zed Books/Dhaka: University Press.

Jancar, Barbara, 1981. 'Women in the Yugoslav National Liberation Movement: An Overview', *Studies in Comparative Communism*, vol. 14, pp. 143–164.

Jaquette, Jane S., 1991. 'Introduction', pp. 1–17 in Jane S. Jaquette, ed., *The Women's Movement in Latin America: Feminism and the Transition to Democracy*. Boulder, CO: Westview Press.

Jones, Ann, 1991. *Women Who Kill*. London: Gollancz.

Justicia y Paz, Comision Intercongregacional [Justice and Peace, Intercongrational Commission], 1994. *Justicia y Paz*, vol. 7, no. 2, Bogota.

Kacic, Biljana, ed., 1997. *Women and the Politics of Peace*. Zagreb: Centre for Women's Studies.

Kanter, Rosabeth Moss, 1977. *Men and Women of the Corporation*. New York: Basic Books.

Kaplan, Gisela, 1997. 'Comparative Europe: Feminism and Nationalism: The European Case', pp. 3–40 in Lois A. West, ed., *Feminist Nationalism*. London: Routledge.

Karadzic, Vuk Stefanovic, 1818. *Srpski rjecnik: Istumacen nemackijem i latinskijem rijecima* [*Serbian German–Latin Dictionary*]. Belgrade: Stamparije Kralevine Jugoslavije, 1935.

Kaushik, Sushila, 1995. *Panchayati Raj in Action: Challenges to Women's Role*. New Delhi: Fredrich Ebert Siftung.

King, Martin Luther, 1964. *Why We Can't Wait*. New York: New American Library.

King, Ynestra, 1989. 'Afterword: If I Can't Dance Your Revolution, I'm Not Coming', pp. 281–298 in Adrienne Harris & Ynestra King, eds, *Rocking the Ship of State: Towards a Feminist Peace Politics*. Boulder, CO: Westview Press.

Klein, Viola, 1946. *The Feminine Character: History of an Ideology*. London: Routledge and Kegan Paul.

Kolb, Deborah M. & Gloria G. Coolidge, 1988. 'Her Place at the Table: A Consideration of Gender Issues in Negotiation', *Harvard Program on Negotiation Working Paper Series*; reprinted, pp. 261–278 in William J. Breslin & Jeffrey Z. Rubin, eds, 1995. *Negotiation Theory and Practice*. Cambridge, MA: Program on Negotiation at Harvard Law School.

Kommisjonen for de Europæiske Fællesskaber, 1987. Euro-barometer: den Offentlige Mening i det Europæiske Fællesskab. Nr. 28, December.

Kuhn, Thomas, 1962. *The Structure of Scientific Revolutions*. Chicago, IL: University of Chicago Press.

Kumar, Krishna, 1997. 'The Nature and Focus of International Assistance for Rebuilding War-torn Societies', pp. 1–38 in Krishna Kumar, ed., *Rebuilding Societies after Civil War: Critical Roles for International Assistance*. Boulder, CO: Lynne Rienner.

Lerner, Gerda, 1986. *The Creation of Patriarchy*. Oxford: Oxford University Press.

Licht, Sonja & Slobodan Draculic, 1996. 'When the Word for Peacenik was Woman: War and Gender in the Former Yugoslavia', pp. 111–141 in Barbara Weinert, Metta Spencer & Slobodan Draculic, eds, *Women in Post-communism*, vol. 2. Greenwich, CT & London: JAI Press.

Liga Internacional por los Derechos y la Liberación de los Pueblos, Seccion Colombiana [International League for the People's Rights and Liberation, Colombian Section], 1990. *El Camino de la niebla* [*The Foggy Road*], vols 2 & 3. Bogota: LIDERLIP.

Liga Internacional por los Derechos y la Liberación de los Pueblos, Seccion Colombiana, 1991. *Proceso a la impunidad de crimenes de lesa humanidad en America Latina, 1989–1991* [*Case against the Impunity of Crimes against Humanity in Latin America 1989 – 1991*], Bogota: LIDERLIP.

Lippa, Richard, A., 1990. *Introduction to Social Psychology*. Belmont, CA: Wadsworth.

Little, Alan & Laura Silber, 1995. *Yugoslavia: Death of a Nation*. New York: Penguin.

Loraux, Nicole, 1989. *Les Expériences de Tirésias: Le féminin et l'homme grec*. Paris: Gallimard.

Lord, Albert, 1960. *The Singer of Tales*. Cambridge, MA: Harvard University Press.

Lord, Audre, 1997. 'Age, Race, Class, and Sex: Women Redefining the Difference', pp. 374–380 in Anne McClintock, Aamir Mufti & Ella Shohat, eds, *Dangerous Liaisons: Gender, Nation, and Postcolonial Perspectives*. Minneapolis, MN: University of Minnesota Press.

Lyotard, Jean-François, 1978. *The Postmodern Condition: A Report on Knowledge*. Minneapolis, MN: University of Minnesota Press.

Macksound, Mona, 1993. *Helping Children Cope with Stresses of War*. New York: UNICEF.

MacLean, J., 1987. *Prolonging the Agony: The Human Cost of Low Intensity Warfare in El Salvador*. London: El Salvador Committee for Human Rights.

Marcellino, Alex, Everett M. Ressler & Joanne Marie Tortorici, 1993. *Children in War: A Guide to the Provision of Services* (NYHQ/G0013). New York: UNICEF.

Marlowe, David, 1983. 'The Manning of the Force and the Structure of the Battle: Men and Women', in Robert K. Fullinwider, ed., *Conscripts and Volunteers: Military Requirements, Social Justice, and the All-Volunteer Force*. Totowa, NJ: Rowman & Allenheld.

Marr, Andrew, 1998. 'One year on, has Britain changed?' *Guardian Weekly*, 30 August, p. 13.

Martinez, Thomas Eloy, 1997. 'Slaughter, Then Silence in Colombian Villages', *International Herald Tribune*, 18 June.

Mason, Gregory, 1995. 'Some Implications of Postmodernism for the Field of Peace Studies', *Peace and Change*, vol. 20, no. 1, pp. 120–131.

Maunaguru, Sitralega, 1995. 'Gendering Tamil Nationalism: The Construction of "Woman" in Projects of Protest and Control', pp. 158–175 in Pradeep Jeganathan & Qadri Ismail, eds, *Unmaking the Nation: The Politics of Identity and History in Modern Sri Lanka*. Colombo: Social Scientists' Association.

Maynard, Kimberly A., 1997. 'Rebuilding Community: Psychosocial Healing, Reintegration, and Reconciliation at the Grassroots Level', pp. 203–226 in Krishna Kumar, ed., *Rebuilding Societies after Civil War: Critical Roles for International Assistance*. Boulder, CO & London: Lynne Rienner.

Mead, George H., 1934. *Mind, Self and Society: From the Standpoint of a Social Behaviourist*, edited and with an introduction by Charles W. Morris. Chicago, IL: Chicago University Press.

Meznaric, Silva, 1994. 'Gender as an Ethno-marker: Rape, War and Identity in the Former Yugoslavia', pp. 76–97 in Valentine M. Moghadam, ed., *Identity Politics and Women: Cultural Reassertion and Feminism in International Perspective*. Boulder, CO: Westview Press.

Milic, Ancelka, 1993. 'Women and Nationalism in the Former Yugoslavia', pp. 109–123 in Nanette Funk & Magda Mueller, eds, *Gender Politics and Post-Communism*. London & New York: Routledge.

Miller, Errol, 1991. *Men at Risk*. Kingston: Jamaica Publishing House.

Miller, Errol, 1994. *Marginalization of the Black Male*. Kingston: Canoe Press.

Minh-ha, Trink T., 1997. 'Not You/Like You: Postcolonial Women and the Interlocking Questions of Identity and Difference', pp. 415–419 in Anne McClintock, Aamir Mufti & Ella Shohat, eds, *Dangerous Liaisons: Gender, Nation, and Postcolonial Perspectives*. Minneapolis, MN: University of Minnesota Press.

Mohanty, Bidyut, 1999. 'Panchyat Raj Institutions and Women', pp. 19-33 in Bharati Ray and Aparna Basu, eds, *From Independence Towards Freedom, Indian Women Since 1947*. New Delhi: Oxford University Press.

Molyneux, Maxine, 1985. 'Mobilization without Emancipation: Women's Interests, the State, and Revolution in Nicaragua', *Feminist Studies*, vol. 11, no. 2, pp. 227–254.

Montgomery, Tommi Sue, 1982. *Revolution in El Salvador: Origin and Evolution*. Boulder, CO: Westview Press.

Moreno, Florentino, 1991. *Infancia y guerra en Centroamerica* [*Childhood and War in Central America*]. San José: FLACSO.

Mossé, Claude, 1983. *La femme dans la Grèce antique*. Paris: Albin Michel.

Mostov, Julie, 1995. '"Our Women"/"Their Women": Symbolic Boundaries, Territorial Markers and Violence in the Balkans', *ProFemina*, no. 3, pp. 210–219.

Mumtaz, Khawar, 1996. 'The Gender Dimension in Sindh's Ethnic Conflict', pp. 144–163 in Kumar Rupesinghe & Khawar Mumtaz, eds, *Internal Conflicts in South Asia*. London: Sage.

Newport, Frank, 1995. 'Majority Still Approves Use of Atom Bombs on Japan in World War II', *Gallup Poll Monthly*, August, p. 2.

Nikolic-Ristanovic, V. et al., 1995. *Zene, nasilje i rat* [*Women, Violence and War*]. Belgrade: Institut za kriminoloska i socioloska istrazivanja.

Osorio Perez, Floraldina, 1993. *La Violencia del silencio: Desplazados del campo a la ciudad* [*The Violence of Silence: Displaced from the Countryside to the City*]. Bogota: CODHES, Universidad Javeriana.

Pandey, Gyanendra, ed., 1993. *Hindus and Others: The Question of Identity in India Today*. New Delhi: Viking, Penguin.

Pantel, Pauline Schmitt, ed., 1992. *From Ancient Goddesses to Christian Saints*, vol. 1 in Georges Duby & Michelle Perrot, eds, *A History of Women in the West*. Cambridge, MA: Belknap Press of Harvard University Press.

Papic, Zarana, 1999. 'Strategies of Women's Resistance: Women and Women's Networks in Serbia', in Sabrina P. Ramet, ed., *Gender Politics in the Western Balkans: Women, Society and Politics in Yugoslavia and the Yugoslav Successor States*. University Park, PA: Pennsylvania State University Press.

Parker, Robert, 1983. *Miasma: Pollution and Purification in Early Greek Religion*. Oxford and New York: Oxford University Press.

Pearce, Jenny, 1990. *Colombia: Inside the Labyrinth*. London: Latin America Bureau.

Pécaut, Daniel, 1987. *Orden y violencia: Colombia 1930–1954* [*Order and Violence: Colombia 1930–1954*], vols 1 & 2. Bogota: Siglo Veintiuno Editores.

Pecic, Vesna V., 1991. 'The Impact of Reforms on the Status of Women in Yugoslavia', paper presented at the Regional Seminar on the Impact of Economic and Political Reform on the Status of Women in Eastern Europe and USSR: The Role of National Machinery. Vienna.

Peeler, John A., 1992. 'Elite Settlements and Democratic Consolidation: Colombia, Costa Rica, and Venezuela', pp. 81–112 in John Higley & Richard Gunther, eds, *Elites and Democratic Consolidation in Latin America and Southern Europe*. Cambridge: Cambridge University Press.

Pérez, Diego, 1993. 'Los aspectos sicosociales de la violencia politica' ['Psychosocial Aspects of Political Violence'], *UTOPIAS*, no. 8.

Pettman, Jan Jindy, 1996. *Worlding Women: A Feminist International Politics*. St Leonards, Australia: Allen and Unwin.

Popov, Nebojsa, ed., 1990. *Kosovski cvor: Dresiti ili seci? [The Kosovo Knot: To Unravel or to Cut? Report of the Independent Commission]*. Titograd: Pobjeda.

Procuraduría General de la Nación [Attorney General's office], 1994. *III Informe sobre derechos humanos en Colombia [Third Report on Human Rights in Colombia]*. Bogota: Procuraduria General de la Nacion.

Proenza, Anne, 1997. 'Thousands Flee Fighting in Colombia', *Guardian Weekly*, 1 June, p. 13.

Reardon, Betty A., 1985. *Sexism and the War System*. New York: Syracuse University Press.

Reardon, Betty A., 1993. *Women and Peace: Feminist Visions of Global Security*. Albany, NY: State University of New York Press.

Reddock, Rhoda Elizabeth, 1994. *Women, Labour & Politics in Trinidad & Tobago: A History*. Kingston: Ian Randle Publishers.

Renan, Ernest, 1882. 'What is a Nation?', pp. 8–22 in Homi K. Bhabha, ed., 1990. *Nation and Narration*. London: Routledge.

Restrepo, Luis Alberto, 1992. 'The Crisis of the Current Political Regime and its Possible Outcomes', pp. 273–292 in Charles Bergquist, Ricardo Penaranda & Gonzalo Sanchez, eds, *Violence in Colombia: The Contemporary Crisis in Historical Perspective*. Washington, DC: SR Books.

Rihtman, Dunja Auguctin, ed., 1996. *Konji, zene, ratovi [Horses, Women, Wars]*. Zagreb: Druga.

Rosellini, Michèle, Suzanne Saïd & Danièle Auger, 1979. *Aristophane: Les femmes et la cité*. Fontenay-aux-roses: E. N. S.

Rubenstein, Richard E. & Jarle Crocker, 1994. 'Challenging Huntington', *Foreign Policy*, no. 96, pp. 113-128.

Ruddick, Sara, 1983. 'Pacifying the Forces: Drafting Women on the Interests of Peace', *Signs: Journal of Women in Culture and Society*, vol. 8, no. 3, pp. 471–490.

Ruddick, Sara, 1989a. *Maternal Thinking: Toward a Politics of Peace*. Boston, MA: Beacon Press.

Ruddick, Sara, 1989b. 'The Rationality of Care', pp. 229–254 in Jean Bethke Elshtain & Sheila Tobias, eds, *Women, Militarism, and War: Essays in History, Politics, and Social Theory*. Lanham, MD: Rowman & Littlefield.

Sánchez, Gonzalo, 1992. 'The Violence: An Interpretative Synthesis', pp. 75-124 in Charles Bergquist, Ricardo Penaranda, Gonzalo Sanchez, eds, *Violence in*

Colombia: The Contemporary Crisis in Historical Perspective. Washington, DC: SR Books.

Sarkar, Tanika, 1996. 'Hindu Women: Politicization Through Communalism', pp. 131–143 in Kumar Rupesinghe & Khawar Mumtaz, eds, *Internal Conflicts in South Asia*. London: Sage.

Sayer, Andrew, 1997. 'Essentialism, Social Constructionism, and Beyond', *The Sociological Review*, vol. 45, no. 3, pp. 453–487.

Segal, Lynne, 1987. *Is the Future Female? Troubled Thoughts on Contemporary Feminism*. New York: Peter Bendrick Books.

Sellström, Tor & Lennart Wohlgemuth, 1996. 'Historical Perspective: Some Explanatory Factors', vol. 1 in David Millwood, ed., *The International Response to Conflict and Genocide: Lessons from the Rwanda Experience*. Copenhagen: Joint Evaluation of Emergency Assistance to Rwanda.

Sharp, Gene, 1973. *The Politics of Nonviolent Action*. Boston, MA: Porter Sargent.

Showalter, Elaine, 1988. 'Feminist Criticism in the Wilderness', pp. 330–353 in David Lodge, ed., *Modern Criticism and Theory*. London: Longman.

Sivard, R.L., 1996. *World Military and Social Expenditures* (16th edition). Washington, DC: World Priorities.

Skjeie, Hege, 1991a. 'The Rhetoric of Difference: On Women's Inclusion into Political Elites', *Politics and Society*, no. 2, pp. 233–263.

Skjeie, Hege, 1991b. 'From Movements to Governments: Two Decades of Norwegian Feminist Influence', *New Left Review*, no. 187, May/June, pp. 79–102.

Skjeie, Hege, 1992. *The Political Meaning of Gender*. Oslo: Institute for Social Research.

Skjelsbæk, Inger, 1997. *Gendered Battlefields: A Gender Analysis of Peace and Conflict*. Oslo: International Peace Research Institute, PRIO Report 6/97.

Sklevicky, Lydia, 1980. 'Ka antropologiji zena' ['Towards the Anthropology of Women'], *Review of Sociology*, no. 10, pp. 29–46.

Sklevicky, Lydia, 1984. *'Zene i moc'* ['Women and Power'], unpublished PhD thesis. Zagreb: Department of Philosophy, University of Zagreb.

Sklevicky, Lydia, ed., 1987. *Zene i drustvo* [*Woman and Society*]. Zagreb: Sociologists' Association of Croatia.

Sklevicky, Lydia, 1996a. 'Pokret i poredak' ['The Movement and the Order'], pp. 107–115 in Dunja Auguctin Rihtman, ed., *Konji, zene, ratori* [*Horses, Women, Wars*]. Zagreb: Druga.

Sklevicky, Lydia, 1996b. 'Organizacijiska struktura AFZ' ['The Organizational Structure of the AFZ'], pp. 115–154 in Dunja Auguctin Rihtman, ed., *Konji, zene, ratori* [*Horses, Women, Wars*]. Zagreb: Druga.

Sklevicky, Lydia & Zarana Papic, eds, 1983. *Antropologija zene* [Anthropology of Woman]. Belgrade: Prosveta.

Slapsak, Svetlana, 1994. 'The Mechanism of Producing Stereoptypes' (Part 1), pp. 11–31 in *Ogledi obezbriznosti* [*Essays on Carelessness*]. Belgrade: Apatridi – Radio B 92.

Slapsak, Svetlana, 1996. 'Between the Vampire Husband and the Mortal Lover', pp. 201–224 in Barbara Weiner, Metta Spencer & Slobodan Drakulic, eds, *Women in Post-Communism*, vol. 2. London: JAI Press.

Slapsak, Svetlana, 1997a. '"What Are Women Made Of?" Inventing Women in the Yugoslav Area', pp. 358–373 in Gisela Brinker-Gabler & Sidonie Smith, eds, *Writing New Identities: Gender, Nation, Immigration in Contemporary Europe*. Minneapolis, MN: University of Minnesota Press.

Slapsak, Svetlana, 1997b. 'The Mechanism of Producing Stereoptypes' (Part 2), pp. 41–59 in *Ratni Kandid* [*Wartime Candide*]. Belgrade: Rat i mir – Radio B 92.

Smith, Anthony D., 1971. *Theories of Nationalism*. London: Duckworth.

Smith, Anthony D., 1986. *The Ethnic Origins of Nations*. Oxford: Basil Blackwell.

Smith, Anthony, 1987. *The Ethnic Origin of Nations*. Oxford: Basil Blackwell.

Smith, Dan, 1997a. 'Language and Discourse in Conflict and Conflict resolution', *Current Issues in Language and Society*, vol. 4, no. 3, pp. 190-214.

Smith, Dan, 1997b. *The State of War and Peace Atlas*. London: Penguin.

Smith, Dan & Øyvind Østerud, 1995. *Nation-State, Nationalism and Political Identity*. Arena Working Paper No. 3 (Oslo, Advanced Research on the Europeanisation of the Nation-State, University of Oslo).

South Asia Regional Perspective, 1994. *South Asia Vision and Perspective*. Lahore: Mubashir Hasan.

Spender, Dale, 1982. *Women of Ideas and What Men Have Done to Them*. London: Routledge and Kegan Paul.

Steihm, Judith, 1983. 'The Protector, the Protected, and the Defended', in Judith Stiehm, ed., *Women and Men's Wars*. Oxford: Pergamon Press.

Stiglmayer, Alexandra, ed., 1996. *Mass Rape: The War against Women in Bosnia-Herzegovina*. Foreword by Roy Gutman. Lincoln, NE: University of Nebraska Press.

Styrkársdóttir, Audur, 1986. 'From Social Movement to Political Party: The New Women's Movement in Iceland', pp. 140–157 in Drude Dahlerup, ed., *The New Women's Movement: Feminism and Political Power in Europe and the USA*. London: Sage.

Tax, Meredith, 1993. 'Five Women Who Won't Be Silenced', *The Nation*, 10 May, pp. 624–625.

Tax, Meredith & Marjorie Agosin, 1995. *The Power of the Word: Culture, Censorship, and Voice*. New York: Women's World.

Tickner, Ann J., 1992. *Gender in International Relations: Feminist Perspectives on Achieving Global Security*. New York: Columbia University Press.

Tickner, Ann J., 1994. 'Feminist Perspectives on Peace and World Security in the Post-Cold War Era', pp. 43–54 in Michael T. Klare, ed., *Peace and World Security Studies: A Curriculum Guide*. Boulder, CO: Lynne Rienner.

Tishkov, Valery, 1997. *Ethnicity, Nationalism and Conflict in and after the Soviet Union: The Mind Aflame*. London: Sage.

Tolstoy, Leo, 1987. *Writings on Civil Disobedience and Nonviolence*. Philadelphia, PA: New Society Publishers.

Tomin, Svetlana, 1995. 'Radmila S. Petrovic (1908–1932)', *ProFemina*, no. 3, pp. 72–103.

Tomin, Svetlana & Svetlana Slapsak, 1996. 'Knjizevna proslost: kontinuitet i diskontinuitet – Julka Chlapec-Djordjevic' ['Literary Past: Continuity and Discontinuity – Julka Chlapec Djordjevic'], *ProFemina*, no. 5 & 6, pp. 81–104.

Trujillo, Elsa Blair, 1993. *Las Fuerzas armadas: Una mirada civil* [*The Armed Forces: A Civilian View*]. Bogota: Cine.

United Nations, 1948. 'Universal Declaration on the Human Rights' in Centre for Human Rights, Geneva, ed., 1993. *Human Rights: A Compilation of International Instruments*, vol. 1, ST/HR/1/Rev.4. New York: United Nations.

United Nations, 1966. 'International Covenant on Civil and Political Rights' in Centre for Human Rights, Geneva, ed., 1993. *Human Rights: A Compilation of International Instruments*, vol. 1, ST/HR/1/Rev.4. New York: United Nations.

United Nations, 1985. *The Nairobi Forward-looking Strategies for the Advancement of Women*. Adopted by the World Conference to Review and Appraise the Achievements of the United Nations Decade for Women: Equality, Development and Peace, Nairobi, 15–16 July 1985. New York: United Nations.

United Nations, 1988. *Access to Information and Education for Peace*. Report of the Secretary-General, 29 December 1987, E/CN.6/1988/5. New York: United Nations.

United Nations, 1989a. *Full Participation of Women in the Construction of Their Countries and in the Creation of Just Social and Political Systems*. Report of the Secretary-General, 20 January 1989, E/CN.6/1989/7. New York: United Nations.

United Nations, 1989b. *Progress at the National, Regional and International Levels in the Implementation of the Nairobi Forward-looking Strategies for the Advancement of Women*. Report of the Secretary-General, E/CN.6/1990/5. New York: United Nations.

United Nations, 1990. *Equality in Political Participation and Decision-making*. Report of the Secretary-General, 13 December 1989, E/CN.6/1990/2. New York: United Nations.

United Nations, 1992. *Equal Participation in All Efforts to Promote International Cooperation, Peace, and Disarmament*. Report of the Secretary-General, 12 December 1991, E/CN.6/1992/10. New York: United Nations.

United Nations, 1993a. *Women and the Peace Process*. Report of the Secretary-General, 28 December 1992, E/CN.6/1993/4. New York: United Nations.

United Nations, 1993b. *The Nairobi Forward-looking Strategies for the Advancement of Women*, DPI/926-41761. New York: United Nations.

United Nations, 1995a. *Looking Back Moving Forward: Second Review and Appraisal of the Implementation of the Nairobi Forward-looking Strategies for the Advancement of Women*, E.95.IV. New York: United Nations.

United Nations, 1995b. *Internally Displaced Persons*. Report of the representative of the Secretary-General, Mr Francis M. Deng (E/CN.4/1995/50). New York: United Nations.

United Nations, 1995c. *Participation of Women in Political Life and Decision-making*. Report of the Secretary-General, E/CN.6/1995/12. New York: United Nations.

United Nations, 1995d. *Peace: Women in International Decision-making*. Report of the Secretary-General, E/CN.6/1995/12. New York: United Nations.

United Nations, 1995e. *The World's Women 1995: Trends and Statistics*, E.95.XVII.2. New York: United Nations.

United Nations, 1996a. *The Beijing Declaration and the Platform for Action*. Fourth World Conference on Women, Beijing, China, 4–15 September 1995, DPI/1766/Wom. New York: United Nations, Department of Public Information.

United Nations, 1996b. 'The Beijing Declaration', pp. 5–8 in *Report of the Fourth World Conference of Women*, A/CONF.177/20. New York: United Nations.

United Nations, 1996c. 'Platform for Action of the Fourth World Conference on Women', pp. 9–135 in *Report of the Fourth World Conference of Women*, A/CONF.177/20. New York: United Nations.

United Nations, 1996d. *Convention on the Elimination of All Forms of Discrimination against Women*. New York: United Nations.

United Nations, 1996e. *Implementation of the Outcome of the Fourth World Conference on Women*. Report of the Secretary-General, A/51/322. New York: United Nations.

United Nations/Department for Policy Coordination and Sustainable Development/Branch for the Advancement of Women, 1995. *Women 2000: The Role of Women in United Nations Peace-keeping*. Vienna: United Nations/Centre for Social Development and Humanitarian Affairs/Branch for the Advancement of Women.

United Nations Centre for Social Development and Humanitarian Affairs, 1992. *Women in Politics and Decision-making in the Late Twentieth Century*. Dordrecht: Martinus Nijhoff.

United Nations Division for the Advancement of Women, 1994. *Gender and the Agenda for Peace*. Expert Group Meeting in New York, 5–9 December, GAP/1994/WP.6.

United Nations Economic and Social Council, 1994. 'Situation of Human Rights in the Territory of the Former Yugoslavia'. Report submitted by Mr Tadeusz Mazowiecki, Special Rapporteur of the Commission on Human Rights, 21 February, E/CN.4/1994/110

UNDAW & PRIO, Oslo, 1996. *Political Decision-making and Conflict Resolution: The Impact of Gender Difference*. Expert Group Meeting in Santo Domingo, Dominican Republic, 7–11 October 1996, EGM/PRDC/1996/REP.1. New York: United Nations Division for the Advancement of Women.

United Nations High Commissioner for Refugees, 1993. *The State of World's Refugees: The Challenge of Protection*. Harmondsworth: Penguin.

United Nations International Research and Training Institute for the Advancement of Women, 1995. *Gender Concepts in Developing Planning: Basic Approach*, INSTRAW/Ser.B/50. Santo Domingo: INSTRAW.

Uprimny & Vargas Castaño, 1990. 'La palabra y la sangre: Violencia, legalidad y guerra sucia' ['The Word and the Blood: Violence, Legality and Dirty War'], pp. 118–130 in German Palacio, ed., *La Irrupcion del paraestado: Ensayos sobre la crisis colombiana* [*The Irruption of the Para-state: Essays on the Colombian Crisis*]. Bogota: ILSA & CEREC.

Uyangoda, Jayadeva, 1996. 'Militarization, Violent State, Violent Society: Sri Lanka', in Kumar Rupesinghe & Khawar Mumtaz, eds, *Internal Conflicts in South Asia*. London: Sage.

Walby, Sylvia, 1990. *Theorizing Patriarchy*. Oxford: Basil Blackwell.

Wall, Victor D. Jr. & Marcia L. Dewhurst, 1991. 'Mediator Gender: Communication Differences in Resolved and Unresolved Mediations', *Mediation Quarterly*, vol. 9, no. 1, pp. 63–85.

Wangerud, Lina, 1998. *The Second Face of Democracy: Women's Representation in the Swedish Parliament*.

Warnock, Kitty, 1995. 'Arms to Fight, Arms to Protect: Women Speak Out about Conflict', unpublished paper presented in Oslo, 19 June, at a PANOS seminar on the project 'Arms to Fight – Arms to Protect'.

War Resisters' League, 1981. *Calendar*. Brussels: War Resisters' League.

Weber, Max, 1947. *The Theory of Social and Economic Organization*. New York: Free Press.

Weber, Max, 1980 [1962]. *Basic Concepts in Sociology*. Secaucus, NJ: Citadel Press.

Weedon, Chris, 1987. *Feminist Practice and Poststructuralist Theory*. Oxford: Basil Blackwell.

West, Candace & Don H. Zimmerman, 1991. 'Doing Gender', pp. 7–13 in Judith Lorber & Susan A. Farrell, eds, *The Social Construction of Gender*. Newbury Park, CA: Sage.

Whitworth, Sandra, 1991. 'Gender in the IPPF and the ILO: A Feminist Analysis of International Relations', dissertation, Ottawa: Carleton University.

Wilcox, Clyde, Lara Hewitt & Dee Allsop, 1996. 'The Gender Gap in Attitudes Toward the Gulf War: A Cross-National Perspective', *Journal of Peace Research*, vol. 3, no. 1, pp. 67–82.

Wilde, Alexander, 1978. 'Conversations among Gentlemen: Oligarchical Democracy in Colombia', pp. 28–81 in Juan Linz & Alfred Stephan, eds, *The Breakdown of Democratic Regimes: Latin America*. Baltimore, MD: Johns Hopkins University Press.

Wills, Virginia, 1991. 'Public Life: Women Make a Difference', Expert Group Meeting on the Role of Women in Public Life, Vienna, 21–24 May, EGM/RWPL/1991/WP.1/Rev.1.

Winslow, Anne, ed., 1995. *Women, Politics, and the United Nations*. Westport, CT: Greenwood Press.

Zajevic, Staca, 1994. *Zene za mir* [*Women for Peace*]. Belgrade: Women in Black.

Zalewski, Marysia, 1995. 'Well, What is the Feminist Perspective on Bosnia?', *International Affairs*, vol. 71, no. 2, pp. 339–356.

Zeitlin, Froma, 1996. *Playing the Other: Gender and Society in Classical Greek Literature*. Chicago, IL: University of Chicago Press.

Index